Corner House

SOCIAL SCIENCE REPRINTS

General Editor MAURICE FILLER

"BOOTS AND SADDLES"

G. A. Custer.

"BOOTS AND SADDLES"

OR LIFE IN DAKOTA WITH GENERAL CUSTER

BY

ELIZABETH B. CUSTER

WITH PORTRAIT AND MAP

CORNER HOUSE PUBLISHERS
WILLIAMSTOWN, MASSACHUSETTS 01267
1974

FIRST PUBLISHED 1885

REPRINTED 1969

BY

CORNER HOUSE PUBLISHERS

2nd Reprinting 1974

F
665
. C93
1974

Standard Book Number: 0-87928-006-9

Printed in the United States of America

𝔇𝔢𝔡𝔦𝔠𝔞𝔱𝔢𝔡

TO

MY HUSBAND

THE ECHO OF WHOSE VOICE HAS BEEN MY INSPIRATION

PREFACE.

ONE of the motives that have actuated me in recalling these simple annals of our daily life, has been to give a glimpse to civilians of garrison and camp life—about which they seem to have such a very imperfect knowledge.

This ignorance exists especially with reference to anything pertaining to the cavalry, which is almost invariably stationed on the extreme frontier.

The isolation of the cavalry posts makes them quite inaccessible to travellers, and the exposure incident to meeting warlike Indians does not tempt the visits of friends or even of the venturesome tourist. Our life, therefore, was often as separate from the rest of the world as if we had been living on an island in the ocean.

Very little has been written regarding the domestic life of an army family, and yet I cannot believe that it is without interest; for the innumerable questions that are asked about our occupations, amusements, and mode of house-keeping, lead me to hope that the actual answers to these queries contained in this little story will be acceptable. This must also be my apology for entering in some instances so minutely into trifling perplexities and events, which went to fill up the sum of our existence.

E. B. C.

148 East 18th Street,
New York City.

CONTENTS.

OUTLINE MAP
of portions of
MONTANA & DAKOTA

10 30 50
100 Miles

Copyright, 1885, by HARPER & BROTHERS.

WYOMING

MONTANA

DAKOTA

MINNESOTA

Milk River

Ft. Assiniboine

Ft. Maginnis

Ft. Lewis

Ft. Peck

MISSOURI R.

Ft. Buford

Big Horn

River

Henry's Landing

Myers

Big Horn

Ft. Custer

Ft. C. F. Smith

Ft. Keogh

Powder R.

Yellowstone R.

NORTHERN PACIFIC R. R.

BISMARCK

Ft. Ab. Lincoln

Ft. Rice

Ft. Yates

Carrington

Ft. Seward

James R.

MISSOURI R.

Yankton

MISSISSIPPI R.

ST. PAUL

Duluth

BOOTS AND SADDLES.

CHAPTER I.

CHANGE OF STATION.

GENERAL CUSTER graduated at West Point just in time to take part in the battle of Bull Run. He served with his regiment—the 5th Cavalry—for a time, but eventually was appointed aide-de-camp to General McClellan. He came to his sister's home in my native town, Monroe, Michigan, during the winter of 1863, and there I first met him. In the spring he returned to the army in Virginia, and was promoted that summer, at the age of twenty-three, from captain to brigadier-general. During the following autumn he came to Monroe to recover from a flesh-wound, which, though not serious, disabled him somewhat. At that time we became engaged. When his twenty days' leave of absence had expired he went back to duty, and did not return until a few days before our marriage, in February, 1864.

We had no sooner reached Washington on our wedding-journey than telegrams came, following one another in quick succession, asking him to give up the rest of his leave of absence, and hasten without an hour's delay to the front. I begged so hard not to be left behind that I finally prevailed. The result was that I found myself in a few hours on the extreme wing of the Army of the Potomac, in an isolated Virginia farm-house, finishing my honeymoon alone. I had so besought him to allow me to come that I did not dare own to myself the desolation and fright I felt. In the preparation for the hurried raid which my husband had been ordered to make he had sent to cavalry head-quarters to provide for my safety, and troops were in reality near, although I could not see them.

The general's old colored servant, Eliza, comforted me, and the Southern family in the house took pity upon my anxiety. It was a sudden plunge into a life of vicissitude and danger, and I hardly remember the time during the twelve years that followed when I was not in fear of some immediate peril, or in dread of some danger that threatened. After the raid was ended, we spent some delightful weeks together, and when the regular spring campaign began I returned to Washington, where I remained until the surrender and the close of the war.

After that we went to Texas for a year, my husband still acting as major-general in command of Volunteers. In 1866 we returned to Michigan, and the autumn of the same year found us in Kansas, where the general assumed charge of the 7th (Regular) Cavalry, to which he had been assigned, with the rank of lieutenant-colonel in the Regular Army. We remained in Kansas five years, during which time I was the only officer's wife who always followed the regiment. We were then ordered, with the regiment, to Kentucky. After being stationed in Elizabethtown for two years, we went to Dakota in the spring of 1873.

When orders came for the 7th Cavalry to go into the field again, General Custer was delighted. The regiment was stationed in various parts of the South, on the very disagreeable duty of breaking up illicit distilleries and suppressing the Ku-klux. Fortunately for us, being in Kentucky, we knew very little of this service. It seemed an unsoldierly life, and it was certainly uncongenial; for a true cavalryman feels that a life in the saddle on the free open plain is his legitimate existence.

Not an hour elapsed after the official document announcing our change of station had arrived before our house was torn up. In the confusion I managed to retire to a corner with an atlas, and surreptitiously look up the territory to which we were going. I hardly liked to own that I had forgotten its location. When my finger traced our route from Kentucky almost up to the border of the British Possessions, it seemed as if we were going to Lapland.

From the first days of our marriage, General Custer celebrated every order to move with wild demonstrations of joy. His exuberance of spirits always found expression in some boyish pranks, before he could set to work seriously to prepare for duty. As soon as the officer announcing the order to move had disappeared, all sorts of wild hilarity began. I had learned to take up a safe position on top of the table; that is, if I had not already been forcibly placed there as a spectator. The most disastrous result of the proceedings was possibly a broken chair, which the master of ceremonies would crash, and, perhaps, throw into the kitchen by way of informing the cook that good news had come. We had so few household effects that it was something of a loss when we chanced to be in a country where they could not be replaced. I can see Eliza's woolly head now, as she thrust it through the door to reprimand her master, and say, " Chairs don't grow on trees in these yere parts, gen'l." As for me, I was tossed about the room, and all sorts of jokes were played upon me before the frolic was ended. After such participation in the celebration, I was almost too tired with the laughter and fun to begin packing.

I know that it would surprise a well-regulated mover to see what short work it was for us to prepare for our journeys. We began by having a supply of gunny-sacks and hay brought in from the stables. The saddler appeared, and all our old traps that had been taken around with us so many years were once more tied and sewed up. The kitchen utensils were plunged into barrels, generally left uncovered in the hurry; rolls of bedding encased in waterproof cloth or canvas were strapped and roped, and the few pictures and books were crowded into chests and boxes. When these possessions were loaded upon the wagon, at the last moment there always appeared the cook's bedding to surmount the motley pile. Her property was invariably tied up in a flaming quilt representing souvenirs of her friends' dresses. She followed that last instalment with anxious eyes, and, true to her early training, grasped her red bandanna, containing a few last things, while the satchel she scorned to use hung empty on her arm.

In all this confusion no one was cross. We rushed and gasped through the one day given us for preparation, and I had only time to be glad with my husband that he was going back to the life of activity that he so loved. His enforced idleness made it seem to him that he was cumbering the earth, and he rejoiced to feel that he was again to have the chance to live up to his idea of a soldier. Had I dared to stop in that hurried day and think of myself all the courage would have gone out of me. This removal to Dakota meant to my husband a reunion with his regiment and summer campaigns against Indians; to me it meant months of loneliness, anxiety, and terror. Fortunately there was too much to do to leave leisure for thought.

Steamers were ready for us at Memphis, and we went thither by rail to embark. When the regiment was gathered together, after a separation of two years, there were hearty greetings, and exchanges of troublous or droll experiences; and thankful once more to be reunited, we entered again, heart and soul, into the minutest detail of one another's lives. We went into camp for a few days on the outskirts of Memphis, and exchanged hospitalities with the citizens. The bachelors found an elysium in the society of many very pretty girls, and love-making went on either in luxurious parlors or in the open air as they rode in the warm spring weather to and from our camp. Three steamers were at last loaded and we went on to Cairo, where we found the trains prepared to take us into Dakota.

The regiment was never up to its maximum of twelve hundred men, but there may have been eight or nine hundred soldiers and as many horses. The property of the companies—saddles, equipments, arms, ammunition, and forage—together with the personal luggage of the officers, made the trains very heavy, and we travelled slowly. We were a week or more on the route. Our days were varied by the long stops necessary to water the horses, and occasionally to take them out of the cars for exercise. My husband and I always went on these occasions to loose the dogs and have a frolic and a little visit with our own horses. The youth and gamins of the village gathered about us as if we had been some travelling show. While on the journey one of our family had a birthday. This was always a day of frolic and fun, and even when we were on the extreme frontier, presents were sent for into the States, and we had a little dinner and a birthday cake. This birthday that came during the journey, though so inopportune, did not leave utterly without resources the minds of those whose ingenuity was quickened by affection. The train was delayed that day for an unusually long time; our colored cook, Mary, in despair because we ate so little in the "twenty-minutes-for-refreshments" places, determined on an impromptu feast. She slyly took a basket and filled it at the shops in the village street. She had already made friends with a woman who had a little cabin tucked in between the rails and the embankment, and there the never absent "eureka" coffee-pot was produced and most delicious coffee dripped. Returning to the car stove, which she had discovered was filled with a deep bed of coals, she broiled us a steak and baked some potatoes. The general and I were made to sit down opposite each other in one of the compartments. A board was brought, covered with a clean towel, and we did table-legs to this impromptu table. We did not dare move, and scarcely ventured to giggle, for fear we should overturn the laden board in our laps. For dessert, a large plate of macaroons, which were an especial weakness of mine, was brought out as a surprise. Mary told me, with great glee, how she had seen the general prowling in the bakers' shops to buy them, and described the train of small boys who followed him when he came back with his brown paper parcel. "Miss Libbie," she said, "they thought a sure enough gen'l always went on horseback and carried his sword in his hand."

We were so hungry we scarcely realized that we were anything but the embodiment of picturesque grace. No one could be otherwise than awkward in trying to cut food on such an uncertain base, while Mary had taken the last scrap of dignity away from the general's appearance by enveloping him in a kitchen towel as a substitute for a napkin. With their usual independence and indifference to ceremony, troops of curious citizens stalked through the car to stare at my husband. We went on eating calmly, unconscious that they thought the picture hardly in keeping with their pre-conceived ideas of a commanding officer. When we

thanked Mary for our feast, her face beamed and shone
with a combination of joy at our delight and heat from
the stove. When she lifted up our frugal board and
set us free, we had a long stroll, talking over other
birthdays and those yet to come, until the train was
ready to start.

CHAPTER II.

A BLIZZARD.

AFTER so many days in the car, we were glad to stop on an open plain about a mile from the town of Yankton, where the road ended.

The three chief considerations for a camp are wood, water, and good ground. The latter we had, but we were at some distance from the water, and neither trees nor brushwood were in sight.

The long trains were unloaded of their freight, and the plains about us seemed to swarm with men and horses. I was helped down from the Pullman car, where inlaid woods, mirrors, and plush surrounded us, to the ground, perfectly bare of every earthly comfort. The other ladies of the regiment went on to the hotel in the town. The general suggested that I should go with them, but I had been in camp so many summers it was not a formidable matter for me to remain, and fortunately for what followed I did so. The household belongings were gathered together. A family of little new puppies, some half-grown dogs, the cages of mocking-birds and canaries, were all corralled safely in a little stockade made of chests and trunks, and we set ourselves about making a temporary home. The general and a number of soldiers, composing the headquarters detail, were obliged to go at once to lay out

the main camp and assign the companies to their places.
Later on, when the most important work was done, our
tents were to be pitched. While I sat on a chest waiting, the air grew suddenly chilly, the bright sun of the
morning disappeared, and the rain began to fall. Had
we been accustomed to the climate we would have
known that these changes were the precursors of a
snow-storm.

When we left Memphis, not a fortnight before, we
wore muslin gowns and were then uncomfortably
warm; it seemed impossible that even so far north
there could be a returned winter in the middle of
April. We were yet to realize what had been told us
of the climate—that there were "eight months of winter and four of very late in the fall." On the bluffs
beyond us was a signal-station, but they sent us no
warning. Many years of campaigning in the Indian
Territory, Kansas, Colorado, and Nebraska, give one an
idea of what the weather can do; but each new country has its peculiarities, and it seemed we had reached
one where all the others were outdone. As the afternoon of that first day advanced the wind blew colder,
and I found myself eying with envy a little half-fin-
ished cabin without an enclosure, standing by itself.
Years of encountering the winds of Kansas, when our
tents were torn and blown down so often, had taught
me to appreciate any kind of a house, even though it
were built upon the sand as this one was. A dug-out,
which the tornado swept over, but could not harm, was
even more of a treasure. The change of climate from
the extreme south to the far north had made a number

of the men ill, and even the superb health of the general had suffered. He continued to superintend the camp, however, though I begged him from time to time as I saw him to give up. I felt sure he needed a shelter and some comfort at once, so I took courage to plan for myself. Before this I had always waited, as the general preferred to prepare everything for me. After he had consented that we should try for the little house, some of the kind-hearted soldiers found the owner in a distant cabin, and he rented it to us for a few days. The place was equal to a palace to me. There was no plastering, and the house seemed hardly weatherproof. It had a floor, however, and an upper story divided off by beams; over these Mary and I stretched blankets and shawls and so made two rooms. It did not take long to settle our few things, and when wood and water were brought from a distance we were quite ready for house-keeping, except that we lacked a stove and some supplies. Mary walked into the town to hire or buy a small cooking-stove, but she could not induce the merchant to bring it out that night. She was thoughtful enough to take along a basket and brought with her a little marketing. Before she had come within sight of our cabin on her return, the snow was falling so fast it was with difficulty that she found her way.

Meanwhile the general had returned completely exhausted and very ill. Without his knowledge I sent for the surgeon, who, like all of his profession in the army, came promptly. He gave me some powerful medicine to administer every hour, and forbade the

general to leave his bed.   It was growing dark, and
we were in the midst of a Dakota blizzard.   The snow
was so fine that it penetrated the smallest cracks, and
soon we found white lines appearing all around us,
where the roof joined the walls, on the windows and
under the doors.   Outside the air was so thick with the
whirling, tiny particles that it was almost impossible to
see one's hand held out before one.   The snow was
fluffy and thick, like wool, and fell so rapidly, and seemingly from all directions, that it gave me a feeling of
suffocation as I stood outside.   Mary was not easily
discouraged, and piling a few light fagots outside the
door, she tried to light a fire.   The wind and the muf-
fling snow put out every little blaze that started, however, and so, giving it up, she went into the house and
found the luncheon-basket we had brought from the
car, in which remained some sandwiches, and these
composed our supper.

The night had almost settled down upon us when the
adjutant came for orders.   Knowing the scarcity of
fuel and the danger to the horses from exposure to the
rigor of such weather after their removal from a warm
climate, the general ordered the breaking of camp.   All
the soldiers were directed to take their horses and go
into Yankton, and ask the citizens to give them shelter
in their homes, cow-sheds, and stables.   In a short time
the camp was nearly deserted, only the laundresses, two
or three officers, and a few dismounted soldiers remaining.   The towns-people, true to the unvarying western
hospitality, gave everything they could to the use of
the regiment; the officers found places in the hotels.

The sounds of the hoofs of the hurrying horses flying by our cabin on their way to the town had hardly died out before the black night closed in and left us alone on that wide, deserted plain. The servants, Mary and Ham, did what they could to make the room below-stairs comfortable by stopping the cracks and barricading the frail door. The thirty-six hours of our imprisonment there seems now a frightful nightmare. The wind grew higher and higher, and shrieked about the little house dismally. It was built without a foundation, and was so rickety it seemed as it rocked in a great gust of wind that it surely would be unroofed or overturned. The general was too ill for me to venture to find my usual comfort from his re-assuring voice. I dressed in my heaviest gown and jacket, and remained under the blankets as much as I could to keep warm. Occasionally I crept out to shake off the snow from the counterpane, for it sifted in between the roof and clapboards very rapidly. I hardly dared take the little phial in my benumbed fingers to drop the precious medicine for fear it would fall. I realized, as the night advanced, that we were as isolated from the town, and even the camp, not a mile distant, as if we had been on an island in the river. The doctor had intended to return to us, but his serious face and impressive injunctions made me certain that he considered the life of the general dependent on the medicine being regularly given.

During the night I was startled by hearing a dull sound, as of something falling heavily. Flying down the stairs I found the servants prying open the frozen and snow-packed door, to admit a half dozen soldiers who, becoming bewildered by the snow, had been saved by the faint light we had placed in the window. After that several came, and two were badly frozen. We were in despair of finding any way of warming them, as there was no bedding, and, of course, no fire, until I remembered the carpets which were sewed up in bundles and heaped in one corner, where the boxes were, and which we were not to use until the garrison was reached. Spreading them out, we had enough to roll up each wanderer as he came. The frozen men were in so exhausted a condition that they required immediate attention. Their sufferings were intense, and I could not forgive myself for not having something with which to revive them. The general never tasted liquor, and we were both so well always we did not even keep it for use in case of sickness.

I saw symptoms of that deadly stupor which is the sure precursor of freezing, when I fortunately remembered a bottle of alcohol which had been brought for the spirit-lamps. Mary objected to using the only means by which we could make coffee for ourselves, but the groans and exhausted and haggard faces of the men won her over, and we saw them revive under the influence of the fiery liquid. Poor fellows! They afterwards lost their feet, and some of their fingers had also to be amputated. The first soldier who had reached us unharmed, except from exhaustion, explained that they had all attempted to find their way to town, and the storm had completely overcome them. Fortunately one had clung to a bag of hard-tack, which was all they had had to eat. At last the day came, but so darkened by the snow it seemed rather a twilight. The drifts were on three sides of us like a wall. The long hours dragged themselves away, leaving the general too weak to rise, and in great need of hot, nourishing food. I grew more and more terrified at our utterly desolate condition and his continued illness, though fortunately he did not suffer. He was too ill, and I too anxious, to eat the fragments that remained in the luncheon-basket. The snow continued to come down in great swirling sheets, while the wind shook the loose window-casings and sometimes broke in the door. When night came again and the cold increased, I believed that our hours were numbered. I missed the voice of the courageous Mary, for she had sunk down in a corner exhausted for want of sleep, while Ham had been completely demoralized from the first. Occasionally I melted a little place on the frozen window-pane, and saw that the drifts were almost level with the upper windows on either side, but that the wind had swept a clear space before the door. During the night the sound of the tramping of many feet rose above the roar of the storm. A great drove of mules rushed up to the sheltered side of the house. Their brays had a sound of terror as they pushed, kicked, and crowded themselves against our little cabin. For a time they huddled together, hoping for warmth, and then despairing, they made a mad rush away, and were soon lost in the white wall of snow beyond. All night long the neigh of a distressed horse, almost human in its appeal, came to us at intervals. The door was pried open once, thinking it might be some suffering fellow-creature in distress. The strange, wild eyes of the horse peering in for help, haunted me long afterwards. Occasionally a lost dog lifted up a howl of distress under our window, but before the door could be opened to admit him he had disappeared in the darkness. When the night was nearly spent I sprang again to the window with a new horror, for no one, until he hears it for himself, can realize what varied sounds animals make in the excitement of peril. A drove of hogs, squealing and grunting, were pushing against the house, and the door which had withstood so much had to be held to keep it from being broken in.

It was almost unbearable to hear the groans of the soldiers over their swollen and painful feet, and know that we could do nothing to ease them. To be in the midst of such suffering, and yet have no way of ameliorating it; to have shelter, and yet to be surrounded by dumb beasts appealing to us for help, was simply terrible. Every minute seemed a day; every hour a year. When daylight came I dropped into an exhausted slumber, and was awakened by Mary standing over our bed with a tray of hot breakfast. I asked if help had come, and finding it had not, of course, I could not understand the smoking food. She told me that feeling the necessity of the general's eating, it had come to her in the night-watches that she would cut up the large candles she had pilfered from the cars, and try if she could cook over the many short pieces placed close together, so as to make a large flame. The result was hot coffee and some bits of the steak she had brought from town, fried with a few slices of potatoes. She could not resist telling me how much better she could have done had I not given away the alcohol to the frozen men!

The breakfast revived the general so much that he began to make light of danger in order to quiet me. The snow had ceased to fall, but for all that it still seemed that we were castaways and forgotten, hidden under the drifts that nearly surrounded us. Help was really near at hand, however, at even this darkest hour. A knock at the door, and the cheery voices of men came up to our ears. Some citizens of Yankton had at last found their way to our relief, and the officers, who neither knew the way nor how to travel over such a country, had gladly followed. They told us that they had made several attempts to get out to us, but the snow was so soft and light that they could make no headway. They floundered and sank down almost out of sight, even in the streets of the town. Of course no horse could travel, but they told me of their intense anxiety, and said that fearing I might be in need of immediate help they had dragged a cutter over the drifts, which now had a crust of ice formed from the sleet and the moisture of the damp night air. Of course I declined to go without the general, but I was more touched than I could express by their thought of me. I made some excuse to go up-stairs, where, with my head buried in the shawl partition, I tried to smother the sobs that had been suppressed during the terrors of our desolation. Here the general found me, and though comforting me by tender words, he still reminded me that he would not like any one to know that I had lost my pluck when all the danger I had passed through was really ended.

The officers made their way over to camp, for they were anxious and uncertain as to what might have happened to the few persons remaining there. I had been extremely troubled, for each of the soldiers for whom we had been caring had, with a trooper's usual love of the sensational, told us of frozen men and of the birth of babies to the laundresses. These stories had reached town through stragglers, until we imagined from the exaggeration that enough newly - born children might be found to start a small orphan asylum. The officers soon returned with the story reduced to one little stranger who had come safely into this world in the stormy night, sheltered by a tent only. No men were frozen, fortunately, though all had suffered. The soldier detailed to take care of the general's horses found his way back with them, and in his solemn voice told us that in spite of every effort, sharing his blankets and holding the little things through the storm, the thorough-bred puppies had frozen one by one. There was one little box-stove in camp which the officers brought back, accompanied by its owner, an old and somewhat infirm officer.

In the midst of all this excitement, and the reaction from the danger, I could not suppress my sense of the ludicrous when I saw the daintiest and most exquisite officer of "ours," whom last I remembered careering on his perfectly equipped and prancing steed before the admiring eyes of the Memphis belles, now wound up with scarfs and impromptu leggings of flannel; his hat tied down with a woollen comforter; buffalo gloves on his hands; and clasping a stove-pipe, necessary for the precious stove.

Some of the officers had brought out parcels containing food, while our brother, Colonel Tom Custer, had struggled with a large basket of supplies. In a short time another officer appeared at our door with a face full of anxiety about our welfare. He did not tell us what we afterwards learned from others, that, fearing the citizens would give up going to us, and knowing that he could not find the way alone over a country from which the snow had obliterated every landmark, he had started to go the whole distance on the railroad. Coming to a long bridge he found the track so covered with ice that it was a dangerous footing; the wind blew the sleet and snow in his face, almost blinding him, but nothing daunted, he crawled over on his hands and knees, and continuing to use the track as his guide, stopped when he thought he might be opposite our cabin, and ploughed his way with difficulty through the drifts.

When the officers had returned to town, we made a fire in the little stove which had been put up-stairs, as the pipe was so short. We ensconced our visitor, to whom the stove belonged, near by. He was a capital fireman; we divided our bedding with him, and put it on the floor, as close as possible to the fire. The shawl and blanket partition separated our rooms, but did not seem to deaden sound, and at night I only lost consciousness of the audible sleeping of our guest after I had dropped the point of a finger in my ear. He was the one among us who, being the oldest of our circle, and hav-

ing had a varied experience, was an authority on many
subjects. He had peculiar and extreme ideas on some
questions. We listened out of respect, but we all drew
the line at following some of his advice, and over one
topic there was general revolt. He disbelieved entirely
in the external or internal use of water, and living as we
did in countries where the rivers were flowing mud, and
the smaller streams dried up under the blazing sun, his
would have been a convenient system, to say the least.
Unfortunately, our prejudices in favor of cleanliness increased with the scarcity of water. Bathing became
one of the luxuries as well as one of the absolute neces-
sities of life. From being compelled to do with very
little water, we had learned almost to take a bath in a
thimble, and to this day I find myself pouring the water out of a pitcher in a most gingerly manner, so strong
is the power of habit—even now with the generous
rush of the unstinted Croton at my disposal. The theory of our venerable friend on the danger of bathing
was fortified with many an earnest argument, and the
advantages of his improved system of dry rubbing set
out elaborately in his best rhetoric. Nevertheless, taking a bath with the palm of the hand was combated to
the last by his hearers. When I had heard him arguing
previously I had rather believed it to be the vagary of
the hour. I had proof to the contrary the next morning after the storm, for I was awakened by a noise of
vigorous friction and violent breathing, as of some one
laboring diligently. I suddenly remembered the doc-
trine of our guest, and realized that he was putting theory into practice. As softly as I awakened my husband,

and tried to whisper to him, he was on nettles instantly, hearing the quiver of laughter in my voice. He feared I might be heard, and that the feelings of the man for whom he had such regard might be wounded. He promptly requested me to smother my laughter in the blankets, and there I shook with merriment, perhaps even greater because of the relief I experienced in finding something to counteract the gloom of the preceding hours. And if I owned to telling afterwards that the old officer's theory and practice were one, it could not be called a great breach of hospitality, for he gloried in what he called advanced ideas, and strove to wear the martyr's crown that all pioneers in new and extreme beliefs crowd on their heads.

Our friend remained with us until the camp was inhabitable and the regular order of military duties was resumed. Paths and roads were made through the snow, and it was a great relief to be again in the scenes of busy life. We did not soon forget our introduction to Dakota. After that we understood why the frontiersman builds his stable near the house; we also comprehended then when they told us that they did not dare to cross in a blizzard from the house to the stable-door without keeping hold of a rope tied fast to the latch as a guide for their safe return when the stock was fed. Afterwards, when even our cool-headed soldiers lost their way and wandered aimlessly near their quarters, and when found were dazed in speech and look, the remembrance of that first storm, with the density of the down-coming snow, was a solution to us of their bewilderment.

CHAPTER III.

WESTERN HOSPITALITY.

THE citizens of Yankton, endeavoring to make up for the inhospitable reception the weather had given us, vied with one another in trying to make the regiment welcome. The hotel was filled with the families of the officers, and after the duties of the day were over in camp, the married men went into town. We were called upon, asked to dine, and finally tendered a ball. It was given in the public hall of the town, which, being decorated with flags and ornamented with all the military paraphernalia that could be used effectively, was really very attractive. We had left gas far behind us, and we had not the mellow, becoming light of wax-candles, but those Western people were generous about lamps, as they are about everything else, and the hall was very bright.

The ladies had many trials in endeavoring to make themselves presentable. We burrowed in the depths of trunks for those bits of finery that we had supposed would not be needed again for years. We knew the officers would do us credit. Through all the sudden changes of fashion, which leave an army lady when she goes into the territories quite an antediluvian in toilet after a few months, the officer can be entirely serene.

He can be conscious that he looks his best in a perfect-ly fitting uniform, and that he is never out of date.

The general and I went into the hotel and took a room for the night of the ball. Such good-humor, con-fusion, and jolly preparations as we had, for the young officers came to borrow the corner of our glass to put on the finishing touches, carrying their neckties, studs, sleeve-buttons, and gloves in their hands. The aigret had been taken from the helmet and placed across their broad chests, brightening still more their shining new uniforms. I remember with what pride the "plebs" called our attention to the double row of buttons which the change in the uniform now gave to all, without regard to rank. The lieutenants had heretofore only been allowed one row of buttons, and they declared that an Apollo even could not do justice to his figure with a coat fastened in so monotonous and straight up-and-down a manner.

Yankton, like all new towns, was chiefly settled with newly - married people, who ornamented their bits of front yards with shining new perambulators. The mothers had little afternoon parades, proud enough to trundle their own babies. If any one's father ever came from the States to a Western town, we all felt at liberty to welcome his gray hairs. There were but few young girls, but that night must have been a memora-ble one for them. All the town, and even the country people, came to the ball. The mayor and common council received us, and the governor opened the fes-tivities. We crossed to the hotel to our supper. We were asked to sit down to the table, and the abundance

of substantials proved that our hosts did not expect
us to nibble. The general was, of course, taken possession of by the city fathers and mothers. Finding
among them a woman he knew I would appreciate, he
placed me beside her at supper. I had but little time
to eat, for she was not only clever and brave, but
very interesting in her description of the dangers and
hardships she had endured during the ten years of
her pioneering. The railroad had been completed
but a short time, and before that the life was wild
enough. She sat quietly among these people in her
simple stuff gown, honored and looked up to. Though
not even elderly, she was still almost the oldest citizen
and an authority in the history of the country. All
classes and conditions came to the ball, for Yankton
was not yet large enough to be divided into cliques;
besides, the rough and hazardous life these people had
shared endeared them to one another.

The days after this passed very rapidly. The officers
were already getting the command into condition to
begin the long march of five hundred miles that lay before us. Before we left, the general, desiring to return
some of the civilities of the citizens, gave the governor
and his staff a review. The wide plain on which our
camp was located was admirably adapted to the display
of troops. My heart swelled with pride to see our
grand regiment all together once more and in such fine
condition. When the review was closing, and that part
came where the officers leave their companies and, joining, ride abreast to salute the commanding officer, the
general could hardly maintain the stereotyped, motion-

less quiet of the soldier—the approach of this fine body of men made him so proud of his command.

All were well mounted; the two years' station in the South had given them rare opportunities to purchase horses. The general, being considered an excellent judge, had, at the request of the officers, bought several from the stables of his Kentucky friends. He told me that if a colt failed a quarter of a second in making certain time expected, the owner was disappointed and willing to sell him at a merely nominal sum. So it came about that even the lieutenants, with their meagre pay, owned horses whose pedigree was unending. There were three officers belonging to each of the twelve companies; some were detailed on duty elsewhere, but those remaining, with the adjutant, surgeon, quartermaster, and commissary, made a long line of brilliantly caparisoned and magnificently formed men mounted on blood-horses. No wonder that the moment they saluted the general, he jumped from the saddle to congratulate them, and show them his pride in their soldierly appearance.

The governor and his staff were not chary in their expressions of admiration. It was a great event in the lives of the citizens, and the whole town was present. Every sort of vehicle used on the frontier came out, filled to overflowing, and many persons walked. The music of the band, the sun lighting up the polished steel of the arms and equipments, the hundreds of spirited horses going through the variety of evolutions which belong to a mounted regiment, made a memorable scene for these isolated people. Besides, they felt

the sensation of possession when they knew that these
troops had come to open the country and protect those
more adventurous spirits who were already finding that
a place into which the railroad ran was too far East for
them.

One day we were all invited to take luncheon on
board the steamer that had been chartered to take the
regimental property up the river to Bismarck.   The
owner of the boat was very hospitable, and champagne
flowed freely as he proposed old-fashioned toasts.   The
officers and ladies of the regiment received with pleasure all this politeness, and since these occasions were
rare in the lives of those of us who lived always on the
outskirts of civilization, we were reluctant to go home.
My horse had been sent away by some mistake, and the
general accepted the offer of the host to drive me out
to camp, he riding for a time beside the carriage, and
then, with his usual restlessness, giving rein to his horse
for a brisk gallop.   It was not long before I discovered
that the uncertain swaying of the vehicle from side to
side, and the hazardous manner in which we skirted the
deep gullies, was due to the fact that our friend was
overcome with hospitality.

Trying to talk intelligently, and to appear not to notice the vagaries of the driver, and at the same time to
control my wandering eyes as they espied from afar a
dangerous bit of road, I spent a very uncomfortable
hour.   Fortunately the "dear Polly" was most demure
in harness, and possibly having been left before that to
find her own way under similar circumstances, she did
not attempt to leap with the carriage over ditches, as

her gay owner invited her to do. When we came up within shouting distance of the general, I cried out, in what I meant to seem like playful menace; but he had taken in the situation, and seeing that Polly was to be trusted, he mischievously laughed back at me and flew over the country. Finally we neared our little cabin, and my last fear came upon me. Mary had spread the clothes-line far and wide; it was at the rear of the house, but my escort saw no door, and Polly soon wound us hopelessly up in the line and two weeks' washing, while she quietly tried to kick her way through the packing-boxes and wood-piles! Mary and Ham extricated me, and started the old nag on the road homeward, and I waved a relieved good-bye to the retreating carriage.

Only such impossible wives as one reads of in Sunday-school books would have lost the opportunity for a few wrathful words. I was not dangerous, though, and the peals of laughter from my husband, as he described my wild eyes peering out from the side of the carriage, soon put me into a good-humor. Next day I was called to the steps, and found that Polly's owner had discovered that we had a door. He said an off-hand "How d'ye?" and presented a peace-offering, adding, "My wife tells me that I was hardly in a condition to deliver a temperance lecture yesterday. As what she says is always true, I bring my apologies." Ham carried in the hamper, and though I urged our guest to remain, he did not seem quite at ease and drove away.

While we were at Yankton, something happened that

filled us with wonder. The Indians from the reservation near brought in reports that came through other tribes of the Modoc disasters. It was a marvel to the general to find that at that distance north news could come to us through Indian runners in advance of that we received by the telegraph.

CHAPTER IV.

CAVALRY ON THE MARCH.

WHEN the day came for us to begin our march, the sun shone and the towns-people wished us good-luck with their good-bye.

The length of each day's march varied according to the streams on which we relied for water, or the arrival of the boat. The steamer that carried the forage for the horses and the supplies for the command was tied up to the river-bank every night, as near to us as was possible. The laundresses and ladies of the regiment were on board, except the general's sister, Margaret, who made her first march with her husband, riding all the way on horseback. As usual, I rode beside the general. Our first few days were pleasant, and we began at once to enjoy the plover. The land was so covered with them that the hunters shot them with all sorts of arms. We counted eighty birds in the gunny-sack that three of the soldiers brought in. Fortunately there were several shot-guns in the possession of our family, and the little things, therefore, were not torn to pieces, but could be broiled over the coals of the camp-fire. They were so plump that their legs were like tiny points coming from beneath the rounded outline that swept the grass as they walked. No butter was needed in cooking them, for they were very fat. Some of the officers had not left behind them all of their epicurean tastes, and preferred to have the birds cooked when they were decidedly "gamy." In this way they secured the privilege of taking their odoriferous luncheon quite apart from the others. The general had invited two officers besides his brother Tom, and his brother-in-law, Mr. Calhoun, to mess with him. We had a tableful, and very merry we were, even in the early morning. To joke before day-light seems impossible, but even at breakfast peals of laughter went up from the dining-tent.

One of the officers was envied, and we declared he got more to eat than the rest, because he insisted upon "carving the hash;" while to cut meat for all our hungry circle, as the general did at the other end of the table, took many precious moments. One of our number called us the "Great Grab Mess," and some one slyly printed the words in large black letters on the canvas that covered the luncheon-hamper, which was usually strapped at the back of our travelling-carriage. How gladly we gathered about that hamper when the command halted at noon ! How good the plover and sand-wiches tasted, while we quenched our thirst with cold coffee or tea ! Since we were named as we were, we all dared to reach over and help ourselves, and the one most agile and with the longest arms was the best fed.

No great ceremony is to be expected when one rises before four, and takes a hurried breakfast by the light of a tallow-candle ; the soldiers waiting outside to take down the tent, the servants hastily and suggestively rattling the kettles and gridiron as they packed them, made it an irresistible temptation for one hungry to "grab."

We had a very satisfactory little cook-stove. It began its career with legs, but the wind used to lift it up from the ground with such violence it was finally dismembered, and afterwards placed flat on the ground. Being of sheet-iron it cooled quickly, was very light, and could be put in the wagon in a few moments after the morning meal was cooked. When we came out from breakfast the wagon stood near, partly packed, and bristling with kitchen utensils; buckets and baskets tied outside the cover, axe and spade lashed to the side, while the little stove looked out from the end. The mess-chest stood open on the ground to receive the dishes we had used. At a given signal the dining-tent went down with all those along the line, and they were stowed away in the wagons in an incredibly short time. The wagon-train then drew out and formed in order at the rear of the column.

At the bugle-call, "boots and saddles," each soldier mounted and took his place in line, all riding two abreast. First came the general and his staff, with whom sister Margaret and I were permitted to ride; the private orderlies and headquarters detail rode in our rear; and then came the companies according to the places assigned them for the day; finally the wagon-train, with the rear-guard. We made a long drawn-out cavalcade that stretched over a great distance. When we reached some high bluff, we never tired of watching the command advancing, with the long line of supply wagons, with their white covers, winding around bends in the

road and climbing over the hills. Every day the breaking of camp went more smoothly and quickly, until, as
the days advanced, the general used to call me to his
side to notice by his watch how few moments it took
after the tents were ordered down to set the whole ma-
chinery for the march in motion ; and I remember the
regiment grew so skilful in preparation that in one campaign the hour for starting never varied five minutes
during the whole summer.

The column was always halted once during the day's
march to water the horses, then the luncheons were
brought forth. They varied decidedly ; sometimes an
officer took from his pocket a hard biscuit wrapped in
his handkerchief ; the faithful orderly of another took
his chief's sandwiches from his own haversack and
brought them to him, wherever he was. Often a provident officer, as he seated himself to his little "spread"
on the grass, was instantly surrounded by interested
visitors, who, heedless ever of any future, believed that
the world owed them a living and they were resolved to
have it.

When the stream was narrow, and the hundreds of
horses had to be ranged along its banks to be watered,
there was time for a nap. I soon acquired the general's
habit of sleeping readily. He would throw himself
down anywhere and fall asleep instantly, even with the
sun beating on his head. It only takes a little training
to learn to sleep without a pillow on uneven ground and
without shade. I learned, the moment I was helped
out of the saddle, to drop upon the grass and lose myself
in a twinkling. No one knows what a privilege it is to

be stretched out after being cramped over the horn of a lady's saddle for hours, until she has experienced it. I think I never got quite over wishing for the shade of a tree; but there was often a little strip of shadow on one side of the travelling wagon, which was always near us on the journey. I was not above selfishly appropriating the space under the wagon, if it had not been taken by somebody else. Even then I had to dislodge a whole collection of dogs, who soon find the best places for their comfort.

We had a citizen-guide with us, who, having been long in the country, knew the streams, and the general and I, following his instructions, often rode in advance as we neared the night's camp. It was always a mild excitement and new pleasure to select camp. The men who carried the guidons for each company were sent for, and places assigned them. The general delighted to unsaddle his favorite horse, Dandy, and turn him loose, for his attachment was so strong he never grazed far from us. He was not even tethered, and after giving himself the luxury of a roll in the grass, he ate his dinner of oats, and browsed about the tent, as tame as a kitten. He whinnied when my husband patted his sleek neck, and looked jealously at the dogs when they all followed us into the tent afterwards.

After tramping down the grass, to prevent the fire from spreading, my husband would carry dry sticks and underbrush, and place them against a fallen tree. That made an admirable back-log, and in a little while we had a glorious fire, the general having a peculiar gift of starting a flame on the wildest day. The next thing

was to throw himself down on the sod, cover his eyes
with his white felt hat, and be sound asleep in no time.
No matter if the sun beat down in a perfect blaze, it
never disturbed him.   The dogs came at once to lie beside him.   I have seen them stretched at his back and
curled around his head, while the nose and paws of one
rested on his breast.   And yet he was quite unconscious
of their crowding.   They growled and scrambled for
the best place, but he slept placidly through it all.

When the command arrived, the guidons pointed out
the location for each company; the horses were unsaddled and picketed out; the wagons unloaded and the
tents pitched.   The hewing of wood and the hauling
of water came next, and after the cook-fires were
lighted, the air was full of savory odors of the soldiers'
dinner.   Sometimes the ground admitted of pitching
the tents of the whole regiment in two long lines facing each other; the wagons were drawn up at either
end, and also at the rear of the two rows of tents;
they were placed diagonally, one end overlapping the
other, so as to form a barricade against the attack of
Indians.   Down the centre of the company street large
ropes were stretched, to which the horses were tied at
night; our tents were usually a little apart from the
rest, at one end of the company street, and it never
grew to be an old story to watch the camp before us.
After I had changed my riding-habit for my one other
gown, I came out to join the general under the tent-fly,
where he lay alternately watching the scene and reading one of the well-thumbed books that he was never
without.   I always had sewing—either a bit of needle-

work that was destined to make our garrison quarters more attractive, or more often some necessary stitches to take in our hard-worn clothes. As we sat there it would have been difficult for a stranger seeing us to believe that it was merely the home of a day.

Our camps along the river were much alike, and each day when we entered the tent our few things were placed exactly as they were the day before. The only articles of furniture we had with us were two folding-chairs, a bed, a wash-bowl, with bucket and tin dipper, and a little mirror. This last, fastened to the tent-pole, swayed to and fro with the never-ceasing wind, and made it a superfluous luxury, for we learned to dress without it. The camp-chairs were a great comfort: they were made by a soldier out of oak, with leather back, seat and arms, the latter so arranged with straps and buckles that one could recline or sit upright at will. I once made a long march and only took a camp-stool for a seat; I knew therefore what an untold blessing it was to have a chair in which to lean, after having been sitting in the saddle for hours.

We had tried many inventions for cot-beds that folded, but nothing stood the wear and tear of travel like the simple contrivance of two carpenter's horses placed at the right distance apart, with three boards laid upon them. Such a bed was most easily transported, for the supports could be tied to the outside of the wagon, while the boards slipped inside before the rest of the camp equipage was packed.

An ineffaceable picture remains with me even now of those lovely camps, as we dreamily watched them by the fading light of the afternoon. The general and I used to think there was no bit of color equal to the delicate blue line of smoke which rose from the camp-fire, where the soldiers' suppers were being cooked. The effect of light and shade, and the varying tints of that perfect sky, were a great delight to him. The mellow air brought us sounds that had become dear by long and happy association—the low notes of the bugle in the hands of the musician practising the calls; the click of the currycomb as the soldiers groomed their horses; the whistle or song of a happy trooper. And even the irrepressible accordeon at that distance made a melody. It used to amuse us to find with what persistent ingenuity the soldiers smuggled that melancholy instrument. No matter how limited the transportation, after a few days' march it was brought out from a roll of blankets, or the teamster who had been bribed to keep it under the seat, produced the prized possession. The bay of the hounds was always music to the general. The bray of the mules could not be included under that head but it was one of those "sounds from home" to which we had become attached. Mingling with the melodies of the negro servants, as they swung the blacking-brushes at the rear of the tents, were the buoyant voices of the officers lying under the tent-flies, smoking the consoling pipe.

The twilight almost always found many of us gathered together, some idling on the grass in front of the camp-fire, or lounging on the buffalo robes. The one with the best voice sang, while all joined in the chorus.

We all had much patience in listening to what must

necessarily be "twice-told tales," for it would have taken the author of "The Arabian Nights" to supply fresh anecdotes for people who had been so many years together. These stories usually varied somewhat from time to time, and the more Munchausen-like they became the more attentive was the audience.

The territories are settled by people who live an intense, exaggerated sort of existence, and nothing tame attracts them. In order to compel a listener, I myself fell into the habit of adding a cipher or two to stories that had been first told in the States with moderate numbers. If the family overheard me, their unquenchable spirit of mischief invariably put a quietus on my eloquence. In fact I was soon cured of temptation to amplify, by the repeated asides of my deriding family, "Oh, I say, old lady, won't you come down a hundred or two?" Sometimes, when we were all gathered together at evening, we improved the privilege which belongs to long-established friendships of keeping silent. The men yielded to the soporific influence of tobacco, in quiet content, knowing that nothing was expected of them if they chose not to talk. My husband and I sometimes strolled through the camp at twilight, and even went among the citizen teamsters that are employed for the march, when they were preparing their evening meal.

These teamsters mess together on the march as the officers do, with rarely more than four or five in the circle. One of the number buys the supplies, takes charge of the rations, and keeps the accounts. The sum of expenses is divided at the end of the month, and each pays his portion. They take turns in doing the cooking, which, being necessarily simple, each can bear a share of the labor. Sometimes we found a more ambitious member of the mess endeavoring to rise superior to the tiresome hard-tack; he had bared his brawny arms and was mixing biscuit on the tail-board of the wagon, let down for the purpose. He whistled away as he moulded the dough with his horny hands, and it would have seemed that he had a Delmonico supper to anticipate.

We had not left Yankton far behind us before we were surprised to see one of its most hospitable citizens drive up; he acknowledged that he had missed us, and described the tameness of life after the departure of the cavalry as something quite past endurance. We were so stupid as not to discover, until after he had said the second good-bye, that he really wanted to join us on the march; still, had he kept on, I am sure his endurance would have been tested, for while I do not remember ever to have been discouraged before in all our campaigning, I was so during the storm that followed. The weather suddenly changed, and we began our march with a dull, gray morning and stinging cold. The general wound me up in all the outside wraps I had until I was a shapeless mass of fur and wool as I sat in the saddle. We could talk but little to each other, for the wind cut our faces and stiffened the flesh until it ached. My hands became too numb to hold my horse, so I gave him his own way. As we rode along like automatons, I was keeping my spirits up with the thought of the camp we would make in the underbrush of a sheltered valley by some stream, and the coming camp-fire rose brightly in my imagination. We went slowly as the usual time a cavalry command makes is barely four miles an hour. It was a discouraging spot where we finally halted; it was on a stream, but the ice was thick along the edges, and all we could see was the opposite bank, about thirty feet high, so frozen over that it looked like a wall of solid ice. It was difficult to pitch the tent, for the wind twisted and tore the canvas; the ground was already so frozen that it took a long time to drive in the iron pins by which the ropes holding the tents are secured. All the tying and pinning of the opening was of little avail, for the wind twisted off the tapes and flung the great brass pins I had brought on purpose for canvas far and wide.

No camp-fire would burn, of course, in such a gale, but I remembered thankfully the Sibley stove that we always carried. The saddler had cut a hole in the roof of the tent for the pipe, and fastened zinc around it to make it safe from fire. I shall never think about a Sibley stove without gratitude, nor cease to wonder how so simple an invention can be the means of such comfort. It is only a cone of sheet-iron, open at the top and bottom; the broader part rests on the ground, while the little pipe fits on the top. The wood is put through a door cut in the side; only billets can be used, for the aperture is of course small. It requires almost constant attention to keep the insatiable little thing filled, but it never occurs to one, where half a dozen are huddled together, to ask who shall be the fireman, and there is equal division of labor. The stove is so light that, in marching, the pipe is removed and a rope run through the openings, which enables it to be tied underneath the wagon, beside the bucket which is always suspended there to be used to water the horses.

The general was busy in the adjutant's tent, so I sent for the sergeant, who was our factotum, and asked him to hunt up the Sibley stove. I felt disheartened when he told me it had been forgotten.* I could have gone to the next tent where a provident officer had put his up, but I felt in too disagreeable a humor to inflict myself on any one, and so crept into bed to keep warm. It was an unmistakable fit of sulks, and I was in the valley of humiliation next morning, for I knew well how difficult it is to have ladies on the march, and how many obstacles the general had surmounted to arrange for my coming. My part consisted in drilling myself to be as little trouble as I could. I had really learned, by many a self-inflicted lesson, never to be too cold or too hot, and rarely allowed a thought of hunger if we were where no supplies could be had. It was a long struggle, but I finally learned never to drink between meals, as it is always difficult to get water on a march. I can remember being even mortified at dropping my whip, for I wished to be so little trouble that every one would be unconscious of my presence, so far as being an inconvenience was concerned. The cold of Dakota overcame me on that one day, but it was the last time I succumbed to it.

---

* It was afterwards recovered.

CHAPTER V.

CAMPING AMONG THE SIOUX.

OUR march took us through the grounds set apart by the Government for the use of the Sioux Indians at peace with our country. We had not made much progress before we began to see their graves. They do not bury their dead, but place them on boards lashed to the limbs of trees, or on high platforms raised from the ground by four poles perhaps twenty feet. The body is wound round and round with clothing or blankets, like a mummy, and inside the layers are placed fire-arms, tobacco, and jerked beef, to supply them on the imaginary journey to the happy hunting-grounds. In the early morning, when it was not quite light, as we filed by these solitary sepulchres, it was uncanny and weird, and the sun, when it came, was doubly welcome. Our first visitor from Agency Indians was Fool-dog, a Sioux chief. He was tall, commanding, and had really a fine face. When he was ready to go home he invited us to come to his village before we left on our next march. At twilight my husband and I walked over. The village was a collection of tepees of all sizes, the largest being what is called the Medicine Lodge, where the councils are held. It was formed of tanned buffalo-hides, sewed together with buckskin thongs, and

stretched over a collection of thirty-six poles. These
poles are of great value to the Indians, for in a sparsely
timbered country like Dakota it is difficult to find suitable trees. It is necessary to go a great distance to pro-
cure the kind of sapling that is light and pliable and
yet sufficiently strong for the purpose. The poles are
lashed together at the tops and radiate in a circle below.
The smoke was pouring out of the opening above, and
the only entrance to the tepee was a round aperture
near the ground, sufficiently large to allow a person to
crawl in. Around the lodge were poles from which
were suspended rags; in these were tied their medi-
cines of roots and herbs, supposed to be a charm to keep
off evil spirits. The sound of music came from within;
I crept tremblingly in after the general, not entirely
quieted by his keeping my hand in his, and whispering
something to calm my fears as I sat on the buffalo robe
beside him. In the first place, I knew how resolute the
Indians were in never admitting one of their own wom-
en to council, and their curious eyes and forbidding expressions towards me did not add to my comfort. The
dust, smoke, and noise in the fading light were not re-
assuring. Fool-dog arose from the circle of what composed their nobility, and solemnly shook hands with the
general; those next in rank followed his example.
The pipe was then smoked, and the general had to take
a whiff when it came his turn. Fortunately we escaped
the speeches, for we had not brought an interpreter.

Coming out of the light into this semi-darkness, with
the grotesque figures of the plebeians, as they danced
around their chiefs and contorted their bodies to the

sound of the Indian drum and minor notes of the singers, made it something unearthly in appearance; their painted faces, grunts and grins of serious mirth as they wheeled around the tepee, made me shiver. How relieved I felt when the final pipe was smoked and the good-bye said! The curious eyes of the squaws, who stood in the vicinity of the lodge, followed us, as they watched me clinging to the general's arm while we disappeared, in the direction of camp, through the thickening gloom.

As we went farther north the twilights became longer, and I was greatly deceived by having so much daylight. Every morning, when the reveille sounded, in attempting to obey its summons I found myself actually mystified from excessive drowsiness, and I announced my resolve to go to bed at dark—as was often my custom on previous marches—when I was informed that we had marched into a land where daylight continues into the night hours. The general, who was always looking at the curious effects in the heavens, delighted in the clearness of the atmosphere and the myriads of stars that seemed to far outnumber all we had ever seen in other skies. All the strange phenomena of northern climes revealed themselves to us day by day. The sun and moon dogs, the lunar rainbows, and sometimes three perfect arcs of brilliant color formed directly above us in the heavens as we made our day's march through spring showers. The storms came down in great belts of rain sometimes, and if the country were level enough we could look ahead on the plain and see where the storm was crossing. This enabled us to halt in time to escape a perfect sheet of pouring rain which fell like a wall of water directly before us. Once we found ourselves in the midst of it, and not knowing then the peculiarities of such storms, we took our drenching philosophically, and believed that it was like too many others that had kept us soaked to the skin for hours. Seeing the sun shining in advance on the plain, the general and I put spurs to our horses and rode out of the storm to perfectly dry ground. The sun came down on us so hotly that we were soon enveloped in a halo of steam from our drying clothes.

The history of one day's march was that of many; they were varied by small misfortunes over which we amused ourselves, but which were very serious affairs to the melancholy Ham. He had cooked by fireplaces in Kentucky, but never having lived out-doors before, he gained his experience by hard trials. The little sheet-iron cooking-stove which we considered such a treasure, was placed in the kitchen-tent on stormy nights, and the bit of pipe, put through a hole in the canvas, had an elbow so that it could be turned according to the direction of the wind.

One day, after camp was re-established, the general saw the smoke pouring out of the opening of the kitchen-tent, and hurried to see what was the matter. It was one of those days when the Dakota winds, like those of Kansas, blow in all directions; poor Ham was barely visible in the dense smoke inside the tent. "Why don't you turn the pipe?" the general called, above the tempest; and Ham shouted back, "Giniril, I did; see whar she's p'intin' now?" His master's sides shook with laughter, for sure enough the pipe would have been right if there had been any uniformity in the course of the wind. The general was hungry, but he did not stop to complain; he found a place somewhat sheltered, and digging a hole in the ground, taught the discouraged darkey how to build a fire outside. At last we sat down to a burned, smoky meal, and had to go to bed hungry.

Another day, when there was a small tornado, we began to wonder why dinner was delayed; we looked out, to find the cook-tent blown flat to the ground. The general ran to the rescue, and found Ham interred, as the old-time child stories buried their heroes, "in a pot of grease." He had been thrown among skillets and kettles, and the half-cooked dinner was scattered over him. The general helped him out, and was too much exhausted with laughter over the old fellow's exasperated remarks about "such a low-down country," to mind the delay of the dinner. Indeed, he soothed him by telling him to wait and begin again when the wind went down, as it usually does when the sun sets.

One day we caught sight of our American flag on the other side of the river, floating over a little group of buildings inside a stockade. When they told me that it was a military post, I could hardly believe it possible; it seemed that no spot could be more utterly desolate. Then I remembered having met an officer at Yankton who had told me that was his station. As I looked at his fine face and figure, I could not help thinking how thoroughly some woman would appreciate him. Thinking aloud, I said that I hoped he had "improved each shining hour " of his leave of absence, and was already engaged. He replied that I would see his post as we went up the river, and then might comprehend why he did not dare ask any woman to be his wife. I argued that if some girl grew fond of him, it would little matter to her where she went, if it were only by her husband's side. I confess, however, that when I saw that lonely place, I thought that it would require extraordinary devotion to follow him there. It was an infantry station, and the soldiers' barracks, officers' quarters, and storehouses were huddled together inside a wall made of logs placed perpendicularly and about fifteen feet high. The sand was so deep about this spot that nothing could be made to grow. Constant gusts of wind over the unprotected plain kept little clouds of fine alkaline dust whirling in the air and filling the eyes and mouth ; not a tree was near, as the Missouri—that most uncertain of rivers—kept constantly changing its channel, and the advancing water washed away great hollows in the banks. The post would then have to be moved farther back for safety. The soldiers would be obliged to take up the stockade, and bury the logs as deep as they could to keep them from blowing over. The frail buildings, " built upon the sand " rocked and swayed in the wind.

Beside the forlorn situation of this garrison, no one could go outside to ride or hunt without peril. The warlike Indians considered that side of the river theirs, and roamed up and down it at will. They came in cessantly to the small sliding panel in the gates of the stockade, and made demands, which, if not consented to, were followed by howls of rage and threatening gestures. All that the handful of men could do was to conciliate them as best they could. The company was not full, and possibly, all told, there were but fifty white men against hundreds of Indians. The only variety in their lives was the passing of an occasional steamer in the brief summer. Then settled down the pitiless winter, burying them in snow which never left the ground until late in the spring. The mail only reached them at irregular intervals. They were compelled to live almost entirely on commissary stores, for though living in the midst of game it was too hazardous to attempt to hunt. When we found that one regiment had been seven years on the river, and some of the officers had never taken leave of absence, it seems strange that any one stationed at such a post had not gone stark mad. It makes me proud of women when I recall the fact that the wife of an officer did live in that wretched little post afterwards, and did not complain. The cavalry, turning to look their last at that garrison, thanked the good-fortune that had placed them in a branch of the service where there was the active duty of campaigns to vary a life otherwise so monotonous.

The dogs had almost as hard a time to become accustomed to the vagaries of a Dakota climate as we did. We had to be their nurses and surgeons. In our large pack of hounds there were many that had marked individuality of character. Not many days could be passed in their company before we were noticing new peculiarities not previously observed. The general had a droll fashion, as we rode along, of putting words into their mouths when they got into trouble, fought among themselves, or tried to lord it over one another. One of them had been given us, and had been called by her former owner "Lucy Stone." In vain did we try, out of respect for the life of the useful woman for whom she was named, to rechristen the dog. She would neither listen nor obey if called anything else. I can see her now, sitting deliberately down in the road directly in front of us, and holding up a paw full of cactus thorns. The general would say, "There sits Lucy Stone, and she is saying, 'If you please, sir, since you chose to bring me into a land of bristling earth like this, will you please get down immediately and attend to my foot?'" Her howls and upturned eyes meant an appeal, certainly, and her master would leap to the ground, sit down in the road, and taking the old creature in his arms, begin the surgery. He carried one of those knives that had many adjuncts, and with the tweezers he worked tenderly and long to extract the tormenting cactus needles. Lucy was a complaining old dame, and when the general saw her sit down, like some fat old woman, he used to say that the old madam was telling him that she "would like to drive a bit, if you please." So it often happened that my travelling-wagon was the hospital for an ill or foot-sore dog. The general had to stop very often to attend to the wounded paws, but experience taught the dogs to make their way very skilfully where the cactus grew. A dancing-master, tripping the steps of instruction, could not have moved more lightly than did they. If there were no one near to whom they could appeal in the human way those dumb things have, they learned to draw out the offending thorns with their teeth.

While we were all getting accustomed to the new climate, it was of no use to try to keep the dogs out of my tent. They stood around, and eyed me with such reproachful looks if I attempted to tie up the entrance to the tent and leave them out. If it were very cold when I returned from the dining-tent, I found dogs under and on the camp-bed, and so thickly scattered over the floor that I had to step carefully over them to avoid hurting feet or tails. If I secured a place in the bed I was fortunate. Sometimes, when it had rained, and all of them were wet, I rebelled. The steam from their shaggy coats was stifling; but the general begged so hard for them that I taught myself to endure the air at last. I never questioned the right of the half-grown puppies to everything. Our struggles to raise them, and to avoid the distemper which goes so much harder with blooded than with cur dogs, endeared them to us. When I let the little ones in, it was really comical to hear my husband's arguments and cunningly-devised reasons why the older dogs should follow. A plea was put up for "the hound that had fits;" there was always another that "had been hurt in hunting;" and so on until the tent would hold no more. Fortunately, in pleasant weather, I was let off with only the ill or injured ones for perpetual companions. We were so surrounded with dogs when they were resting after the march, and they slept so soundly from fatigue, that it was difficult to walk about without stepping on them.

My favorite, a great cream-colored stag-hound, was

named "Cardigan." He never gave up trying to be my lap-dog. He was enormous, and yet seemingly unconscious of his size. He kept up a perpetual struggle and scramble on his hind-legs to get his whole body up on my lap. If I pieced myself out with a camp-stool to support him, he closed his eyes in a beatific state and sighed in content while I held him, until my foot went to sleep and I was cramped with his weight. One thing that made me so fond of him was that on one occasion, when he was put in the kennel after an absence, he was almost torn to pieces by the other dogs. He was a brave hound, but he was at fearful odds against so many. Great slices of flesh were torn from his sides, and gaping wounds made by the fang-like teeth showed through his shaggy coat. It was many months before they healed.

Though the stag-hound is gentle with human beings he is a terrible fighter. They stand on their hind-legs and, facing each other, claw and tear like demons. It was always necessary to watch them closely when a new dog, or one that they had not seen for some time, was put in their midst.

I will anticipate a moment and speak of the final fate of Cardigan. When I left Fort Lincoln I askèd some one to look out for his welfare, and send him, as soon as possible, to a clergyman who had been my husband's friend. My request was complied with, and afterwards, when the poor old dog died, his new master honored him by having his body set up by the taxidermist, and a place was given him in one of the public buildings in Minneapolis. I cannot help thinking that he was worthy of the tribute, not only because of the testimony thus given to the friendship of the people for his master, but because he was the bravest and most faithful of animals.

Most of the country passed over in our route belonged to the Indian Reservations, and the Government was endeavoring to teach the tribes settled there to cultivate the soil. They had hunted off most of the game; an occasional jack-rabbit, the plover, and a few wild ducks were all that were left. I must not forget the maddening curlew. It was not good eating, but it was always exciting to see one. There never was a more exasperating bird to shoot. Time and again a successful shot was prophesied, and I was called to be a witness, only to see finally the surprise of the general when the wily bird soared calmly away. I believe no person was able to bring one down during the entire trip.

As we approached an Indian village, the chiefs came out to receive us. There were many high-sounding words of welcome, translated by our guide, who, having lived among them many years, knew the different dialects. The Government had built some comfortable log-houses for them, in many of which I would have lived gladly. The Indians did not care for them, complaining that they had coughs if they occupied a house. A tepee was put up alongside, in which one or two families lived, while little low lodges, looking like the soldiers' shelter-tents, were used for the young men of the circle to sleep in. The tools and stores given by the Government were packed away in the otherwise empty houses.

CHAPTER VI.

A VISIT TO THE VILLAGE OF "TWO BEARS."

A SIOUX chief, called Two Bears, had the most picturesque village that we saw.   The lodges were placed
in a circle, as this was judged the most defensive position; the ponies were herded inside the enclosure at
night.   This precaution was necessary, for the neighboring tribes swept down on them after dark and ran off
the stock if they were not secured.   As we dismounted,
we saw an old man standing alone in the circle, apparently unconscious of everything, as he recounted some
war tale in loud, monotonous tones.   He had no listen-
ers—all were intently watching the approaching regiment; still the venerable Sioux went on as persistently
as if he were looking "upon a sea of upturned faces."
He was the "medicine-man," or oracle, of the tribe,
or possibly the "poet-laureate" of the village, for the
guide told us he sang of the deeds of valor of his people far back in history.

Just outside of the village, the chiefs sat in a circle
awaiting us.   Two Bears arose to welcome the general,
and asked him to go with him to his lodge.   I was asked
to go also and be presented to Miss Two Bears; for she
was too royal in birth to be permitted outside, and it
was not in keeping with the dignity of her rank to

mingle with the others, the guide afterwards explained to us.

The honor of going alone into the tepee was one that I could have foregone, for my courage was much greater if I did my Indian sight-seeing surrounded by the regiment. The general, fearing their *amour propre* might be offended if I declined the invitation, whispered an encouraging word, and we dipped our heads and crept into the tepee. The chief was a dignified old man, wrapped in his blanket, without the usual addition of some portion of citizen's dress which the Indians believe adds to their grandeur. His daughter also was in complete squaw's costume; her feet were moccasined, her legs and ankles wound round with beaded leggings, and she had on the one buckskin garment which never varies in cut through all the tribes. A blanket drawn over her head was belted at her waist. To crown all this, however, she had an open parasol, brought to her, doubtless, as a present by some Indian returning from a council at Washington. She held it with dignity, as if it might be to her as much an insignia of state as the mace of the lord-mayor.

Fortunately they did not ask us to sit down and partake of jerked beef, or to smoke the never-ending pipe, so we soon got through our compliments and returned to the outer entrance of the village.

Here the tribe were assembled, and evidently attired in gala-dress in our honor. We were most interested in the village belle, and the placid manner in which she permitted us to walk around her, gazing and talking her good points over, showed that she expected homage.

She sat on a scarlet blanket spread on the ground, and over her, stretched from poles, was another for an awning. She was loaded with ornaments, row after row of beads about her neck, broad armlets and anklets of brass, pinchbeck rings, and a soft buckskin dress and leggings, heavily embroidered. Her ears were pierced twice—on the side as well as in the lobe—and from these holes were suspended circles of gilt. Her bright eyes, the satin smoothness of her hair, and the clear brown of the skin made a pretty picture. There was no attempt to blend into the brown the bright patch of car-mine on each cheek.

Only extreme youth and its ever attractive charms can make one forget the heavy square shape of Indian faces and their coarse features. It was surprising to see all the other squaws giving up the field to this one so completely. They crouched near, with a sort of "every-dog-must-have-its-day" look, and did not even dispute her sway by making coy eyes as we spoke to them.

There were but few young men. Their absence was always excused by the same reason—they were out hunting. We knew how little game there was, and surmised —what we afterwards found to be true—that they had joined the hostile tribes, and only came in to the distribution of supplies and presents in the fall. A few rods from the village a tripod of poles was set in the ground, and lashed to it the Indian's shield, made of the hide of the buffalo where it is thickest about the neck. There were rude paintings and Indian hieroglyphics covering it. The shield is an heirloom with the Indian, and the one selected to hang out in this manner has always the greatest war record. One of their superstitions is that it keeps away enemies. These nomads had some idea of luxury, for I recollect seeing some of them reclining on a kind of rest made of a framework of pliable rods, over which was stretched buckskin. Afterwards I found how comfortable such contrivances were, for one was given me. The slope is so gradual that you half recline and can read with great ease.

When we had reached camp and were taking our afternoon siesta the same day, with the tent walls raised for air, we were roused by the sound of music. Looking off over the bluffs we saw a large body of Indians approaching on ponies, while squaws and children ran beside them. It was the prompt response of Two Bears to the general's invitation to return his call. The warriors stopped near camp, and dismounting advanced towards us. The squaws unbridled and picketed the ponies, and made themselves comfortable by arranging impromptu shades of the bright blankets. They staked down two corners closely to the ground, and propped up the others with poles stuck in the sod.

When the Indians came up to us, the council was, as usual, begun. The pipe being smoked, Two Bears gave us a eulogy of himself. He then demanded, in behalf of the tribe, payment for the use of the ground on which we were encamped, and also for the grass consumed, though it was too short to get more than an occasional tuft. He ended, as they all do, with a request for food. The general in reply vaguely referred them to the Great Father in payment for the use of their land, but presented them with a beef in return for their hospitality.

Only half satisfied, they stalked away one by one. We watched them at a distance kill and divide the beef. It surprised us to see how they despatched it, and that hardly a vestige of it was left.

Many of the Indians coming from reservations carried papers which they valued and carefully guarded. After burrowing under robe and shirt, something was produced wrapped in layers of soiled cotton cloth. It was a recommendation of them obtained from some officer or Indian agent. This was presented on entering, as their letter of introduction. Most of these papers read very much the same way. Giving the Indian's name, it stated that he had been living on the reservation for a certain length of time, that he was friendly to the whites, etc.

One of our guests that day carried something a little different. He was called "Medicine Jo." Lingering behind the rest, he presented his letter with perfect good faith and great pomposity. Some wag had composed it, and it read something like this:

"Medicine Jo says he is a good Indian, that you can trust him. If he is, he is the first I have ever seen, and in my opinion he, like all the rest, will bear watching."

It was all the general could do to keep his face straight as he handed back to the unconscious owner this little libel on himself.

The interpreter kept constantly before us the fine post that we were approaching, and the last day before we reached there it was visible for a long distance. The atmosphere of Dakota was so deceptive that we imagined ourselves within a few miles of the garrison, when, in reality, there was a march of twenty-nine long miles before us.

Our road led up from the river valley on the high bluffs, and sometimes followed along the backbone of hills from which on either side we looked down a great distance. There was barely room for the travelling-wagon. Occasionally I had been obliged to take refuge from the cold for a little while and drive. Our lead-mules were tiny, quick-moving little dots, and I soon discovered that they were completely demoralized at the sight of an Indian. They could see one in advance long before the driver could. A sudden shying and quick turning of these agile little brutes, a general tangle of themselves in the harness and legs of the wheelers, loud shouts of the driver, and a quick downfall of his foot on the brake, to keep us from overturning, made an exciting *mêlée*.

Nothing would get them righted and started again. They would have to be unharnessed, and the rebellious pair tied to the rear of the wagon until we had gone far beyond the object of terror. Part of the day that we were following the wanderings of the road alongside hills and over the narrow, smooth level of the hill-tops, I was compelled to drive, and I watched anxiously the ears of these wretched little beasts to see if they expressed any sentiment of fright. We came to such steep descents, the brake holding the wheels seemed of no use. Looking down from the wagon on to the mules below us, we appeared to be in the position of flies on a wall.

As we came to one descent more awful than the rest, the general, who was always near, rode up to the carriage and told me not to be afraid, for he would order the wheels manned. The head-quarters escort of over a hundred men, dismounting, attached ropes to the wheels, and held on with all their strength while I went down the steepest declivity I had ever descended. After that I begged to get out, and the general carried me to a bank and set me down where I could watch the repairing of the road.

He took off his coat and joined the soldiers in carrying logs and shovelling earth, for they were obliged to fill up the soft bed of the stream before the command could cross. It took a long time and much patience; but the general enjoyed it all, and often helped when the crossings needed to be prepared. When the logs were all laid, I had to laugh at the energy he showed in cracking a whip he borrowed from a teamster, and shouting to the mules to urge them to pull through where there was danger of their stalling. When the road was completed, I was ready to mount my horse, for it seemed to me preferable to die from accident, surrounded with friends, than to expire alone in the mule-wagon. The ascent was rendered so wet and slippery, the general feared my saddle would turn, and I was once more shut in by myself. The soldiers again manned the wheels to prevent the carriage sliding back, the mules scrambled, and with the aid of language prepared expressly for them, we reached the summit.

The driver had named the lead-mules Bettie and Jane, and when they were over their tempers he petted and caressed them. Their repeated rebellion at last wore out even his patience. One morning I noticed new leaders, but the imperturbable face of the driver gave no hint of his successful plotting. Mary told me, however, that he was worn out with his struggles, and had gone after dark into the herd of mules with Bettie and Jane, and, as he expressed it, "lost them." He selected two more from among those belonging to the wagon-train, and returned triumphant over his premeditated exchange. He carefully reclipped their manes and tails, and disguised them still further with blotches of black paint, to give them a mottled appearance. When the other teamster prepared to harness in the morning, of course he discovered the fraud perpetrated on him. There was no redress then, and he had to take out his wrath in language more forcible than elegant, which the teamsters have adapted expressly for extreme occasions. Our driver told Mary, with a chuckle, that with a command of many hundred men waiting for a teamster to harness, he found "no time for swapping horses."

Burkman, the soldier who took care of our horses, was a middle-aged man, so deliberate in speech and slow in his movements, he seemed as incongruous among the spirited cavalrymen as would be an old-time farmer. Early in the march I had heard him coughing as he groomed the horses. When I asked if he had done anything for his cold, he replied, "Bottle after bottle of stuff, mum, but it don't do no good," so I begged the surgeon to look more carefully into his case. He made an examination, and told me, as the result, that the man

must have only light work and nourishing food. After
that I asked Mary to save everything for Burkman and
make his recovery her especial care. The officers made
fun of me, as they were rather incredulous, and thought
a bit of shamming was being practised on me, but I knew
better. They never failed to comment and smile when
they saw the old defender of his country coming out of
the kitchen-tent, his jaws working and his mouth full,
while he carried all the food his hands would hold. To
tell the truth, he kept up this prescription of nourishing
food long after he had quite recovered.

It became the delight of my husband and the officers
to chaff me about "Old Nutriment," for such was the
sobriquet they gave him. At last, even Mary began
to narrate how he swept everything before him with
voracious, convalescing appetite. "Why, Miss Libbie,"
she said to me one day, "I thought I'd try him with a
can of raw tomatoes, and set them before him, asking
if he was fond of them. And he just drawled out,
'*Always was*,' and the tomatoes were gone in no time."
His laconic answer passed into a proverb with us all,
when invited to partake of anything we liked.

Such a tender heart as that old soldier had! I
had noticed this first in Kentucky. My horse, which I
prized above all that I have ever ridden, died during
my temporary absence from home. I was too greatly
grieved to ask many questions about him, but one day,
some time afterwards, when we were riding through a
charming bit of country, Burkman approached me from
the place where he usually rode behind us, and said,
" I'd like to tell Mrs. Custer there's whar poor Phil lies.

I picked the purtiest place I could find for him." And he had indeed, for the green valley under wide-spreading trees would have gone far to reconcile many a weary human heart to be placed under the sod.

We thought we had made the first step towards savage life when Burkman brought the mother of the one baby of our regiment the dried vertebra of a rattlesnake that he killed, because he had heard that it was the best of anything on which the infant could cut its teeth!

I had made some scarlet flannel shirts for my husband's use on the summer campaign, and he was as much pleased as possible, beginning at once to wear them. Not many days' march proved to me what an error I had made. The bright red color could be seen for miles, when the form itself was almost lost on the horizon. I had to coax to get them away again and replace them with the dark blue that he usually wore. Though I triumphed, I was met with a perfect fusillade of teasing when I presented the red shirts to Burkman. The officers, of course, hearing all the discussion over the subject—as no trifle was too small to interest us in one another's affairs—attacked me at once. If I had been so anxious to protect the general from wearing anything that would attract the far-seeing eye of the vigilant Indian on the coming campaign, why should I be so willing to sacrifice the life of "Old Nutriment?" They made no impression on me, however, for they knew as well as I did that the soldier, though so faithful, was not made of that stuff that seeks to lead a Balaklava charge.

My husband and I were so attached to him, and appreciated so deeply his fidelity, we could not thank the good-fortune enough that gave us one so loyal to our interests.

Before we reached the post we were approaching, the commandant sent out ice for our use, and the despatches of the Associated Press. The general was greatly delighted to get news of events that had occurred all over the world, in this far distant land. We found afterwards that the officers joined in paying for the despatches. The Indians had such a superstition about molesting the wires, that the lines ran through even the most dangerous country. I can hardly say how good it seemed to us to see a telegraph-pole again.

We were not surprised, after seeing the other posts below on the river, that the guide had praised Fort Sully. It was the head-quarters of one of the infantry regiments, and the commanding officer had been at the post long enough to put it in excellent order. It was situated on an open plateau, from which there was an extensive view. Below in the valley the companies had gardens, and they also kept cows, pigs, and chickens. We looked upon all this as an El Dorado, and the thought of remaining long enough at one fort to get any good out of a garden was simply unknown in our vagrant existence.

Our camp was very near the post, on the same open plain, without trees or shelter. We were received with genuine hospitality, and finally all of us invited to luncheon. The ladies came up from the steamer, and the large house was filled with happy people. The post band played outside on the parade-ground while we lunched. We had nine kinds of game on the table. Some of it was new to us—the beaver tail, for instance —but it was so like pork and so fat I could only taste it. We had, in addition, antelope, elk, buffalo tongue, wild turkey, black-tailed deer, wild goose, plover, and duck. The goose was a sort of "fatted calf" for us. The soldiers had caught it while young, and by constantly clipping its wings, had kept it from joining the flocks which its cries often brought circling around the post. At last it began to make the life of the chickens a burden to them, and we arrived in time to enjoy the delicious bird served with jelly made from the tart, wild "bullberries" that grew near the river. The home-made bread, delightful cake, tender ham of the garrison's own curing, and the sweets made with cream, fresh butter, and eggs—three unheard-of luxuries with us—proved that it is possible for army people to live in comfort if they do not belong to a mounted regiment. Still, though they had a band and a good library belonging to the regiment, the thought of being walled in with snow, and completely isolated for eight months of the year, made me shudder. The post was midway between Yankton and Bismarck, each the termination of a railroad, and each two hundred and fifty miles away.

The wife of the commanding officer was known throughout the department for her lovely Christian character, and the contented life she led under all circumstances. I was much amused at her account of her repeated trials in trying to secure a permanent governess. She said all the posts along the river seemed to know intuitively when a new one arrived from the East. The young officers found more imperative duties calling them to Fort Sully than they had dreamed of in a year. Before long the governess began to be abstracted, and watch longingly for the mails. A ring would next appear on the significant first finger, and be the forerunner of a request to allow her to resign her place. This had happened four times when I met our hostess, and though she was glad to furnish the officers with wives, she rather sighed for a woman who, though possessing every accomplishment, might still be so antiquated and ugly that she could be sure to keep her for a time at least.

The commandant had some fine greyhounds, and joining the general with his packs of stag and fox hounds, they had several hunts in the few days that remained. Of course, after so bright a visit and such a feast, it was hard to begin again on the march with baking-powder biscuit and tough beef. The cattle that supplied us with meat were driven along on the march, and killed every other day, and could not be expected to be in very good condition. The interest of our journey, however, made us soon forget all deprivations. Grateful sentiments towards those who had been so kind to us as strangers remained as a memory.

CHAPTER VII.

ADVENTURES DURING THE LAST DAYS OF THE MARCH.

My husband and I kept up our little *détours* by ourselves as we neared the hour for camping each day. One day one of the officers accompanied us. We left the higher ground to go down by the water and have the luxury of wandering through the cottonwood-trees that sometimes fringed the river for several miles. As usual, we had a number of dogs leaping and racing around us. Two of them started a deer, and the general bounded after them, encouraging the others with his voice to follow. He had left his friend with me, and we rode leisurely along to see that the younger dogs did not get lost. Without the least warning, in the dead stillness of that desolate spot, we suddenly came upon a group of young Indian warriors seated in their motionless way in the underbrush. I became perfectly cold and numb with terror. My danger in connection with the Indians was twofold. I was in peril from death or capture by the savages, and liable to be killed by my own friends to prevent my capture. During the five years I had been with the regiment in Kansas I had marched many hundred miles. Sometimes I had to join my husband going across a dangerous country, and the exposure from Indians all those years had been constant. I had been a subject of conversation among the officers, being the only woman who, as a rule, followed the regiment, and, without discussing it much in my presence, the universal understanding was that any one having me in charge in an emergency where there was imminent danger of my capture should shoot me instantly. While I knew that I was defended by strong hands and brave hearts, the thought of the double danger always flashed into my mind when we were in jeopardy.

If time could have been measured by sensations, a cycle seemed to have passed in those few seconds. The Indians snatched up their guns, leaped upon their ponies, and prepared for attack. The officer with me was perfectly calm, spoke to them coolly without a change of voice, and rode quickly beside me, telling me to advance. My horse reared violently at first sight of the Indians, and started to run. Gladly would I have put him to his mettle then, except for the instinct of obedience, which any one following a regiment acquires in all that pertains to military directions. The general was just visible ascending a bluff beyond. To avoid showing fear when every nerve is strung to its utmost, and your heart leaps into your throat, requires superhuman effort. I managed to check my horse and did not scream. No amount of telling over to myself what I had been told, that all the tribes on this side were peaceable and that only those on the other side of the river were warlike, could quell the throbbing of my pulses. Indians were Indians to me, and I knew well that it was a matter of no time to cross and recross on their little tub-like boats that shoot madly down the tide.

What made me sure that these warriors whom we had just met were from the fighting bands was the recollection of some significant signs we had come upon in the road a few days previous. Stakes had been set in the ground, with bits of red flannel fastened on them peculiarly. This, the guide explained, meant warnings from the tribes at war to frighten us from any further advance into their country. Whether because of the coolness of the officer, or because the warriors knew of the size of the advancing column, we were allowed to proceed unharmed. How interminable the distance seemed to where the general awaited us, unconscious of what we had encountered! I was lifted out of the saddle a very limp and unconscious thing.

Encouraged by references to other dangers I had lived through without flinching, I mounted again and followed the leader closely. He took us through some rough country, where the ambitious horses, finding that by bending their heads they could squeeze through, forgot to seek openings high enough to admit those sitting in the saddle. We crashed through underbrush, and I, with habit torn and hands scratched, was sometimes almost lifted up, Absalom-like, by the resisting branches. Often we had no path, and the general's horse, "Vic," would start straight up steep banks after we had forded streams. It never occurred to his rider, until after the ascent was made, and a faint voice arose from the valley, that all horses would not do willingly what his thorough-bred did. He finally turned to look back and tell me how to manage my horse.   I abandoned the bridle when we came to those ascents, and wound my hands in the horse's mane to keep from sliding entirely off, while the animal took his own way.   All this was such variety and excitement I was delighted, and forgot my terror of the morning.

We found a bit of lovely road, which only those who go hundreds of miles under a blazing sun can appreciate fully.   The sunshine came flickering down through the branches of the trees and covered the short grass with checkered light and shade.   Here we dawdled, and enjoyed looking up at the patches of blue sky through great grown-up tree-tops.   It was like a bit of woods at home, where I never thought to be grateful for foliage, but took it as a matter of course.   My husband remembered my having put some biscuit in the leather pocket on my saddle, and invited himself to luncheon at once. We dismounted, and threw ourselves on the ground to eat the very frugal fare.

After resting, we gave ourselves the privilege of a swift gallop over the stretch of smooth ground before us.   We were laughing and talking so busily I never noticed the surroundings until I found we were almost in the midst of an Indian village, quite hidden under a bluff.   My heart literally stood still.   I watched the general furtively.   He was as usual perfectly unmoved, and yet he well knew that this was the country where it was hardly considered that the Indian was overburdened with hospitality.   Oh, how I wished ourselves safely with the column, now so far away!   There were but few occupants of the village, but they glowered and growled, and I could see the venomous glances they cast on us as I meekly followed. I trembled so I could barely keep my seat as we slowly advanced, for the general even slackened his speed, to demonstrate to them, I suppose, that we felt ourselves perfectly at home. He said "How," of course, which was his usual salutation to them. An echoing "how" beside him proved that I still had power of utterance. When we came to one Indian, who looked menacingly at us and doggedly stood in our road, the officer with us declared that I accompanied my "how" with a salaam so deep that it bent my head down to the pommel of my saddle! At all events, I meant, if politeness would propitiate, not to be deficient in that quality at such a critical moment.

In a few moments, which seemed however a lifetime, we saw the reason why the village appeared so empty. Men, women, and children had gone nearly to the top of the bluff, and there, with their bodies hidden, were looking off at a faint cloud of dust in the distance.

My husband, appreciating my terror, quickly assured me it was the 7th Cavalry. Even then, what a stretch of country it seemed between us and that blessed veil of sand, through which we perceived dimly that succor was at hand.

My horse was rather given to snuggling, and pressed so against the general that he made his leg very uncomfortable sometimes. But then, in my terror, it seemed to me an ocean of space was dividing us. I longed for the old Puritan days, when a wife rode on a pillion behind her liege as a matter of course.

I found courage to look back at last. The bluff was crowned with little irregularities, so still they seemed like tufts of grass or stones. They represented many pairs of bead-like eyes, that peered over the country at the advancing troops.

The next day the general thought I might rather not go with him than run the risk of such frights; but I well knew there was something far worse than fears for my own personal safety. It is infinitely worse to be left behind, a prey to all the horrors of imagining what may be happening to one we love. You eat your heart slowly out with anxiety, and to endure such suspense is simply the hardest of all trials that come to the soldier's wife.

I gladly consented to be taken along every day, but there never seemed a time when it was not necessary to get accustomed to some new terror. However, it is only the getting used to it that is so bad. It is the unexpected things that require fresh relays of courage. When a woman has come out of danger, she is too utterly a coward by nature not to dread enduring the same thing again; but it is something to know that she is equal to it. Though she may tremble and grow faint in anticipation, having once been through it, she can count on rising to the situation when the hour actually comes.

The rattlesnakes were so numerous on this march that all Texas and Kansas experience seemed to dwarf in contrast. My horse was over sixteen hands high, but I would gladly have exchanged him for a camelopard when I rode suddenly almost upon a snake coiled in the grass, and looked down into the eyes of the upraised head. We counted those we encountered in one day's journey until we were tired. The men became very expert and systematic in clearing the camp of these reptiles. If we halted at night in the underbrush, they cut and tore away the reeds and grass, and began at once to beat the ground and kill the snakes. When I say that as many as forty were killed in one night, some literal person may ask if I actually saw the bodies of all those "lately slain!" It is not an exaggerated story, however, and one only needs to see hundreds of men pounding and clearing such a place to realize that many snakes could be disposed of in a short time. After that, when the ground was selected for our camp in the low part of the valley, I was loath to lie down and sleep until the soldiers had come up to prepare the ground. My husband used to indulge this little prejudice of mine against making my head a reproduction of Medusa's, and we often sought the high ground for a rest until the command came up.

The guide rode often at the head of the column, and we found him full of information about the country. We began also to listen for a new domestic disclosure every time we approached an Indian village. He was the most married of any man I ever saw, for in every tribe he had a wife. Still this superfluity did not burden him, for the ceremony of tying a marital knot in the far West is simple, and the wives support themselves. Sometimes he gave us new points about making ourselves comfortable in camp. One day I was very grateful to him. We were far in advance of the wagon-train containing the tents; the sun was scorching; not a tree, nor even a clump of bushes was near. In a brief time, however, the guide had returned from the stream, where he had cut some willow saplings, and sticking them in the ground made what he called "wik-a-up." He wove the ends loosely together on top, and over this oval cover he threw the saddle blankets. There was just room enough to crawl into this oven-like place, but it was an escape from the heat of the sun, and I was soon asleep. After I emerged the general took my place. When he had taken his nap the dogs crept in ; so a very grateful family thanked the guide for teaching us that new device.

The bends in the Missouri River are sometimes so long that the steamer with supplies would have to make a journey of sixty miles while we had perhaps only five to march across the peninsula. All the soldiers, officers' servants, teamsters, and other citizen employés took that time to wash their clothes, for we were two days in camp. The creek on which we halted was lined with bending figures, their arms moving vigorously back and forth as they wrung out each article. Later on the camp looked like an animated laundry. From every tent-rope and bush floated the apparel. I had only a small valise for my summer's outfit, but Mary had soon taken out our few things, and around the kitchen-tent was suspended the family linen. As soon as this was dry she folded and pressed it as best she could, and laid it between the mattresses as a substitute for ironing.

All the way up the river the guide was constantly interviewed as to the chances for fishing. He held out promises that were to be realized upon reaching Choteau Creek. We arrived there on one of the resting-days, and camp was no sooner made, and food and water brought, than a great exodus took place.

The general called me to the tent-door to see the deserted camp, and wondered how the soldiers could all have disappeared so quickly. Another problem was, where the fishing-tackle came from! Some had brought rods, even in the restricted space allotted them, but many cut them from the bushes along the river, attaching hooks and lines, while some bent pins and tied them to strings. The soldiers shared so generously with one another that one pole was loaned about while the idle ones watched. I never cared for fishing, but my husband begged me to go with him always, and carried my book and work. I sat under a bush near him, which he covered with a shawl to protect me from the sun, and there we stayed for hours. Officers and men competed alike for the best places by the quiet pools. The general could hardly pay attention to his line, he was so interested watching the men and enjoying their pleasure. His keen sense of the ludicrous took in the comical figures as far as we could see. In cramped and uncomfortable positions, with earnest eyes fixed steadily in one place for hours, they nearly fell into the water with excitement if they chanced to draw out a tiny fish. The other men came from all along the bank to observe if any one was successful.

One of the men near us was a member of the band. He was a perfect reproduction of the old prints of Izaak Walton. The fixedness of his gaze—his whole soul in his eyes—while he was utterly unconscious of any one being near, was too much for the general's equanimity.

He put his head under the canopy made by my shawl, not daring to laugh aloud, for fear he might be heard by the man, and said it was more fun to see that soldier fish than to hear him play on the violin.   No wonder the men enjoyed the sport, for even these little bull-fish, fairly gritty from the muddy water in which they lived, were a great addition to their pork and hard-tack fare.

For once the sun overcame me, and I knew the ignominy of being compelled to own that I was dizzy and faint.   I had not been long in military life before I was as much ashamed of being ill as if I had been a real soldier.   The troops pride themselves on being invulnerable to bodily ailments.   I was obliged to submit to being helped back to camp, and in the cool of the evening watched the return of the fishers, who were as proud of the strings of ugly little things they carried as if they had been pickerel or bass.   Then the blue flame and soft smoke began to ascend from the evening fires, and the odor from the frying supper rose on the air.

In my indolent, weak condition I never knew how I was able to perform such agile pirouettes as I did; but hearing a peculiar sound, I looked down and saw a huge rattlesnake gliding towards me.   I had long ago learned to suppress shrieks, but I forgot all such self-control then.   How I wished myself the Indian baby we had seen the day before—the veritable "baby in the tree-top," for it was tied by buckskin thongs to a limb! There I thought I could rest in peace.   The snake was soon despatched.   The men had left camp so hurriedly in the morning that the usual beating of the ground was omitted, and so I had this unwelcome visitor.

When we camped near a village, the Indians soon appeared. Groups of half a dozen on ponies, with children running after, would come. The ponies were, most of them, dull and sway-backed. It was no wonder, for I have seen four persons on one pony—an Indian and three half-grown boys. No horse could keep its shape loaded down, as those of the Indians usually are, with game and property. These visitors grew to be great trials, for they were inveterate beggars. One day an old Indian, called "The-Man-with-the-Broken-Ear," came riding in, elaborately decorated and on a shapely pony. He demanded to see the chief. The general appeared, assisted him to dismount, and seated him in my camp-chair. The savage leaned back in a grand sort of manner and calmly surveyed us all. I was soon in agonies of anxiety, for Colonel Tom and the young officers lounging near entered the tent. They bowed low, took the hand of the old fellow with profound deference, and, smiling benignly, addressed him. In just as suave a voice as if their words had been genuine flattery, they said, "You confounded old galoot, why are you here begging and thieving, when your wretched old hands are hardly dry from some murder, and your miserable mouth still red from eating the heart of your enemy?" Each one saluted him, and each vied with the other in pouring forth a tirade of forcible expletives, to which he bowed in acknowledgment and shook hands. My terror was that he might understand, for we often found these people as cunning as foxes, sitting stolid and stupid, pretending not to know a word, while they understood the gist of much that was said.

The officers gave this chief tobacco—Perique I think it is called—and so strong that, though I was accustomed to all kinds, I rather avoided the odor of it. We had no whiskey, but if we had kept it, the general obeyed the law of the reservation too strictly to allow it to be given away. He was called to the office-tent a few moments, and in a trice one of the others had emptied the alcohol from the spirit-lamp and offered the cup to the distinguished guest. Putting the great square of Perique into his mouth, with a biscuit beside, he washed it all down with gulps of the burning fluid. His eyes, heretofore dull, sparkled at the sight of the fire-water. The officers said, "How," and he replied, "How." This did not surprise me, for that one word is the Indian toast, and all tribes know it. But my breath almost went out of my body when they asked him if he would have more, and he replied, "You bet." I was sure then that he had understood all the railing speeches and that he would plan a revenge. Loud cries of laughter greeted his reply; but matching their cunning against his, they eventually found that he knew no more English. He had learned these words, without understanding their meaning, at the trader's store on the reservation. He waited around in the tent, hoping for more alcohol, until I was weary of the sight of him; but I was too much afraid of him, limp as he then was, to look bored.

Finally he was lifted out, a tumbled up, disorganized heap of drooping feathers, trailing blanket, and demoralized legs. When once, however, one drunken old foot was lifted over the pony for him, he swung himself into the saddle, and though swaying uncertainly, he managed to ride away.

During the last days of our march we came upon another premonitory warning from the Indians. A pole was found stuck in the trail before us, with a red flag, to which were fastened locks of hair. It was a challenge, and when interpreted meant, that if we persisted in advancing, the hostiles were ready to meet the soldiers and fight them. The officers paid little attention to this, but my heart was like lead for days afterwards.

We encamped that night near what the Indians call "Medicine Rock;" my husband and I walked out to see it. It was a large stone, showing on the flat surface the impress of hands and feet made ages ago, before the clay was petrified. The Indians had tied bags of their herb medicine on poles about the rock, believing that virtue would enter into articles left in the vicinity of this proof of the marvels or miracles of the Great Spirit. Tin cans, spoons, and forks, that they had bought at the Agency, on account of the brightness of the metal, were left there as offerings to an unseen God.

Everything pertaining to the Indians was new and interesting to me. While we were in Kansas the tribes were at war, and we had not the opportunity to see their daily life as we did while passing through the Sioux reservations on the march.

I regretted each day that brought us nearer to the conclusion of our journey, for though I had been frightened by Indians, and though we had encountered cold, storms, and rough life, the pleasures of the trip overbalanced the discomforts.

CHAPTER VIII.

SEPARATION AND REUNION.

The day at last came for our march of five hundred miles to terminate. A rickety old ferryboat that took us over the river made a halt near Fort Rice, and there we established ourselves. Strange to say, the river was no narrower there than it was so many hundred miles below, where we started. Muddy and full of sand-bars as it was, we began bravely to drink the water, when the glass had been filled long enough for the sediment partially to settle, and to take our bath in what at first seemed liquid mud. We learned after a time to settle the water with alum, and we finally became accustomed to the taste.

The commandant at Fort Rice was most hospitable, and his wife charming. The quarters were very ordinary frame buildings, with no modern improvements. They were painted a funereal tint, but one warranted to last. The interior showed the presence of a tasteful woman. She met us as cheerfully as if she were in the luxurious home from which we knew she had gone as a girl to follow a soldier's life. Contrast often helps us to endure, and Dakota was not so bad as their last station in Arizona. The dinner was excellent, and our entertainers were the happy possessors of a good cook.

Rarely do army people have two good servants at the same time on the frontier. Our host and hostess made no apologies, but quietly waited on the table themselves, and a merry time we had over the blunders of the head of the house, who was a distinguished general, in his endeavors to find necessary dishes in the china closet.

A steamer that arrived a day or two after we had reached Fort Rice brought the regimental property, consisting of everything that was not used on the march. Our household effects and trunks were delivered to us in a very sorry condition. They had been carelessly stored on the wharf at Yankton, near the government warehouse, without any covering, during all the storms that drenched us coming up the river. Almost everything was mildewed and ruined. We tried to dry our clothing in the sun. Many a little bit of silken finery that we had cherished since our marriage days, feeling sure that we should never attain to such grandeur again, was suspended from the tent-ropes, stained and dull. Our sister's husband helped her to unpack her clothes and his own soaked uniform. He was dignified and reserved by nature, but on that occasion the barriers were broken. I heard him ask Margaret to excuse him while he went outside the tent to make some remarks to himself that he felt the occasion demanded. There were furious people on all sides, and savage speeches about the thoughtlessness of those who had left our property exposed to snow and rain, when we were no longer there to care for it. I endured everything until my pretty wedding-dress was taken out, crushed and spotted

with mildew. My husband had great control over himself in the small annoyances of life, and was able to repeat again the proverb he had adopted in his boyhood,
"Never cry for spilled milk."   How he could submit
so quietly, when he took out his prized books and the
few pictures I knew that he valued, was a mystery.

All thought began now to centre on the coming events
of the summer.   It was decided that the regiment was
to go out to guard the engineers of the Northern Pacific
Railroad while they surveyed the route from Bismarck
to the Yellowstone River.   The ladies necessarily were
to be left behind.   Now began the summer of my dis-
content.   I longed to remain in Dakota, for I knew it
would take much longer for our letters to reach us if
we went East.   Besides, it was far more comforting to
stay at a military post, where every one was interested
in the expedition, and talked about it as the chief topic
of concern.   I remembered when I had gone East before, during a summer when our regiment was fighting
Indians, and my idea was that the whole country would
be almost as absorbed as we were, how shocked I was
to be asked, when I spoke of the regiment, "Ah, is there
a campaign, and for what purpose has it gone out?"

I was willing to live in a tent alone at the post, but
there were not even tents to be had.   Then we all
looked with envious eyes at the quarters at Fort Rice.
The post was small, and there were no vacant rooms except in the bachelor quarters.   These are so called when
the unmarried men take rooms in the same house and
mess together.   No opportunity was given us to wheedle
them into offering us a place.   Our officers hinted to

them, but they seemed to be completely intimidated regarding women. They received an honest and emphatic "no" when they asked if the ladies of the 7th Cavalry quarrelled. Even then these wary men said "they did not dare to offer to take in any women." They added that there were but three in the post, and no two of them spoke to each other. They thought if we were asked to remain it might be the history of the Kilkenny cats repeated, and they were obdurate.

There was nothing left for us, then, but to go home. It was a sore disappointment. We were put on the steamer that was to take us to Bismarck, a heart-broken little group. I hated Dakota, the ugly river, and even my native land. We were nearly devoured with mosquitoes at once. Only the strongest ammonia on our faces and hands served to alleviate the torment. The journey was wretchedness itself. I had thrown myself on the berth in one of the little suffocating state-rooms, exhausted with weeping, and too utterly overcome with the anguish of parting to know much of the surroundings. I was roused by the gentle hand of a woman, who had forgotten her own troubles to come to me. Ah, even now, when the tears rain down my face at the remembrance of those agonizing good-byes, which were like death each time, and which grew harder with each separation, I think of the sympathy shown me. The sweet, tender eyes of the wives of officers come to me now, and I feel the soft touch of their hands as they came to comfort me, even when their own hearts were wrung. Grief is so selfish, I wonder now that they could have been such ministering angels.

At last the slow, wearisome journey was over, and we went into the little town of Bismarck to take the cars. The Department Commander, returning to his head-quarters, had offered to take charge of us to St. Paul, and was kind enough to share with us the car of the President of the Northern Pacific Railroad, which had been placed at his disposal. There were seven of us and his own personal staff. Another five hundred miles were before us, but in such luxury it hardly seemed that my sister and I were the same two who had been "roughing it" on the march a few days before.

The journey was very quiet and over an uninteresting country, but we ladies had something to occupy our time, as we began to prepare some of our meals, for the untidy eating-houses on the road were almost unendurable. The staff of the Commanding General went out at the stations and foraged for what food they could find to add to our bill of fare. At St. Paul we bade them all good-bye, and soon found ourselves welcomed by dear father and mother Custer, at Monroe. Their hearts were ever with the absent ones.

For several slow, irksome months I did little else than wait for the tardy mails, and count each day that passed a gain. I had very interesting letters from my husband, sometimes thirty and forty pages in length. He wrote of his delight at having again his whole regiment with him, his interest in the country, his hunting exploits, and the renewal of his friendship with General Rosser. The 7th Cavalry were sent out to guard the engineers of the Northern Pacific, while they surveyed the route to the Yellowstone. This party

of citizens joined the command a few days out from
Fort Rice. The general wrote me that he was lying
on the buffalo-robe in his tent, resting after the march,
when he heard a voice outside asking the sentinel which
was General Custer's tent. The general called out,
"Halloo, old fellow! I haven't heard that voice in
thirteen years, but I know it. Come in and welcome!"

General Rosser walked in, and such a reunion as they
had! These two had been classmates and warm friends
at West Point, and parted with sorrow when General
Rosser went into the Southern army. Afterwards they
had fought each other in the Shenandoah Valley time
and time again. Both of them lay on the robe for
hours talking over the campaigns in Virginia. In the
varying fortunes of war, sometimes one had got possession of the wagon-train belonging to the other. I knew
of several occasions when they had captured each other's head-quarters wagons with the private luggage. If
one drove the other back in retreat, before he went into
camp he wrote a note addressing the other as "dear
friend," and saying, "you may have made me take a
few steps this way to-day, but I'll be even with you to-
morrow. Please accept my good-wishes and this little
gift." These notes and presents were left at the house
of some Southern woman, as they retreated out of the
village.

Once General Custer took all of his friend's luggage,
and found in it a new uniform coat of Confederate
gray. He wrote a humorous letter that night thanking
General Rosser for setting him up in so many new
things, but audaciously asking if he "would direct his

tailor to make the coat-tails of his next uniform a little
shorter" as there was a difference in the height of the
two men.   General Custer captured his herd of cattle
at one time, but he was so hotly pursued by General
Rosser that he had to dismount, cut a whip, and drive
them himself until they were secured.

To return to the Yellowstone expedition. The hour
for starting never varied more than a few moments
during the summer, and it was so early the civilians
connected with the engineering party could not become reconciled to it.   In the afternoon my husband
sometimes walked out on the outskirts of camp, and
threw himself down in the grass to rest with his dogs
beside him.

It was a source of amusement to him if he accidentally overheard the grumbling. His campaigning dress
was so like that of an enlisted man, and his insignia of
rank so unnoticeable, that the tongues ran on, indifferent to his presence.   Sometimes, in their growling, the
civilians accused him of having something on his conscience, and declared that, not being able to sleep himself, he woke every one else to an unearthly reveille.
At this he choked with laughter, and to their dismay
they discovered who he was.

I remember his telling me of another occasion, when
he unavoidably heard a soldier exclaim, "There goes
taps, and before we get a mouthful to eat, reveille
will sound, and 'Old Curley' will hike us out for the
march." The soldier was slightly discomfited to find
the subject of his remarks was within hearing.

The enlisted men were constantly finding new names

for the general, which I would never have known—
thereby losing some amusement—if Mary had not occasionally told me of them. A favorite was "Jack," the
letters G. A. C. on his valise having served as a suggestion.

When the expedition returned from the Yellowstone,
a despatch came to me in Michigan, saying the regiment had reached Fort Lincoln in safety. Another soon
followed, informing me that my husband was on his
way home. The relief from constant anxiety and suspense, together with all the excitement into which I
was thrown, made me almost unfit to make preparation to meet him. There was to be an army reunion
in the city nearest us, and in my impatience I took
the first train, thinking to reach there in advance of
General Custer. As I walked along the street, looking
into shop-windows, I felt, rather than saw, a sudden
rush from a door, and I was taken off my feet and set
dancing in air. Before I could resent what I thought
was an indignity, I discovered that it was my husband, who seemed utterly regardless of the passers-by.
He was sunburnt and mottled, for the flesh was quite
fair where he had cut his beard, the growth of the summer. He told me the officers with whom he had travelled in the Pullman car had teased him, and declared
that no man would shave in a car going at forty miles
an hour, except to prepare to meet his sweetheart. I
was deeply grateful, though, for I knew the fiery tint
of the beard, and infinitely preferred the variegated
flesh tints of his sunburnt face.

CHAPTER IX.

OUR NEW HOME AT FORT LINCOLN.

In a few days we were ready to return to Dakota, and very glad to go, except for leaving the old parents.

The hardest trial of my husband's life was parting with his mother. Such partings were the only occasions when I ever saw him lose entire control of himself, and I always looked forward to the hour of their separation with dread.

For hours before we started, I have seen him follow his mother about, whispering some comforting word to her; or, opening the closed door of her own room, where, womanlike, she fought out her grief alone, sit beside her as long as he could endure it. She had been an invalid for so many years that each parting seemed to her the final one. Her groans and sobs were heartrending. She clung to him every step when he started to go, and exhausted at last, was led back, half fainting, to her lounge.

The general would rush out of the house, sobbing like a child, and then throw himself into the carriage beside me completely unnerved. I could only give silent comfort. My heart bled for him, and in the long silence that followed as we journeyed on, I knew that his thoughts were with his mother. At our first stop he was out of the cars in an instant, buying fruit to send back to her. Before we were even unpacked in the hotel, where we made our first stay of any length, he had dashed off a letter. I have since seen those missives. No matter how hurriedly he wrote, they were proofs of the tenderest, most filial love, and full of the prophecies he never failed to make, of the reunion that he felt would soon come.

After long debates with her parents, we had captured a young lady who was to return with us. She was a "joy forever," and submitted without a word to the rough part of our journey. After we left St. Paul, the usual struggle for decent food began. Some of the officers returning from leave of absence had joined us, and we made as merry over our hardships as we could. When we entered the eating-houses, one young member of our party, whom we called the "butter fiend," was made the experimenter. If he found the butter too rancid to eat undisguised, he gave us a hint by saying, under his breath, "this is a double-over place." That meant that we must put a layer of bread on top of the butter to smother the taste.

The general was so sensitive when living in civilization that the heartiest appetite would desert him if an allusion to anything unpleasant or a reference to suffering was made at the table. But he never seemed to be conscious of surroundings when "roughing it." Of course I had learned to harden myself to almost anything by this time, but I can see the wide-open eyes of our girl friend when she saw us eat all around any foreign ingredients we found in our food. She nearly

starved on a diet consisting of the interior of badly-
baked potatoes and the inside of soggy rolls.

One of the eating-places on the road was kept in
a narrow little house, built on a flat car. Two men
presided, one cooking and the other waiting on the
table. We were laboriously spearing our food with
two tined forks, and sipping the muddy coffee with a
pewter spoon, when I heard with surprise the general
asking for a napkin. It seemed as foreign to the place
as a finger-bowl. The waiter knew him, however, and
liked him too well to refuse him anything; so he said,
"I have nothing but a towel, general." "Just the thing,
just the thing," repeated my husband, in his quick, jolly way. So the man tied a long crash towel under his
chin, and the general ate on, too indifferent to appearances to care because the tableful of travellers smiled.

When we finally reached the termination of the road
at Bismarck, another train was about starting back to
St. Paul. The street was full of people, wildly expost-
ulating and talking loudly and fiercely. It appeared that
this was the last train of the season, as the cars were
not to run during the winter. The passengers were
mostly Bismarck citizens, whose lawless life as gam-
blers and murderers had so outraged the sentiments of
the few law-abiding residents that they had forced them
to depart. We could see these outlaws crowding at the
door, hanging out of the windows, swearing and mena-
cing, and finally firing on the retreating crowd as the
cars passed out of town. I was inclined to remain a
fixture in our car; to step down into such a *melée* was
too much for my courage. The general made allow-

ance for my fears, and we were quietly slipped out on the other side of the depot, hurried into the ambulance, and driven to the river.

The ice was already thick enough to bear our weight part way over; then came a swift rushing torrent of water which had to be crossed in a small boat. Some of the soldiers rowed, while one kept the huge cakes of floating ice from our frail boat with a long, iron-pointed pole. As I stepped into the little craft, I dropped upon the bottom and hid my eyes, and no amount of reference to dangers I had encountered before induced me to look up. The current of the Missouri is so swift it is something dreadful to encounter. We were lifted out upon the ice again, and walked to the bank. Once more on shore, I said to myself, here will I live and die, and never go on that river again.

Our brother, Colonel Tom, met us, and drove us to our new home. In the dim light I could see the great post of Fort Lincoln, where only a few months before we had left a barren plain. Our quarters were lighted, and as we approached, the regimental band played "Home, Sweet Home," followed by the general's favorite, "Garryowen."

The general had completely settled the house before he left for the East, but he had kept this fact secret, as a surprise. Our friends had lighted it all, and built fires in the fireplaces. The garrison had gathered to welcome us, and Mary had a grand supper ready. How we chattered and gloried over the regiment having a home at last. It seemed too good to believe that the 7th Cavalry had a post of its own, with room for the half of the regiment assigned to duty there. In other garrisons, when we had come in late in the fall from campaigns, the officers, in order to get places for themselves, had been obliged to turn some one else out. There is a disagreeable, though probably necessary law in the army regulations, which directs officers to take their quarters according to rank.

Fort Lincoln was built with quarters for six companies. The barracks for the soldiers were on the side of the parade-ground nearest the river, while seven detached houses for officers faced the river opposite. On the left of the parade-ground was the long granary and the little military prison, called the "guard-house." Opposite, completing the square, were the quartermaster and commissary storehouses for supplies and the adjutant's office. Outside the garrison proper, near the river, were the stables for six hundred horses. Still farther beyond were the quarters for the laundresses, easily traced by the swinging clothes-lines in front, and dubbed for this reason "Suds Row." Some distance on from there were the log-huts of the Indian scouts and their families, while on the same side also was the level plain used for parades and drill. On the left of the post was the sutler's store, with a billiard-room attached. Soon after the general arrived he permitted a citizen to put up a barber-shop, and afterwards another built a little cabin of cotton-wood, with canvas roof for a photographer's establishment.

The post was located in a valley, while just back of us stretched a long chain of bluffs. On the summit of a hill, nearly a mile to the left, was a small infantry garrison, which had been established some time, and now belonged to our post. When we went to return the visits of the infantry ladies, the mules dragged the ambulance up the steep hill with difficulty. We found living in this bleak place—in small, shabbily built quarters, such as a day-laborer would consider hardly good enough for his family—delicate women and children, who, as usual, made no complaint about their life. Afterwards we were much indebted to one of the ladies, who, determined to conquer fate, varied our lives and gave us something to look forward to, by organizing a reading-club that met every week. She had sent to the East, before the trains ceased running, for the new books.

This little post had been built before the railroad was completed, and the houses were put together with as few materials as possible. There was no plastering, but the ceilings and partitions were of thick paper made for the purpose. When narrow mouldings of wood were tacked over the joined places, and all of it painted, the effect was very pretty. When it was torn and ragged it looked poverty-stricken enough. In one set of quarters there chanced to be so many children and so little room that the parents had invented a three-story bed, where the little ones could be all stowed at night. While we were calling there one day, I sat talking with the cheerful little mother, and wondering how she could be so bright. Everything in garrison life was, of course, new to my girl friend, and I discovered she was trying to smother a laugh. She commanded a view of the inner door. One of the children, who had been beating the wall and crying to enter, had finally made prelimi-

nary preparations. She had thrust through a hole in
the paper partition each article of her little wardrobe,
even to her shoes, and was putting the first rosy foot
through after them. When the mother discovered this
she laughed heartily, and gave us thus an opportunity
to join her.

Our own post was somewhat sheltered by the bluffs
behind; but though our quarters were plastered, the unseasoned lumber warped, and it was a struggle to keep
warm. The wood with which we were provided was
far from dry, and much of it of that kind that burns
quickly but sends out little heat. It seemed to require
the entire time of one man to keep up the fires. It
was thus a blessed thing for the poor fellow whose duty
it was, for he had never been able to remain long with
his company at a time. He had an uncontrollable habit
of drinking. Most of the time he belonged to the band
of prisoners who are taken out of the guard-house every
day, under a sentinel, to police the garrison and cut the
wood. Mary gave them the coffee and whatever else was
left from the table every day. This seemingly worthless fellow told Mary that he believed he could "keep
straight" if Mrs. Custer would get the general to remit
his sentence and let him come to us to keep the fires.
So he came, and was occasionally sober for some time.
He learned to go through the house with his arms full
of wood when he was quite drunk. He really had too
much heart to cause me trouble, and used to say, " Mary,
I am pretty full, but don't let Mrs. Custer know it, for
I told her I would not do so again, and I don't like to
make her feel bad." So Mary spied out the land before

him and opened his doors. After he had tried her patience long, she finally lost her temper on finding that he had swallowed all the Worcestershire sauce and her bottle of pain-killer. She held out the can of kerosene oil to him, and asked if he would not add that to his dram, and began such a berating that he hurried off to escape from the violence of her tongue.

The soldiers asked the general's permission to put up a place in which they could have entertainments, and he gave them every assistance he could. They prepared the lumber in the saw-mill that belonged to the post. The building was an ungainly looking structure, but large enough to hold them all. The unseasoned cottonwood warped even while the house was being built, but by patching and lining with old torn tents, they managed to keep out the storm. The scenery was painted on condemned canvas stretched on a frame-work, and was lifted on and off as the plays required. The footlights in front of the rude stage were tallow-candles that smoked and sputtered inside the clumsily cobbled casing of tin. The seats were narrow benches, without backs. The officers and ladies were always invited to take the front row at every new performance, and after they entered, the house filled up with soldiers. Some of the enlisted men played very well, and used great ingenuity in getting up their costumes. The general accepted every invitation, and enjoyed it all greatly. The clog-dancing and negro character songs between the acts were excellent. Indeed, we sometimes had professionals, who, having been stranded in the States, had enlisted.

A regiment is recruited from all classes and conditions of men. Occasionally accident revealed the secret
that there were fugitives from justice in the ranks. If
they changed their names, they found no place where
they were so hidden from every one they ever knew as
in a regiment that is always on duty in the territories.
It came to pass sometimes that a man of title, who had
"left his country for his country's good," wore the government blue as a disguise, and served as a trooper for
want of anything better to do. Among the men who
sent word they would be glad to help me about the
house when we were settling—either as a carpenter, a
saddler to sew carpets, or a blacksmith to put up stoves
—there were several with histories. Though they were
strictly military with the general, observing the rule of
never speaking unless spoken to, they sought the first
opportunity to tell me their troubles. These were invariably domestic difficulties, until I began to think
our regiment was "a city of refuge" for outraged
husbands. It would eventually be found out that
these men had run away and enlisted under assumed
names, when driven desperate by the scoldings of a
turbulent wife. Time, and the loneliness of a soldier's life, would soften their woes, and they began at
last to sigh even for the high-pitched voice of the deserted woman. The general felt as badly as I did when
I carried their stories to him, begging him to get them
discharged. He had a little fashion, however, of asking
me to remember that about this, as about every other subject that we ever discussed, "there were always two sides
to a question." My sympathy for the soldiers in trou-

ble was of little avail, for the law compelling them to serve the five years out was irrevocable. All I could do was to write letters at their solicitation, revealing their identity and asking for a reconciliation.

My husband's duties extended over a wide range. If the laundresses had a serious difficulty, he was asked to settle it. They had many pugilists among them, and the least infringement of their rights provoked a battle in which wood and other missiles filled the air. Bandaged and bruised, they brought their wrongs to our house, where both sides had a hearing. The general had occasionally to listen and arbitrate between husband and wife, when the laundress and her soldier husband could not agree. I was banished from the room, while he heard their story and gave them counsel. In the same way he listened to whatever complaints the soldiers made. Some of them came into our quarters on one occasion with a tin cup of coffee for the general to taste, and determine whether he agreed with them that it was too poor to drink. From that time on, after every Sunday morning inspection, the general went with all the officers to visit the kitchens, as well as the barracks of each company, and every troop commander was called upon to pass criticisms on the cleanliness of the quarters and the wholesomeness of the food.

CHAPTER X.

INCIDENTS OF EVERY-DAY LIFE.

THE companies each gave a ball in turn during the winter, and the preparations were begun long in advance. There was no place to buy anything, save the sutler's store and the shops in the little town of Bismarck, but they were well ransacked for materials for the supper. The bunks where the soldiers slept were removed from the barracks, and flags festooned around the room. Arms were stacked and guidons arranged in groups. A few pictures of distinguished men were wreathed in imitation laurel leaves cut out of green paper. Chandeliers and side brackets carved out of cracker-box boards into fantastic shapes were filled with candles, while at either end of the long room great logs in the wide fireplaces threw out a cheerful light.

The ball opened, headed by the first-sergeant. After this the officers and their wives were invited to form a set at one end of the room, and we danced several times. One of the men whose voice was clear and loud sang the calls. He was a comical genius, and improvised new ways of calling off. When the place came in the quadrille to " Turn your partners," his voice rose above the music, in the notes of the old song, " Oh swing those girls, those pretty little girls, those girls you left behind you !" This was such an inspiration to the fun-

lovers that the swinging usually ended in our being
whirled in the air by the privileged members of our
family.

The soldiers were a superb lot of men physically.
The out-door life had developed them into perfect specimens of vigorous manhood. After the company tailor
had cut over their uniforms, they were often the perfection of good fitting. The older soldiers wore, on the
sleeves of their coats, the rows of braid that designate
the number of years in the service. Some had the army
badges of the corps in which they fought during the
war, while an occasional foreign decoration showed that
they had been brave soldiers in the fatherland. We
were escorted out to the supper-room in the company-
kitchen in advance of the enlisted men. The general
delighted the hearts of the sergeant and ball-managers
by sitting down to a great dish of potato-salad. It was
always well-flavored with the onion, as rare out there,
and more appreciated than pomegranates are in New
York. We ladies took cake, of course, but sparingly,
for it was also a great luxury.

When we returned to watch the dancing, the general
was on nettles for fear we should be wanting in tact, and
show our amusement by laughing at the costumes of the
women. There was but a sprinkling of them: several
from Bismarck and a few white servants of the officers.
Each company was allowed but three or four laundresses. The soldier was obliged to ask permission to marry, and his engagement was a weary waiting sometimes.
In order to get a vacancy for his sweetheart, he had to
await the discharge of some other soldier from the com-

pany, whose wife held the appointment of laundress.
These women were at the ball in full force, and each
one brought her baby. When we removed our wraps in
the room of the first-sergeant we usually found his bed
quite full of curly-headed infants sleeping, while the
laundress mothers danced. The toilets of these women
were something marvellous in construction. In low
neck and short sleeves, their round, red arms and well-
developed figures wheeled around the barracks all night
long. Even the tall Mexican laundress, hereafter spe-
cially mentioned, would deck herself in pink tarletan
and false curls, and notwithstanding her height and co-
lossal anatomy, she had constant partners.

The little Dutch woman, who loved her husband
more devotedly after each beating, and did not dance
with any one else, was never absent from the balls.
Her tiny little figure was suspended between heaven
and earth while her tall soldier whirled her around the
long hall in the endless German waltz. Some officer
would whisper slyly in my ear, as she bowed and
smiled in passing, "Do you see the get-up of 'Old
Trooble Agin?'" She had long before earned this
sobriquet, when coming to me for help out of her
misfortunes, beginning each story of woe with "Trooble agin." Wherever we were, when the orders were
issued for a campaign, she soon appeared claiming sympathy. No one could feel at such a time more than I
the truth of her preface, for if we were to be left behind, it was, indeed, "Trouble again."

The pack of hounds were an endless source of delight
to the general. We had about forty: the stag-hounds

that run by sight, and are on the whole the fleetest and most enduring dogs in the world, and the fox-hounds that follow the trail with their noses close to the ground. The first rarely bark, but the latter are very noisy. The general and I used to listen with amusement to their attempts to strike the key-note of the bugler when he sounded the calls summoning the men to guard mount, stables, or retreat. It rather destroyed the military effect to see, beside his soldierly figure, a hound sitting down absorbed in imitation. With lifted head and rolling eyes there issued from the broad mouth notes so doleful they would have answered for a *misericordia.*

The fox-hounds were of the most use in the winter, for the hunting was generally in the underbrush and timber along the river. I never tired of watching the start for the hunt. The general was a figure that would have fixed attention anywhere. He had marked individuality of appearance, and a certain unstudied carelessness in the wearing of his costume that gave a picturesque effect, not the least out of place on the frontier. He wore troop-boots reaching to his knees, buckskin breeches fringed on the sides, a dark navy blue shirt with a broad collar, a red necktie, whose ends floated over his shoulder exactly as they did when he and his entire division of cavalry had worn them during the war. On the broad felt hat, that was almost a sombrero, was fastened a slight mark of his rank.

He was at this time thirty-five years of age, weighed one hundred and seventy pounds, and was nearly six feet in height. His eyes were clear blue and deeply set, his hair short, wavy, and golden in tint. His mustache was long and tawny in color; his complexion was florid, except where his forehead was shaded by his hat, for the sun always burned his skin ruthlessly.

He was the most agile, active man I ever knew, and so very strong and in such perfect physical condition that he rarely knew even an hour's indisposition.

Horse and man seemed one when the general vaulted into the saddle. His body was so lightly poised and so full of swinging, undulating motion, it almost seemed that the wind moved him as it blew over the plain. Yet every nerve was alert and like finely tempered steel, for the muscles and sinews that seemed so pliable were equal to the curbing of the most fiery animal. I do not think that he sat his horse with more grace than the other officers, for they rode superbly, but it was accounted by others almost an impossibility to dislodge the general from the saddle, no matter how vicious the horse might prove. He threw his feet out of the stirrups the moment the animal began to show his inclination for war, and with his knees dug into the sides of the plunging brute, he fought and always conquered. With his own horses he needed neither spur nor whip. They were such friends of his, and his voice seemed so attuned to their natures, they knew as well by its inflections as by the slight pressure of the bridle on their necks what he wanted. By the merest inclination on the general's part, they either sped on the wings of the wind or adapted their spirited steps to the slow movement of the march. It was a delight to see them together, they were so in unison, and when he talked to them, as though they had been human beings, their intelligent eyes seemed to reply.

As an example of his horsemanship he had a way of escaping from the stagnation of the dull march, when it was not dangerous to do so, by riding a short distance in advance of the column over a divide, throwing himself on one side of his horse so as to be entirely out of sight from the other direction, giving a signal that the animal understood, and tearing off at the best speed that could be made. The horse entered into the frolic with all the zest of his master, and after the race the animal's beautiful, distended nostrils glowed blood-red as he tossed his head and danced with delight.

In hunting, the general rode either Vic or Dandy. The dogs were so fond of the latter, they seemed to have little talks with him. The general's favorite dog, Blücher, would leap up to him in the saddle, and jump fairly over the horse in starting. The spirited horses, mounted by officers who sat them so well, the sound of the horn used for the purpose of calling the dogs, their answering bay, the glad voices, and "whoop-la" to the hounds as the party galloped down the valley, are impressions ineffaceable from my memory. They often started a deer within sound of the bugle at the post. In a few hours their shouts outside would call me to the window, and there, drooping across the back of one of the orderlies' horses, would be a magnificent black-tailed deer. We had a saddle of venison hanging on the wood-house almost constantly during the winter. The officers', and even the soldiers', tables had this rarity to vary the monotony of the inevitable beef.

After these hunts the dogs had often to be cared for. They would be lame, or cut in the chase, through the tangle of vines and branches. These were so dense it was a constant wonder to the general how the deer could press through with its spreading antlers. The English hounds, unacquainted with our game, used to begin with a porcupine sometimes. It was pitiful, though for a moment at first sight amusing, to see their noses and lips looking like animated pin-cushions. There was nothing for us to do after such an encounter but to begin surgery at once. The general would not take time to get off his hunting-clothes nor go near the fire until he had called the dog into his room and extracted the painful quills with the tweezers from his invaluable knife. I sat on the dog and held his paws, but quivered even when I kept my head averted. The quills being barbed cannot be withdrawn, but must be pulled through in the same direction in which they entered. The gums, lips, and roof of the mouth were full of little wounds, but the dogs were extremely sagacious and held very still. When the painful operation was over they were very grateful, licking the general's hand as he praised them for their pluck.

Sometimes, when the weather was moderate, and I rode after the fox-hounds, one of them separated himself from the pack, and came shaking his great, velvet ears and wagging his cumbrous tail beside my horse. The general would call my attention to him, and tell me that it was our latest surgical patient, paying us his bill in gratitude, "which is the exchequer of the poor."

Among the pack was an old hound that had occasional fits. When he felt the symptoms of an attack he left the kennel at the rear of the house, came round to the front-door, and barked or scratched to get in. My husband knew at once that the dog was going to suffer, and that instinct had taught him to come to us for help. Rover would lie down beside the general until his hour of distress, and then solicit the ever-ready sympathy with his mournful eyes. The general rubbed and cared for him, while the dog writhed and foamed at the mouth. He was always greatly touched to see the old hound, when he began to revive, try to lift the tip of his tail in gratitude.

With the stag-hounds, hunting was so bred in the bone that they sometimes went off by themselves, and even the half-grown puppies followed. I have seen them returning from such a hunt, the one who led the pack holding proudly in his mouth a jack-rabbit.

The wolves in their desperate hunger used to come up on the bluffs almost within a stone's-throw of our quarters. It was far from pleasant to look out of the window and see them prowling about. Once when the stag-hounds were let out of the kennel for exercise, they flew like the winds over the hills after a coyote. The soldier who took care of them could only follow on foot, as the crust on the snow would not bear the weight of a horse. After a long, cold walk he found the dogs standing over the wolf they had killed. When he had dragged it back to our wood-shed he sent in to ask if the general would come and see what the dogs had done unaided and alone, for he was very proud of them.

As the family all stood talking over the size of the

coyote and its fur, I said, triumphantly, "Now, I shall have a robe!" It was enough for them, and they made no end of sport about my planning a robe out of one small skin. After we had all gone into the house, the soldier, who was not accustomed to hear such badgering, went in to Mary, and indignantly exclaimed, "Be jabers, and they'll not tease her about that long!" After that, during the winter, he walked frequently over the plain with the dogs, and when they had started a trail and run almost out of sight, he patiently followed until he reached the spot where they had brought down the game. Even in that bitter weather he brought in enough foxes, swifts, and coyotes to make me a large robe. When it was made up, I triumphantly placed myself on it, and reminded my family of their teasing, and the time, so lately past, when I had been an object of jest to them.

The weather seemed to grow colder and colder as the winter advanced — from 20° to 30° below zero was ordinary weather. The officers were energetic enough to get up sleighs, even with all the difficulties they had to encounter. There was no lumber at the post except unseasoned cotton-wood. The man who could get a packing-box for the body of his sleigh was a Crœsus. The carpenter cut and sawed the edges into scallops and curves; the rudest bobs were ironed by the company blacksmith; and the huge tongue of an army wagon was attached to the frail egg-shell. The wood-work was painted black, and really the color and shape reminded one of a little baby hearse. Sister Margaret and I disliked sleighing even under favorable circumstances, but that made no sort of difference; we were expected to go twice a day, and try in turn each new sleigh.

My husband found a sketch in some of the illustrated papers, which he thought such a fitting representation of us that he added some lines and drew some applicable features to the picture, and wrote underneath, " Margaret and Libbie *enjoying* a sleigh-ride !" (two wretched, shivering beings, wrapped in furs, sit with their feet in a tub of ice-water, while a servant rings a dinner-bell over their heads). When we were thus taken out, as a sacrifice we were enveloped in so many wraps we had literally to be carried and dropped into the sleigh, and after hot bricks were adjusted to our feet, we assumed the martyr look that women understand how to take on when persuaded against their will, and off we flew. It made no impression if we were speechless — the dearth of women made the men far from critical. Sometimes we went to the Hart River, which empties into the Missouri, and which we were not afraid to drive over, as it was frozen solid. And yet it should be understood that we preferred to go and be frozen rather than stay at home and be comfortable, for we were a band of friends sharing the same isolation, and each took comfort in contributing to the enjoyment of the rest.

One sort of sleighing we really did enjoy. One of the officers got up a long sleigh, using the bed of an army wagon for the box. He was his own coachman, and stood in front driving an excellent four-in-hand. We all placed ourselves in the straw and robes, and nothing of the whole party was visible except two rows of " tip tilted," rosy-tinted noses peeping out from under fur caps

and gay mufflers. If any one rashly left a seat to play
some prank it was never regained. The space closed up
instantly, and it was a choice of standing for the rest of
the distance, or uncomfortably sitting on the spurs, arc-
tics, or buffalo over-shoes of the others. Another of
our number tried driving tandem ; and as his horses
were very fleet and his sleigh very frail, it was a study
from first to last how soon we should gather up the
fragments of our scattered selves from the white plain
over which we flew at eagle speed.

When the thermometer went down to 45° below
zero, the utmost vigilance was exercised to prevent
the men from being frozen. The general took off
all the sentinels but two, and those were encased
in buffalo overcoats and shoes, and required to walk
their beat but fifteen minutes at a time. There were
no wells or cisterns, and the quartermaster had no
means of supplying the post with water, except with a
water-wagon that required six mules to haul it around
the garrison. The hole in the river through which the
water was drawn was cut through five feet of ice. It
was simply dreadful on those bitter days to see the
poor men whose duty it was to distribute the supply.
My husband used to turn away with a shudder from
the window when they came in sight, and beg me not
to talk of a matter that he was powerless to remedy.
The two barrels at the kitchen-door were all that we
could have, and on some days the men and wagon could
not go around at all. We husbanded every drop, and
borrowed from a neighbor, if any neighbor was fortunate enough not to have used all his supply.

CHAPTER XI.

THE BURNING OF OUR QUARTERS.—CARRYING THE MAIL.

WE had hardly finished arranging our quarters when, one freezing night, I was awakened by a roaring sound in a chimney that had been defective from the first. Women have such a rooted habit of smelling smoke and sending men on needless investigating trips in the dead of night, that I tried to keep still for a few moments. The sound grew too loud to be mistaken, and I awakened my husband. He ran up-stairs and found the room above us on fire. He called to me to bring him some water, believing he could extinguish it himself. While I hurried after the water, there came such a crash and explosion that my brain seemed to reel from fright. I had no thought but that my husband was killed. Nothing can describe the relief with which I heard his voice calling back to my agonized question as to his safety. His escape was very narrow; the chimney had burst, the whole side of the room was blown out, and he was covered with plaster and surrounded with fallen bricks. The gas from the petroleum paper put on between the plastering and the outer walls to keep out the cold had exploded. The roof had ignited at once, and was blown off with a noise like the report of artillery. The sentinel at the guard-house fired his carbine as an alarm. The general ran to one of the lower windows, and with his powerful voice that he could throw so far called for the guard. Then we hurried to the room occupied by our girl-friend. The plastering falling on her bed from the burning roof was the first hint she had of the danger. It was unsafe for her to stop to gather her clothes, and wrapping a blanket about her we sent her to our sister next door.

In an incredibly short time the men were swarming about the house. The general had buttoned his vest, containing his watch and purse, over his long night-dress, and unconscious of his appearance, gave just as cool orders to the soldiers as if it were at drill. They, also, were perfectly cool, and worked like beavers to remove our things; for with no engine and without water it was useless to try to save the house. The general stood upon the upper landing and forbade them to join him, as it was perilous, the floors being then on fire. He had insisted upon my going out of the house, but I was determined not to do so until he was safe. When I did leave I ran in my night-dress over the snow to our sister's. The house burned very quickly. Fortunately it was a still, cold night, and there was no wind to spread the flames. Except for this the whole garrison must have been burned.

When the morning came we went to inspect the heap of household belongings that had been carried out on the parade-ground. It was a sorry collection of torn, broken, and marred effects! Most of my clothes were gone. Our poor girl-friend looked down into her trunk, empty except for one tarlatan party gown. I had lost silver and linen, and what laces and finery I had. The

only loss I mourned, as it was really irreparable, was
a collection of newspaper clippings regarding my husband that I had saved during and since the war.   Besides these I lost a little wig that I had worn at a fancy-
dress ball, made from the golden rings of curly hair cut
from my husband's head after the war, when he had
given up wearing long locks.

The fire served one purpose after all.   Before it occurred I had always been a trial to Mary because I cared
so little for dress and really owned so few ornaments.
When the servants gathered together after that to boast
of the possessions of their several mistresses, as is customary with the colored people, who so love display, Mary
was armed with an excuse for me.   I used to hear of her
saying, "You jist orter seed what Miss Libbie had afo'
the fire;" and then she would describe in detail elegant
apparel that I had never even thought of having.   Long
afterwards I heard of the comments of one of our number, who loved the loaves and fishes of this life beyond
everything.   In vain she accumulated and had the proud
satisfaction of out-doing every one in the number of her
dresses.   Mary managed to slip into her kitchen on some
feigned errand, and drawing upon her imagination re-
lated how much richer Miss Libbie's possessions were
before the fire.   I had a hearty laugh by myself when I
heard that the Miss Flora McFlimsey of our circle, worn
out with the boasting of the cook, was heard to exclaim,
"I wish I might have seen for myself all the gorgeous-
ness described.   I am tired to death of hearing about
'befo' the fire.'"

The general selected another set of quarters next to

his brother's, and thither removed the remnants of our household goods. He begged me not to go near the house, or attempt to settle, until I had recovered from the fright of the fire and of his imperilled life the night before. We were all busy enough trying to fit our things upon our little friend. Her purse, with abundance to buy a new outfit, was burned, and it would be weeks before she could receive a remittance from home by our slow mails. Next day, as she sat among us in borrowed apparel, several sizes too large, she had a surprise. A huge clothes-basket was handed in at the door, with a note addressed to her, begging her to consider herself, what the garrison had long felt that she was, "the daughter of the regiment." The basket contained everything that the generous hearts of friends could suggest. Not content with this, another was sent on the next day, with a further supply of things bought in the store at Bismarck. She objected to the acceptance, and tears rose in her eyes at the thoughtfulness; but there were no names signed to the note, so we would not heed remonstrances. Every one came with needles and thimbles, and the scissors flew.

I was too much absorbed in this scheme to ask many questions about the new quarters. When I did inquire, the general put me off by saying that in a few days I should begin to settle. The second evening after the fire he sent for me, and asked if I would come and consult with him about some arrangement of the furniture, as he was too busy to come after me. I started at once, but Mary, ever thoughtful of my appearance, and deep in the mystery that followed, urged me to put on my

other gown. I was unwillingly put into it, and went
to the new house to find both sets of quarters lighted
throughout, and the band playing "Home, Sweet Home."
My husband, meeting me, led me in, and to my utter
surprise I found the whole place completely settled, a
door cut through into Colonel Tom's quarters, and the
garrison assembled at the general's invitation for the
house-warming. The pantry was full of good things to
eat that Mary had prepared for the supper. Every one
tried, by merry frolic and dancing, to make me forget
the catastrophe, and the general, bubbling over with fun,
inspired me to join. Then he told me to what subter-
fuges he had resorted to get the house ready, and repeated to me again that it was never worth while to
"cry over spilled milk."

The life of the enlisted men was very dull during the
cold weather. In the summer they had mounted drill
and parades, and an occasional scout, to vary the life.
They got very little good out of their horses in the winter. An hour in the morning and another in the afternoon were spent every day in grooming them. The
general took me down to the stables sometimes to watch
the work. Each horse had the name given to him by
his rider printed in home-made letters over his stall.
Some of the men were so careful of their horses that
they were able to keep them for service during the five
years of their enlistment. The daily intercourse of
horse and rider quickened the instinct of the brute, so
that he seemed half human. Indeed, I have seen an old
troop-horse, from whose back a raw recruit had tumbled,
go through the rest of the drill as correctly as if mount

ed by a well-trained soldier. Many of the soldiers love and pet their dumb beasts, and if the supply of grain gives out on a campaign they unhesitatingly steal for them, as a mother would for a starving child.

Beside every stall hung the saddle and equipments of the trooper, and the companies vied with one another in keeping them in perfect condition. Some of the horses' coats shone like satin under the busy currycomb of an attached master. The captain of a company and his first-sergeant soon discovered the faults of a horse. When the preparations for a campaign began, it was really laughable to hear the ingenious excuses why an apparently sound horse should be exchanged for another from the fresh supply.

In the same way a soldier who was hopelessly worthless was often transferred to another company. The officers who had been the recipient of the undesirable soldier would come to the general to complain. I could not always keep a straight countenance when the injured captain narrated his wrongs. One told of what desperate need he had been in for a tailor. He had been proffered this man with many eulogies by a brother officer, and the final recommendation given which insured the acceptance of this seemingly generous offer was, "He has made clothes for *me*." Not until the transfer was effected, and a suit of clothes ruined for the captain, was he told by his would-be liberal friend the whole story, which was, "Oh yes! he made clothes for me, but, *I forgot to add*, I couldn't wear them."

The general sympathized with the impatience of the enlisted men in their dull life, which drove the sergeants to solicit as a privilege the transportation of the mail. For a man of my husband's temperament it was easy to understand that danger was more endurable than the dead calm of barrack life. The telegraph lines were frequently down, and except for the courage of the sergeants we should have been completely isolated from the outside world. With four mules and the covered body of a government wagon on bobs, they went over a trackless waste of snow for two hundred and fifty miles. Occasionally there were huts that had once been stage stations, where they could stop, but it was deadly perilous for them to leave the telegraph line, no matter through what drifts they were compelled to plunge.

The bewilderment of a snow-storm comes very soon. An officer lying in the hospital, quite crazed from having been lost in attempting to cross a parade-ground only large enough for the regiment in line, was a fearful warning to these venturesome men. If the mail sergeant did not appear when he was due—at the end of two weeks—the general could scarcely restrain his anxiety. He was so concerned for the man's safety that he kept going to the window and door incessantly. He spoke to me so often of his fears for him that I used to imagine he would, for once, express some of his anxiety when the sergeant finally appeared to report; but military usage was too deeply bred in the bone of both, and the report was made and received with the customary repressed dignity of manner. However, I have seen my husband follow the man to the door, and tell him that he had felt great concern about him, and renew his directions to take every precaution for his safety. How thankful I used to be that I was not hedged in with a soldier's discipline, but that I could follow the faithful old trooper and tell him how the general had worried about him, and how thankful we all were for his safe return.

It did not take long for the garrison to discover the poor mules, with their tired, drooping heads and wilted ears, dragging the mail-sleigh into the post. Every officer rushed to the adjutant's office for his mail. It was a great event and the letters were hailed with joy. An orphan, and having no brothers and sisters, I must have been the only one who was contented not to get any. For my world was there. An officer's wife who could hardly wait for news from her lonely, delicate mother in the East used to say pathetically, realizing the distance that intervened, that no one knew what it was to be married to a husband and a mother at the same time.

As soon as the mail was distributed, the general buried himself with the newspapers. For several days after he agreed with me that an old engraving, called "My Husband," was a faithful likeness of him at such a time (the picture represented a man sitting in a chair, completely hidden, except his crossed legs and his hands, and clasping an outspread paper). As soon as the contents were devoured, he cut from the illustrated papers comic pictures, and adding to them some doggerel, sent them in to our witty neighbor as illustrating some joke that had transpired against her. With other papers, by a little drawing he transposed the figures and likenesses of some of the officers who had been placed previously in some ludicrous position. Adding marginal comments, he left the pictures uppermost where they were sure to be seen by the persons for whom they were intended, when they came in as usual to look over the papers and magazines in his room. A clever lady in a neighboring garrison, speaking of the arrival of the mail, described how voraciously she seized the new reading matter and closeted herself for hours to read up in advance of the others. She felt that "having exhausted every other topic she must coach up on something new."

In spite of the great risks and dangers of the mail-carriers, their journeys were accomplished without serious accident. I used to hear occasionally that the sergeant had levied such a heavy tax upon the citizens of Bismarck, when he brought small parcels through for them, that he had quite a little sum of money for himself by spring.

CHAPTER XII.

PERPLEXITIES AND PLEASURES OF DOMESTIC LIFE.

The climate of Dakota was so fine that those who had been poisoned by malaria in the South became perfectly well after a short residence there. Sickness was of rare occurrence, and because of its infrequency it drew forth lavish sympathy. In the autumn a beautiful little girl, the daughter of the sutler, was brought into the garrison dying with diphtheria. There was no law, like the city ordinance, compelling a warning placard to be placed on the door, and it would have been of no avail in keeping her friends away. When I begged the heart-broken mother to turn from the last breath of her idol, it seemed to me her lot was too hard for human endurance. Every sorrow seemed much worse out there, where we were so unaccustomed to suffering.

As I looked at the little waxen body prepared for burial, lying so like a pretty flower, I did not wonder at the mother's grief and despair. She was a thousand miles from Eastern friends; her husband was absent on business, and she among strangers. At another time, when a young mother was caring for her newly-born babe, the little toddling brother was unfortunately exposed to the cold, and fell violently ill with pneumonia.

Every lady came daily to help care for him, and at last the officers' repeatedly proffered services were accepted for night nursing. I remember watching and admiring the tenderness of a handsome, dashing young fellow as he walked the floor with the feverish little sufferer, or rocked him patiently until dawn. And when I saw him often afterwards gliding about in the dance, or riding beside some pretty girl, I used to think to myself that I could tell his sweetheart something good about him. We were all like one family—every one was so quick to sympathize, so ready to act if trouble came.

After the trains had been taken off, and winter had fairly set in, the young mother, whom we all loved, was in despair about clothing for her little ones. We had reached a land where there were no seamstresses, no ready-made clothing, and nothing suitable for children. Money did no good, though our friend had abundance of that, but busy fingers were needed. The ladies quietly arranged, as a surprise, a sewing-bee. We impressed our brother Tom into our service, and taught him to use the sewing-machine. A laughing crowd dropped scissors and thimbles at parade-time and followed to the door to watch him hurry on his belt and sabre and take his place—the quintessence then of everything military and manly. A roomful of busy women, cutting, basting, making button-holes, and joining together little garments, soon had a passable outfit for the brave mother's little ones, and even a gown for her own sweet self. I do not remember ever seeing anything quite so Dutchy and cumbersome, however, as those little children dressed in the cobbled-out woollen clothes our ignorant fingers had fashioned.

A woman on the frontier is so cherished and appreciated, because she has the courage to live out there, that there is nothing that is not done for her if she be gracious and courteous. In twenty little ways the officers spoiled us: they never allowed us to wait on ourselves, to open or shut a door, draw up our own chair, or to do any little service that they could perform for us. If we ran to the next house for a chat, with a shawl thrown over our heads, we rarely got a chance to return alone, but with this undignified head-covering were formally brought back to our door! I wonder if it will seem that we were foolishly petted if I reveal that our husbands buttoned our shoes, wrapped us up if we went out, warmed our clothes before the fire, poured the water for our bath out of the heavy pitcher, and studied to do innumerable little services that a maid would have done for us in the States.

I don't think it made us helpless, however. In our turn we watched every chance we could to anticipate their wants. We did a hundred things we would not have remembered to do had not the quickly passing time brought nearer each day those hours of separation when we would have no one to do for. I am sure I never saw more tender men than the officers. One learned to conceal the fact that one was ailing or fatigued, for it made them so anxious. The eyes of sister Margaret's husband come to me now, full of intense suffering for his wife, as she silently read her home letters telling of our mother Custer's failing strength. She suppressed her weeping until they had retired and she believed him asleep. She found her mistake when his gentle hands stole softly to her cheeks to feel if they were moistened with tears.

So seldom did we hear of an officer's unkindness to his wife, that a very old legend used to be revived if a reference to anything of the kind was needed. Before the war some officer wished to measure the distance of a day's march, and having no odometer elected his wife to that office. The length of the revolution of a wheel was taken, a white handkerchief tied to a spoke, and the madam was made to count the rotations all day long. The story seldom failed to fire the blood of the officers when it was told. They agreed that nothing but a long life among Indians, and having the treatment of the squaw before him, would cause a man to act with such brutality.

Domestic care sat very lightly on me. Nothing seemed to annoy my husband more than to find me in the kitchen. He determinedly opposed it for years, and begged me to make a promise that I would never go there for more than a moment. We had such excellent servants that my presence was unnecessary most of the time, but even in the intervals when our fare was wretched he submitted uncomplainingly rather than that I should be wearied. A great portion of the time my life was so rough that he knew it taxed me to the utmost, and I never forgot to be grateful that I was spared domestic care in garrison. We had so much company that, though I enjoyed it, I sometimes grew weary. When the winter came and there was little to do

officially, my husband made every preparation for our
receptions: ordered the supplies, planned the refresh-
ment, and directed the servants. The consequence was
that I sometimes had as enjoyable a time as if I had
been entertained at some one else's house. To prove
how much pleasure I had, I recall a speech that the
family kept among a collection of my *faux pas*. They
overheard me saying to some of our guests, "Don't go
home, we are having such a good time." Afterwards
the tormenting home circle asked me if it would not
have been in a little better taste to let the guests say
that!

We had such a number of my husband's family in
garrison that it required an effort occasionally to prevent our being absorbed in one another. A younger
brother came on from Michigan to visit us, and our
sister Margaret's husband had a sister and brother at
the post. Sometimes we found that nine of us were
on one side of the room deeply interested in conversation. Something would rouse us to a sense of our
selfishness, and I was the one sent off to look out the
quiet ones at the hop who needed entertaining. If I
chanced to be struggling to teach new steps in dancing
to feet unaccustomed to anything but march or drill,
or strove to animate the one whom all pronounced a
bore, the family never failed to note it. They played
every sly trick they could to disconcert and tease me.
I did not submit tamely. As soon as I could, I made
my way to them, and by threats and intimidations scattered them to their duty!

At the hops the officers waited long and patiently for

the women to dance with them; sometimes the first waltz they could get during the evening would not come before midnight. I think it would have been very hard for me to have kept a level head with all the attention and delightful flattery which the ordinary manners of officers convey, if I had not remembered how we ladies were always in the minority. The question whether one was old or young, pretty or plain, never seemed to arise with them. I have seen them solicit the honor of taking a grandmamma to drive, and even to ride as gallantly as if she were young and fair. No men discover beauty and youth more quickly, but the deference they feel for all women is always apparent.

It seemed very strange to me that with all the value that is set on the presence of the women of an officer's family at the frontier posts, the book of army regulations makes no provision for them, but in fact ignores them entirely! It enters into such minute detail in its instructions, even giving the number of hours that bean-soup should boil, that it would be natural to suppose that a paragraph or two might be wasted on an officer's wife! The servants and the company laundresses are mentioned as being entitled to quarters and rations and to the services of the surgeon. If an officer's wife falls ill she cannot *claim* the attention of the doctor, though it is almost unnecessary to say that she has it through his most urgent courtesy. I have even known a surgeon, who from some official difficulty was not on friendly terms with an officer, go personally and solicit the privilege of prescribing through the illness of his wife, whom he knew but slightly.

The officers used sportively to look up the rules in the army regulations for camp followers, and read them out to us as they would the riot act! In the event of any question being raised regarding our privileges, we women really came under no other head in the book which is the sole authority for our army. If we put down an emphatic foot, declaring that we were going to take some decisive step to which they were justly opposed as involving our safety, perhaps, we would be at once reminded, in a laughingly exultant manner, of the provision of the law. The regulations provide that the commanding officer has complete control over all *camp followers*, with power to put them off the reservation or detain them as he chooses. Nevertheless, though army women have no visible thrones or sceptres, nor any acknowledged rights according to military law, I never knew such queens as they, or saw more willing subjects than they govern.

CHAPTER XIII.

A "STRONG HEART" DANCE!

THE Indian scouts employed by our government and living at our post belonged to a tribe called the Arickarees. This tribe was small, and though not strong enough in numbers to attack the more powerful Sioux, there was implacable enmity between them, and a constant desire for revenge. During the preceding summer a band of Sioux came to Fort Lincoln, and drew the scouts belonging to the infantry garrison out of their quarters by some cunningly devised pretext. No sooner did they appear than they were fired upon by the Sioux. They fought all day, and finally the Rees succeeded in driving their enemies away. All this took place right at the post, where the firing could be seen from the windows. It was not known how many Sioux were killed, for all tribes make extraordinary exertions to carry their dead from the field. Four only were left. After some months the Sioux, for some reason best known to themselves, sent word that they were coming for a treaty. The Rees prepared to receive them with what they termed a "Strong Heart" dance. A message inviting the garrison was sent by them, through the interpreter, and we hailed with relief the variety in our existence this spectacle would afford. Indian life was still a novelty to us, for we had not been with any peaceable tribe before coming into Dakota. We stowed ourselves away in long sleighs which took us to the quarters of the scouts. Their buildings were of logs, and were long and low in construction. Around the walls on the inside were bunks on which were marks showing the quarters assigned to each family. When the outer door closed upon us we could scarcely breathe; the atmosphere was stifling, and loaded with the odor of smoked meat, tanned skins, and killikinick tobacco. The place was lighted by burning logs in a large fireplace, and the deep shadows threw into high-relief the figures that came into the glare of the fire, and produced effects from which Doré might have found material for a most powerful work.

Before the ceremonies began, we women went round the place to see the papooses in their mothers' arms, as they sat in the bunks or on the earthen floor. Each mother held her baby up for our inspection, with as much pride as if there had never been a little one on earth before. The squaws were not permitted to come near the charmed circle in front of the fire, where the mimic orchestra beat their drums; they were allowed to sing at a distance, and joined in the low monotone of the musicians. At regular intervals, as if keeping time, they jerked out a nasal twanging note which was emphasized by the coarse voices of the warriors. The dancers were naked, except for the customary covering over their loins. They had attached to their belts beads and metal ornaments. Some had so fastened to their girdles the feathers from the tail of the wild turkey, that they stood up straight as the savages bent over in the evolutions of the dance. One leg and arm would be painted bright vermilion or blue, and the other a vivid green, with cabalistic characters drawn on them in black. The faces were hideous, being painted in all colors. A few had necklaces of bears' claws, on which they set great value. These hung over the bronze shoulders, the claws pointing into the brown skin of their chests. One, evidently poorer than the rest, had a rudely cut shirt made out of an old ham-bag, on which the trade-mark and name of the manufacturing firm figured conspicuously as his sole decoration. Another, equally poor, wore only the covering over his hips, while suspended by a cord from his neck was a huge tin toy horse. From the scalp-lock of some there was a strip of cloth falling to the ground, on which silver disks made of coins were fastened at close intervals.

In the plait of hair falling to their waists we saw sticks crossed and running through the braid. The interpreter explained that these represented "coups." Our attention was arrested at once by a little four-year-old boy, who, from time to time during the evening, was brought to the circle by his mother, and left to make his little whirling gyrations around the ring of the dancers. It was explained to us that he had won his right to join in the festivities of the tribe when the fight took place the summer before, to settle which this treaty was planned. Of the four Sioux left on the battle-field that day, one, though mortally wounded, was not yet dead when the retreat took place. A Ree squaw, knowing that it would count her child "a coup" if he put another wound in the already dying man, sent him out and incited the child to plunge a knife into the wounded warrior. As a reward he was given the privilege of joining in all celebrations, and the right to wear an eagle feather standing straight from the scalp-lock of his tiny head. We saw the mother's eyes gleam with pride as she watched this miniature warrior admitted among the mature and experienced braves. All the dancers rotated around together for a time, their bodies always bent, and they howled as they moved. In the shadowy gloom, only momentarily made brilliant by the flashes of light from the fire, these grotesque, crouching figures were wild enough for gnomes. Only occasionally, where there was a large mixture of white blood, did we see a well-developed figure. The legs and arms of Indians are almost invariably thin. None of them ever do any manual labor to produce muscle, and their bones are decidedly conspicuous.

We were surprised to observe that though dancing in so small a space, and weaving in and out in countless figures, without an apparent effort to avoid collisions, they never interfered or caught their brandished weapons in the ornaments of one another's toggery. When a warrior wished to speak, he made some sign to the others. They then sat down around him, and the music ceased. He began with a recital of his achievements— Indians never fail to recapitulate these as a preface to each speech. Sometimes the speaker's career was illustrated, and a cotton sheet was unfolded on which were painted a number of primitive figures. He gradually grew more and more earnest; his dull eyes glared as he pointed to the scalps he had taken, which were even then dangling from his belt. Finally the warrior began to give presents, and to receive them in return, as is the custom on those occasions. If he gave a pony, he declared it by throwing down a stick on which were cut notches that signified the gift to the recipient.

After several had told their "coups," for so they designate their deeds of prowess, one bounded with great energy into the circle. He narrated with spirit how he had revenged the death of two of their band by killing the murderer at the last fight at the post. Before any one realized it, an old squaw pushed her way violently into the open space, threw down a roll of calico at his feet, and flung off her leggings and blanket as presents in her gratitude, for it was of her husband and son that he spoke. As she was about to complete the gift by removing her last garment, the interpreter, in consideration for us, hurried her out to her bunk in the darkness, and we saw her no more. Last of all an old Sioux, wrapped in a black mourning blanket, tottered into the circle, and silence settled down on all. He spoke of his son who had been in the fight, and had fallen bravely, but said that before he was killed he had made many Rees "bite the dust," as he then figuratively expressed it. Excited by the story of the courage of his offspring, he tottered back to his place, but his pride soon succumbed to his greater sorrow; he buried his head in his blanket when he sank down to his seat. Hardly had he ceased, before a young Ree leaped into the midst of the warriors, threw off his blanket, and with flashing eye plunged into a hurried enumeration

of his achievements, to prove his courage in days past.
Then, striding up to the bereaved father, he said in exultant, imperious tones, "Boast no longer of the successes
of your dead, I who stand here am he who killed him!"
The father did not even raise his eyes. The Ree
called out to the listening warriors, "Will he not fight
me? I stand ready." The old warrior remained unmoved, even under the insolent words of the aggressor.
Many years of an eventful life had made him too well
versed in, and too subservient to the laws of Indian
warfare, not to know that a "Strong Heart" dance
bound all in inviolable honor not to break the temporary peace; but he knew that once meeting each other
on the open plain there were no restrictions.

When we left the unearthly music, the gloom, and the
barbaric sights, and breathed pure air again, it seemed
as if we had escaped from pandemonium.

One morning soon after that we heard singing, and
found that the squaws were surging down from their
quarters nearly a mile distant. We had not received a
hint of the honor to be conferred, and were mystified
when they all halted in front of our house. They had
come to give us a dance. It was an unusual occurrence,
for the women rarely take part in any but the most
menial services. They were headed by Mrs. Long Back,
the wife of the chief of the scouts. She was distinguished as the leader by a tall dress-hat that had been
the property of some society man when he wore civilian
dress in the States. They began going around after
each other in a jogging, lumbering sort of movement,
and singing a humdrum song in a minor key. Much of

the finery we had seen at the genuine war-dance was
borrowed from the warriors for this occasion. It was
festooned over the figures of the women already well
covered with blankets, and the weight was not calculated
to add materially to their grace. The ranking lady had
a sabre which her chief had received as a present, and
this she waved over the others in command. One woman carried her six-weeks'-old papoose on her back, and
its little, lolling head rolled from side to side as the
mother trotted round and round after the others.

During the dance one of the officers' colored servants
rushed out, and in his excitement almost ran his head
into the charmed precincts. An infuriated squaw, to
whom all this mummery was the gravest and most momentous of concerns, flew at him, brandishing a tomahawk over his head. He had no need to cry, " O, that
this too, too solid flesh would melt !" for his manner of
vanishing was little short of actual evaporation into air.
Neither his master nor any one else saw him for twenty-
four hours afterwards.

When the women stopped their circumvolutions for
want of breath, we appeared on the porch and made
signs of thanks. They received them with placid self-
satisfaction, but the more substantial recognition of the
general's thanks, in the shape of a beef, they acknowledged more warmly.

CHAPTER XIV.

GARRISON LIFE.

THERE were about forty in our garrison circle, and as we were very harmonious we spent nearly every evening together.   I think it is the general belief that the peace of an army post depends very much upon the example set by the commanding officer.   My husband, in the six years previous, had made it very clear, in a quiet way, that he would much prefer that there should be no conversation detrimental to others in his quarters. It required no effort for him to refrain from talking about his neighbors, but it was a great deprivation to me occasionally.   Once in a while, when some one had brought down wrath upon his or her head by doing something deserving of censure, the whole garrison was voluble in its denunciation; and if I plunged into the subject also and gave my opinion, I soon noticed my husband grow silent and finally slip away.   I was not long in finding an excuse to follow him and ask what I had done.   Of course I knew him too well not to divine that I had hurt him in some manner.   Then he would make a renewed appeal to me beginning by an unanswerable plea, "if you wish to please me," and imploring me not to join in discussions concerning any one.   He used to assure me that in his heart he believed

me superior to such things. In vain I disclaimed being
of that exalted order of females, and declared that it
required great self-denial not to join in a gossip. The
discussion ended by his desiring me to use *him* as a
safety-valve if I *must* criticise others. From motives
of policy alone, if actuated by no higher incentive, it
seemed wise to suppress one's ebullitions of anger. In
the States it is possible to seek new friends if the old
ones become tiresome and exasperating, but once in a
post like ours, so far removed, there is no one else to
whom one can turn. We never went away on leave of
absence, and heard ladies in civil life say emphatically
that they did not like some person they knew, and
" never would," without a start of terror. I forgot that
their lives were not confined to the small precincts of a
territorial post, where such avowed enmity is disastrous.

I had very little opportunity to know much of official
matters; they were not talked about at home. Instinct
guided me always in detecting the general's enemies,
and when I found them out, a struggle began between
us as to my manner of treating them. My husband
urged that it would embarrass him if others found out
that I had surmised anything regarding official affairs.
He wished social relations to be kept distinct, and he
could not endure to see me show dislike to any one who
did not like him. I argued in reply that I felt myself
dishonest if I even spoke to one whom I hated. The
contest ended by his appealing to my good-sense, arguing that as the wife of the commanding officer I belonged to every one, and in our house I should be hos-

pitable upon principle. As every one visited us, there
was no escape for me, but I do not like to think now
of having welcomed any one from whom I inwardly
recoiled.

I was not let off on such occasions with any formal
shake of the hand. My husband watched me, and if I
was not sufficiently cordial he gave me, afterwards, in
our bedroom, a burlesque imitation of my manner. I
could not help laughing, even when annoyed, to see him
caricature me by advancing coldly, extending the tips of
his fingers, and bowing loftily to some imaginary guest.
His raillery, added to my wish to please him, had the
effect of making me shake hands so vigorously that I
came near erring the other way and being too demonstrative, and thus giving the impression that I was the
best friend of some one I really dreaded.

As I was in the tent during so many summers, and
almost constantly in my husband's library in our winter
quarters, I naturally learned something of what was
transpiring. I soon found, however, that it would do
no good if I asked questions in the hope of gaining further information. As to curiosity ever being one of
my conspicuous faults, I do not remember, but I do
recollect most distinctly how completely I was taken
aback by an occurrence which took place a short time
after we were married. I had asked some idle question
about official matters, and was promptly informed in a
grave manner, though with a mischievous twinkle of the
eye, that whatever information I wanted could be had by
application to the adjutant-general. This was the ster-
cotyped form of endorsement on papers sent up to the

regimental adjutant asking for information. One incident of many comes to me now, proving how little I knew of anything but what pertained to our own home circle. The wife of an officer once treated me with marked coldness. I was unaware of having hurt her in any way, and at once took my grievance to that source where I found sympathy for the smallest woe. My husband pondered a moment, and then remembered that the husband of my friend and he had had some slight official difficulty, and the lady thinking I knew of it was taking her revenge on me.

When I first entered army life I used to wonder what it meant when I heard officers say, in a perfectly serious voice, "Mrs. —— commands her husband's company." It was my good-fortune not to encounter any such female grenadiers. A circumstance occurred which made me retire early from any attempt to assume the slightest authority. One of the inexhaustible jokes that the officers never permitted me to forget was an occurrence that happened soon after the general took command of the 7th Cavalry. A soldier had deserted, and had stolen a large sum of money from one of the lieutenants. My sympathy was so aroused for the officer that I urged him to lose no time in pursuing the man to the nearest town, whither he was known to have gone. In my interest and zeal I assured the officer that I knew the general would be willing, and he need not wait to apply for leave through the adjutant's office. I even hurried him away. When the general came in I ran to him with my story, expecting his sympathy, and that he would endorse all that I had done. On the contrary, he quietly assured me that he commanded the regiment, and that he would like me to make it known to the lieutenant that he must apply through the proper channels for leave of absence. Thereupon I ate a large piece of humble pie, but was relieved to find that the officer had shown more sense than I, and had not accepted my proferred leave, but had prudently waited to write out his application. Years afterwards, when my husband told me what a source of pride it was to him that others had realized how little I knew about official affairs, and assured me that my curiosity was less than that of any woman he had ever known, I took little credit to myself. It would have been strange, after the drilling of military life, if I had not attained some progress.

The general planned every military action with so much secrecy that we were left to divine as best we could what certain preliminary movements meant. One morning, when it was too cold for anything but important duty, without any explanations he started off with a company of cavalry and several wagons. As they crossed the river on the ice, we surmised that he was going to Bismarck. It seemed that the general had been suspicious that the granaries were being robbed, and finally a citizen was caught driving off a loaded wagon of oats from the reservation in broad daylight. This was about as high-handed an instance of thieving as the general had encountered, and he quietly set to work to find out the accomplices. In a little while it was ascertained that the robbers had concealed their plunder in a vacant store in the principal street of Bismarck.

The general determined to go himself directly to the town, thinking that he could do quickly and without opposition what another might find difficult. The better class of citizens honored him too highly to oppose his plan of action, even though it was unprecedented for the military to enter a town on such an errand. The general knew the exact place at which to halt, and drew the company up in line in front of the door. He demanded the key, and directed the men to transfer the grain to the wagons outside. Without a protest, or an exchange of words even, the troops marched out of the town as quietly as they had entered. This ended the grain thefts.

It was a surprise to me that after the life of excitement my husband had led, he should grow more and more domestic in his tastes. His daily life was very simple. He rarely left home except to hunt, and was scarcely once a year in the sutler's store, where the officers congregated to play billiards and cards. If the days were too stormy or too cold for hunting, as they often were for a week or more at a time, he wrote and studied for hours every day. We had the good-fortune to have a billiard-table loaned us by the sutler, and in the upper room where it was placed, my husband and I had many a game when he was weary with writing.

The general sometimes sketched the outline of my pictures, which I was preparing to paint, for he drew better than I did, and gladly availed himself of a chance to secure variety of occupation.

The relatives of the two young housemaids whom we had in our service regretted that they were missing school, so the general had the patience to teach them. The day rarely passed that Col. Tom, my husband, and I did not have a game of romps. The grave orderly who sat by the hall-door used to be shocked to see the commanding officer in hot pursuit of us up the steps. The quick transformation which took place when he was called from the frolic to receive the report of the officer of the day was something very ridiculous.

Occasionally he joined those who gathered in our parlor every evening. He had a very keen sense of his social responsibilities as post-commander, and believed that our house should be open at all hours to the garrison. His own studious habits made it a deprivation if he gave up much of his time to entertaining. I learned that in no way could I relieve him so much as by being always ready to receive. He grew to expect that I would be in the parlor at night, and plan whatever diversions we had. I managed to slip away several times in the evening, and go to him for a little visit, or possibly a waltz, while the rest danced in the other room. If I delayed going to him while absorbed in the general amusement, a knock at the door announced the orderly carrying a note for me. Those missives always reminded me of my forgetfulness in some ingenious arrangement of words. When I laughed outright over one of these little scraps, our friends begged me to share the fun with them. It was only a line, and read, "Do you think I am a confirmed monk?" Of course they insisted laughingly upon my going at once to the self-appointed hermit.

We spent the days together almost uninterruptedly

during the winter. The garrison gave me those hours and left us alone. My husband had arranged my sewing-chair and work-basket next to his desk, and he read to me constantly. At one time we had read five authorities on Napoleon, whose military career was a never-ending source of interest to him. He studied so carefully that he kept the atlas before him, and marked the course of the two armies of the French and English with pencils of different color. One of his favorite books was a life of Daniel Webster, given him in the States by a dear friend. Anything sad moved him so that his voice choked with emotion, and I have known him lay down the book and tell me he could not go on. One of the many passages in that beautifully written book, which my husband thought the most utterly pathetic of all, was the tribute an old farmer had paid to the dead statesman. Looking down upon the face of the orator for the last time, the old man says, in soliloquy, "Ah, Daniel, the world will be lonesome now you are gone!"

I became so accustomed to this quiet life in the library with my husband that I rarely went out. If I did begin the rounds of our little circle with our girl-friend, whom every one besought to visit them, an orderly soon followed us up. Without the glint of a smile, and in exactly the tone of a man giving the order for a battle, he said, " The general presents his compliments, and would like to know when he shall send the trunks?" I recollect a message of this sort being once brought to us when we were visiting an intimate friend, by the tallest, most formidable soldier in the regiment.

It was a mystery to us how he managed to deliver his errand without moving a muscle of his face. He presented the compliments of the commanding officer, and added, " He sent you these." We did not trust ourselves to look up at his lofty face, but took from his extended hands two bundles of white muslin. There was no mistaking the shape; they were our night-dresses. When we hurried home, and took the general to task for making us face the solemn orderly, he only replied by asking if we had intended to stay forever, pointing to his open watch, and speaking of the terrors of solitary confinement!

It was the custom at guard mount every morning to select the cleanest, most soldierly-looking man for duty as orderly for the post-commander. It was considered the highest honor, and really was something of a holiday, as the man detailed for this duty had but little to do, and then had his night in bed; otherwise, belonging to the guard, and being newly appointed every twenty-four hours, he would have been obliged to break his rest to go on picket duty at intervals all night. There was great strife to get this position, and it was difficult for the adjutant to make the selection. He sometimes carried his examination so far as to try and find dust on the carbines with his cambric handkerchief.

Guard mount in pleasant weather, with the adjutant and officer of the day in full uniform, each soldier perfect in dress, with the band playing, was a very interesting ceremony. In Dakota's severe cold it looked like a parade of animals at the Zoo! All were compelled to wear buffalo overcoats and shoes, fur caps and gloves.

When the orderly removed these heavy outside wraps, however, he stood out as fine a specimen of manhood as one ever sees. His place in our hall was near the stove, and on the table by his side were papers and magazines, many of which were sent by the Young Men's Christian Association of New York. The general had once met the secretary of the society, and in response to his inquiry about reading-matter, he impressed him by a strong statement of what a treasure anything of the kind was at an isolated post.

There was usually a variety of reading-matter, but one day the orderly stole out to the cook with a complaint. He asked for the general's *Turf, Field, and Farm*, or Wilkes's *Spirit of the Times*, which he was accustomed to find awaiting him, and confessed that "those pious papers were too bagoted" for him! He usually sat still all day, only taking an occasional message for the general, or responding to a beckoning invitation from Mary's brown finger at the kitchen-door. There he found a little offering from her of home things to eat. Occasionally, in the evening, the general forgot to dismiss him at taps. After that a warning cough issued from the hall. When this had been repeated several times, my husband used to look up so merrily and say to me it was remarkable how temporary consumption increased after the hour of bedtime had come. When the general had a message to send, he opened his door and rattled off his order so fast that it was almost impossible for one unacquainted with his voice to understand. If I saw the dazed eyes of a new soldier, I divined that probably he did not catch a word. Without the general's noticing it, I slipped through our room into the hall and translated the message to him.

When I returned, and gave my husband the best imitation I could of the manner in which he spoke when hurried, and described the orderly, standing, rubbing his perplexed head over the unintelligible gibberish, he threw himself on the lounge in peals of laughter. While we were in the States, sometimes he was invited to address audiences, but being unaccustomed to public speaking, and easily embarrassed, he made very droll attempts. He realized that he had not the gift of oratory, and I used to wish that he would practise the art. I insisted, that if he continued to speak so fast in public, I would be obliged to stand beside him on the platform as interpreter for his hearers, or else take my position in the audience and send him a sign of warning from there. I proposed to do something so startling that he could not help checking his mad speed. He was so earnest about everything he did, I assured him no ordinary signal would answer, and we finished the laughing discussion by my volunteering to rise in the audience the next time he spoke, and raise an umbrella as a warning to slacken up!

CHAPTER XV.

GENERAL CUSTER'S LITERARY WORK.

WHEN my husband began to write for publication, it opened to him a world of interest, and afterwards proved an unfailing source of occupation in the long Dakota winters. I think he had no idea, when it was first suggested to him, that he could write. When we were in New York, several years before, he told me how perfectly surprised he was to have one of the magazine editors seek him out and ask him to contribute articles every month. And a few days after he said, "I begin to think the editor does not imagine that I am hesitating about accepting his offer because I doubt my ability as a writer, but because he said nothing about payment at first; for to-day," he added, not yet over his surprise at what seemed to him a large sum, "he came again and offered me a hundred dollars for each contribution." We at once seemed to ourselves bonanzas. Many times afterwards we enjoyed intensely the little pleasures and luxuries given us by what his pen added to the family exchequer.

On the frontier, where the commanding officer keeps open house, he has little opportunity to have more than a passing glimpse of his pay accounts, so quickly do they go to settle table expenses. It made very little

difference to us, though; our tastes became more
simple each year that we lived so much out-of-doors.
There was little dress competition in garrison, and in
no way could we enjoy the general's salary more than
in entertaining.

At our first post after the war, the idle tediousness of
the life was in such contrast to the whirl and dash of
the years just passed that the days seemed insupportable to my husband. While there we entertained a
charming officer of the old school. His experience and
age made me venture to speak to him confidentially of
the sympathy I felt for the aimlessness of my husband's
life. I was in despair trying to think of some way in
which to vary the monotony; for though he said little,
I could see how he fretted and chafed under such an
existence. The old officer appreciated what I told him,
and after thinking seriously for a time, urged me to try
and induce him to explore new territory and write de-
scriptive articles for publication. When the actual offer
came afterwards, it seemed to me heaven-sent. I used
every persuasive argument in my power to induce him
to accept. I thought only of its filling up the idle
hours. I believed that he had the gift of a ready writer,
for though naturally reticent, he could talk remarkably
well when started. I had learned to practise a little
stratagem in order to draw him out. I used to begin a
story and purposely bungle, so that, in despair, he would
take it up, and in rapid graphic sentences place the
whole scene before us. Afterwards he was commended
for writing as he talked, and making his descriptions of
plains life "pen pictures."

The general said to me that it was with difficulty he suppressed a smile when his publisher remarked to him that his writing showed the result of great care and painstaking. The truth was, he dashed off page after page without copying or correcting. He had no dates or journal to aid him, but trusted to his memory to take him back over a period of sixteen years. I sat beside him while he wrote, and sometimes thought him too intent on his work to notice my going away. He would follow shortly, and declare that he would not write another line unless I returned. This was an effectual threat, for he was constantly behind, and even out there heard the cry for "copy" which the printer's devil is always represented as making. I never had anything to do with his writing, except to be the prod which drove him to begin. He used to tell me that on some near date he had promised an article, and would ask me solemnly to declare to him that I would give him no peace until he had prepared the material. In vain I replied that to accept the position of "nag" and "torment" was far from desirable. He exacted the promise.

When he was in the mood for writing, we used laughingly to refer to it to each other as "genius burning." At such times we printed on a card, "this is my busy day," and hung it on the door. It was my part to go out and propitiate those who objected to the general shutting himself up to work.

While my father lived, he used to ask me if I realized what an eventful life I was leading, and never ceased to inquire in his letters if I was keeping a journal. When the most interesting portions of our life were passing, each day represented such a struggle on my part to endure the fatigues and hardships that I had no energy left to write a line when the evening came. My husband tried for years to incite me to write, and besought me to make an attempt as I sat by him while he worked. I greatly regret that I did not, for if I had I would not now be entirely without notes or dates, and obliged to trust wholly to memory for events of our life eleven years ago.

When my husband returned from the East in the spring of 1876 he had hardly finished his greeting before he said, "Let me get a book that I have been reading, and which I have marked for you." While he sought it in his travelling-bag I brought one to him, telling him that I had underlined much of it for him, and though it was a novel, and he rarely read novels, he must make this book an exception. What was our surprise to find that we had selected the same story, and marked many of the same passages! One sentiment which the general had enclosed with double brackets in pencil, was a line spoken by the hero, who is an author. He begs the heroine to write magazine articles, assuring her she can do far better than he ever did.

Once, when on leave of absence, the general dined with an old officer, whose high character and long experience made whatever he said of real value. He congratulated my husband on his success as a writer, but added, with a twinkle in his eye, "Custer, they say that your wife wrote the magazine articles." "If they say that," replied my husband, "they pay me the highest compliment that I could possibly receive." "Ah, well," replied the generous friend, " whoever wrote them they certainly reflect great credit on the family." My husband wrote much, but was not a voluble talker. As I have said, most of the entertaining devolved upon me, and the fact that I often spoke of the scenes in his " Life on the Plains " that we had shared together, must have been the reason why some persons listening to the oft-repeated stories ascribed the book to me.

As for my congratulations, the very highest meed of praise I could give him was that he had not taken the opportunity offered in describing his life in the book to defend himself against the unjust charges of his enemies. I had found that they expected and dreaded it, for " the pen is mightier than the sword," and military people are quick to realize it. My husband appreciated my having noticed what he studied to avoid, though while I commended, I frankly owned I could not have been equal to the task of resisting what could not but be a temptation to retaliate.

CHAPTER XVI.

INDIAN DEPREDATIONS.

LONG after the flowers were blooming in the States, the tardy spring began to appear in the far North. The snow slowly melted, and the ice commenced to thaw on the river. For a moment it would be a pleasure to imagine the privilege of again walking out on the sod without peril of freezing. The next instant the dread of the coming campaign, which summer is almost certain to bring to a cavalry command, filled every thought, and made me wish that our future life could be spent where the thermometer not only went down to twenty degrees below zero but remained there.

When I spied the first tiny blade of grass, I used to find myself acting like a child and grinding the innocent green with my heel, back from where it sprang. The first bunch of flowers that the soldiers brought me, long before the ground had begun to take on even a faint emerald tint, were a variety of anemone, a bit of blue set deep down in a cup of outer petals of gray. These were so thick and fuzzy they looked like a surrounding of gray blanket. And well the flowers needed such protection on the bleak hills where they grew. They were a great novelty, and I wanted to go and seek them myself, but my husband gave me the strictest injunction in reply not to step outside the garrison limits. We had received warning only a short time before that the Indians had crawled out of their winter tepees, and we knew ourselves to be so surrounded that it became necessary to station pickets on the high ground at the rear of the post.

On the first mild day my husband and I rode over to the opposite bank of the river, which was considered the safe side. Thinking ourselves secure from danger there, we kept on further than we realized. A magnificent black-tailed deer, startled by our voices and laughter, and yet too well hidden by the underbrush to see us, resorted to a device habitual with deer when they wish to see over an extent of country. He made a leap straight into the air, his superb head turned to us searchingly. He seemed hardly to touch the earth as he bounded away. It was too great a temptation to resist. We did not follow far though, for we had neither dogs nor gun.

Scarcely any time elapsed before an officer and a detachment of men riding over the ground where we had started the deer, but obliged to pursue their way further up the valley as they were on duty, came to a horrible sight. The body of a white man was staked out on the ground and disembowelled. There yet remained the embers of the smouldering fire that consumed him. If the Indians are hurried for time, and cannot stay to witness the prolonged torture of their victim, it is their custom to pinion the captive and place hot coals on his vitals.

The horror and fright this gave us women lasted for

a time, and rendered unnecessary the continued warnings of our husbands about walking outside the line of the pickets. Even with all the admonitions, we began to grow desperate, and chafed under the imprisonment that confined us to a little square of earth month in and month out. One day temptation came suddenly upon us as three of us were loitering on the outskirts of the post. The soldier who drove our travelling-wagon, the imperturbable Burkman, came near. We cajoled him into letting us get in and take ever so short a turn down the valley. Delighted to have our freedom again, we wheedled the good-natured man to go a "little and a little further." At last even he, amiable as he was, refused to be coaxed any longer, and he turned around. We realized then how far away we were; but we were not so far that we could not plainly discover a group of officers on the veranda at our quarters. They were gesticulating wildly, and beckoning to us with all their might. As we drove nearer we could almost see by a certain movement of the lower jaw that the word being framed was one that seems to be used in all climates for extreme cases of aggravation. They were all provoked, and caught us out of the carriage and set us down, after a little salute, for all the world like mothers I have seen who receive their children from narrow escapes with alternate shakings and hugs. It seemed hard to tell whether anger or delight predominated. In vain we made excuses, when order was restored and we could all speak articulately. We were then solemnly sworn, each one separately, never to do such a foolhardy thing again.

The Government had made a special appropriation for rations to be distributed, through the officers, to the suffering farmers throughout Minnesota and Dakota whose crops had been destroyed by grasshoppers. As we were on the side of the river with the warlike Indians, we knew of but one ranch near us. It was owned by an old man who had been several times to the general for assistance. He was a man of extraordinary courage, for he had located his claim too far away from any one to be able to obtain assistance if he needed it. He never left his home except to bring into market the skins that he had trapped, or his crops, when the season was profitable. He was so quaint and peculiar, and so very grateful for the help given him, that my husband wanted me to hear him express his thanks. The next time he came, the door into our room was left open, in order that I might listen to what otherwise he would have been too shy to utter. He blessed the general in the most touching and solemn manner. The tears were in his eyes, and answering ones rose in my husband's, for no old person failed to appeal to his sympathies and recall his own aged parents. Referring to some domestic troubles that he had previously confided to the general, he spoke of their having driven him beyond the pale of civilization when he was old and feeble, and compelled him to take his "dinner of herbs" in a deserted spot. At this point in his narrative the door was significantly shut, and I was thus made aware that the gratitude part was all that I was to be permitted to hear. My husband considered his confidence sacred. We knew that the old man lived a hermit's life, entirely alone the year through. In the blizzards he could not leave his door-step without being in danger of freezing to death. Some time after this a scout brought word that during the spring he had passed the ranch, and nothing was to be seen of the old man. The general suspected something wrong, and took a company himself to go to the place. He found that the Indians had been there, had dismantled and robbed the house, driven off the cattle and horses, and strewn the road with plunder. On the stable floor lay the body of the harmless old man, his silvery hair lying in a pool of blood, where he had been beaten to death. They were obliged to return and leave his death unavenged, for by the time the first news reached us the murderers were far away.

CHAPTER XVII.

A DAY OF ANXIETY AND TERROR.

WHEN the air became milder it was a delight, after our long housing, to be able to dawdle on the piazza. The valley below us was beginning to show a tinge of verdure. Several hundred mules belonging to the supply-wagon train dotted the turf and nibbled as best they could the sprouting grass. Half a dozen citizens lounged on the sod, sleepily guarding the herd, for these mules were hired by the Government from a contractor. One morning we were walking back and forth, looking, as we never tired of doing, down the long, level plain, when we were startled by shouts. We ran to the edge of the piazza, and saw the prisoners, who had been working outside the post, and the guard who had them in charge, coming in at a double-quick. A hatless and breathless herder dashed up to the officer on an unsaddled mule. With blanched face and protruding eyeballs he called out that the Indians were running off the herd.

The general came hastily out, just in time to see a cloud of dust rising through a gap in the bluffs, marking the direction taken by the stampeded mules. Instantly he shouted with his clear voice to the bugler to sound the call, "Boots and saddles," and keep it up until he told him to stop. The first notes of the trumpet had hardly

sounded before the porches of the company quarters
and the parade were alive with men.   Every one, without stopping to question, rushed from the barracks and
officers' quarters to the stables.   The men threw their
saddles on their horses and galloped out to the parade-
ground.   Soldiers who were solely on garrison duty,
and to whom no horse was assigned, stole whatever
ones they could find, even those of the messengers tied
to the hitching-posts.   Others vaulted on to mules
barebacked.   Some were in jackets, others in their flannel shirt-sleeves.   Many were hatless, and occasionally
a head was tied up with a handkerchief.   It was anything but a military-looking crowd, but every one was
ready for action, and such spirited-looking creatures it
is rarely one's lot to see.   Finding the reason for the
hasty summons when they all gathered together, they
could hardly brook even a few moments' delay.

The general did not tarry to give any but brief directions.   He detailed an officer to remain in charge
of the garrison, and left him some hurried instructions.
He stopped to caution me again not to go outside the
post, and with a hasty good-bye flung himself into the
saddle and was off.   The command spurred their horses
towards the opening in the bluff, not a quarter of a
mile away, through which the last mules had passed.
In twenty minutes from the first alarm the garrison
was emptied, and we women stood watching the cloud
of dust that the hoofs of the regimental horses had
stirred as they hurled themselves through the cleft in
the hills.

We had hardly collected our senses before we found

that we were almost deserted. As a rule, there are enough soldiers on garrison duty, who do not go on scouts, to protect the post, but in the mad haste of the morning, and impelled by indignant fury at having the herd swept away from under their very noses as it were, all this home-guard had precipitately left without permission. Fortunately for them, and his own peace of mind regarding our safety, the general did not know of this until he returned. Besides, the officers never dreamed the pursuit would last for more than a mile or so, as they had been so quick in preparing to follow.

After our gasping and wild heart-beating had subsided a little, we realized that, in addition to our anxiety for those who had just left us, we were in peril ourselves. The women, with one instinct, gathered together. Though Indians rarely attack a post directly, the pickets that were stationed on the low hills at the rear of the garrison had been fired upon previously. We also feared that the buildings would be set on fire by the wily, creeping savages. It was even thought that the running off of the herd was but a ruse to get the garrison out, in order to attack the post. Of course we knew that only a portion of the Indians had produced the stampede, and we feared that the remainder were waiting to continue the depredations, and were aware of our depleted numbers.

Huddled together in an inner room, we first tried to devise schemes for secreting ourselves. The hastily-built quarters had then no cellars. How we regretted that a cave had not been prepared in the hill back of

us for hiding the women in emergencies. Our means
of escape by the river were uncertain, as the ferry-boat
was in a shocking condition; besides, the citizens in
charge would very naturally detain the boat upon some
pretext on the safe side of the river. Finally, nervous
and trembling over these conferences, we returned to
the piazza, and tried to think that it was time for the
return of the regiment. Our house being the last in
the line, and commanding an extended view of the
valley, we kept our lookout there. Each of us took
turns in mounting the porch railing, and, held there in
place by the others, fixed the field-glass on the little
spot of earth through which the command had vanished. With a plaintive little laugh, one of our number called out the inquiry that has symbolized all be-
leaguered women from time immemorial, " Sister Anne,
do you see any one coming?"

All of us scanned the horizon unflaggingly. We
knew the Indian mode of taking observation. They
pile a few stones on the brow of the hill after dark;
before dawn they creep up stealthily from the farther
side, and hiding behind the slight protection, watch all
day long with unwearying patience. These little picket
posts of theirs were scattered all along the bluffs. We
scarcely allowed ourselves to take our eyes off them.
Once in a while one of our group on watch called out
that something was moving behind the rocks. Chairs
were brought out and placed beside her, in order that
a second pair of eyes might confirm the statement.
This threw our little shivering group into new panics.

There was a window in the servants' room at the

rear of the house, to and from which we ascended and descended all day long. I do not think the actual fear of death was thought of so much as the all-absorbing terror of capture. Our regiment had rescued some white women from captivity in Kansas, and we never forgot their stories. One of our number became so convinced that their fate awaited us, that she called a resolute woman one side to implore her to promise that, when the Indians came into the post, she would put a bullet through her heart, before she carried out her determination to shoot herself. We sincerely discussed whether, in extreme danger, we could be counted upon to load and fire a carbine.

It would be expected that army women would know a great deal about fire-arms; I knew but few who did. I never even went into the corner of my husband's library, where he kept his stand of unloaded arms, if I could help it. I am compelled to confess that the holster of a pistol gave me a shiver. One of our ladies, however, had a little of the Mollie Pitcher spirit. She had shot at a mark, and she promised to teach us to put in the cartridges and discharge the piece. We were filled with envy because she produced a tiny Remington pistol that heretofore she had carried in her pocket when travelling in the States. It was not much larger than a lead-pencil, and we could not help doubting its power to damage. She did not insist that it would kill, but even at such a time we had to laugh at the vehement manner in which she declared that she could disable the leg of an enemy. She seemed to think that sufficient pluck would be left to finish him afterwards. The officer who had remained in command was obliged to see that the few troopers left were armed, and afterwards he visited the pickets. Then he came to us and tried to quiet our fears, and from that time his life became a burden.

We questioned twenty times his idea as to *where* he thought the command had gone, *when* it would come back, and such other aimless queries as only the ingenuity of frightened women can devise. He was driven almost desperate. In assuring us that he hoped there was no immediate danger, he asked us to remember that the infantry post was near enough to give assistance if we needed it. Alas, that post seemed miles away, and we believed the gulleys that intervened between the two garrisons would be filled with Indians. After a prolonged season of this experience, the officer tried to escape and go to his quarters. We were really so anxious and alarmed that he had not the heart to resist our appeals to him to remain near.

And so that long day dragged away. About five o'clock in the afternoon a faint haze arose on the horizon. We could hardly restrain our uneasy feet. We wanted to run up over the bluff to discover what it meant. We regretted that we had given our word of honor that we would not leave the limits of the post. Soon after the mules appeared, travelling wearily back through the same opening in the bluffs through which so many hours before they had rushed headlong. We were bitterly disappointed to find only a few soldiers driving them, and they gave but little news. When the regiment overtook the stock these men had been detailed to return with the recaptured animals to the garrison; the command had pushed on in pursuit of the Indians.

The night set in, and still we were in suspense. We made a poor attempt to eat dinner; we knew that none of the regiment had taken rations with them, and several of the officers had not even breakfasted. There was nothing for us to do but to remain together for the night.

From this miserable frame of mind we were thrown into a new excitement, but fortunately not of fear: we heard the sound of the band ringing out on the still evening air. Every woman was instantly on the piazza. From an entirely different direction from that in which they had left, the regiment appeared, marching to the familiar notes of "Garryowen."

Such a welcome as met them! The relief from the anxiety of that unending day was inexpressible. When the regiment was nearing the post, the general had sent in an orderly to bring the band out to meet them. He cautioned him to secrecy, because he wished us to have a joyous release from the suspense he knew we had endured.

The regiment had ridden twenty miles out, as hard as the speed of the horses would allow. The general, and one other officer mounted like himself on a Kentucky thorough-bred, found themselves far in advance, and almost up to some of the Indians. They seeing themselves so closely pressed, resorted to the cunning of their race to escape. They threw themselves from their ponies, and plunged into the underbrush of a deep ravine where no horse could follow. The ponies were captured, but it was useless to try any further pursuit. All the horses were fagged, and the officers and men suffering from the want of food and water.

When the herders were questioned next day, it was found that the Indians had started the stampede by riding suddenly up from the river where they had been concealed. Uttering the wildest yells, they each swung a buffalo robe about the ears of the easily excited mules.

An astonishing collection of maimed and halt appeared the next morning; neither men nor officers had been in the saddle during the winter. This sudden ride of so many miles, without preparation, had so bruised and stiffened their joints and flesh that they could scarcely move naturally. When they sat down it was with the groans of old men. When they rose they declared they would stand perpetually until they were again limber and their injuries healed.

As to the officer who had been left behind, he insisted that their fate was infinitely preferable to his. We heard that he said to the others in confidence, that should he ever be detailed to command a garrison where agitated women were left, he would protest and beg for active duty, no matter if his life itself were in jeopardy.

CHAPTER XVIII.

IMPROVEMENTS AT THE POST, AND GARDENING.

The general began, as soon as the snow was off the ground, to improve the post. Young cotton-wood trees— the only variety that would grow in that soil—were transplanted from the river bank. They are so full of sap that I have seen the leaves come out on the logs that had been cut some time and were in use as the framework of our camp-huts. This vitality, even when the roots were dying, deceived us into building hopes that all the trees we planted would live. We soon found by experience, however, that it was not safe to regard a few new leaves as a sure augury of the long life of these trees. It would have been difficult to estimate how many barrels of water were poured around their roots during the summer. A few of them survived, even during the dry season, and we watched them with great interest.

One day my husband called me to the door, with a warning finger to come softly. He whispered to me to observe a bird perched on a branch, and trying to get under the shade of two or three tiny leaflets that were struggling to live. Such a harbinger of hope made us full of bright anticipations of the day when our trees would cast a broad shadow.

No one who has not experienced it can dream what it is to live so many years in a glare as we did. Many of the officers were almost blind from time to time, owing to the reflection of the sand over which they marched, and with which they were surrounded in camp and garrison. I once asked a friend who had crossed the plains several times, what she would prefer above everything else on the march. When she replied, "a tree," I agreed with her that nothing else could have been such a blessing.

My husband felt that any amount of care spent on the poor little saplings would be labor well bestowed. If we were ordered away, he knew that others coming after us, stationed in that dreary waste, would derive the benefit. Several years afterwards I was assured that some one was reaping his sowing, for a large leaf was enclosed to me in an envelope, and a word added to explain that it was from the tree in front of our quarters.

On the opposite side of the Missouri River, except for the scattered underbrush along the banks, there was a stretch of country for eighty miles eastward without a tree, and with hardly a bush. The only one I knew of, on our side of the river, I could not help calling a genuine ancestral tree. It was a burying-place for the Indians. We counted seventeen of them that were lashed to boards and laid across the main branches, and there securely fastened, so that a tornado could not dislodge them. Much as we longed to enjoy what had become by its rarity a novelty, the sitting under the shade of green trees, and hearing the sound of the wind through the foliage, not one of us could be induced to tarry under those sepulchral boughs.

The struggles to make the grass grow on the sandy parade-ground were unceasing. Not only would it have been an improvement to the post, in its general appearance, but it would certainly have added materially to our comfort. How we longed to escape from the clouds of dust that the unceasing wind took up in straight whirling eddies and then wafted in great sheets of murky yellow into our doors and windows, making our eyes smart and throats raw and parched, as alkali sand can do so effectually.

The general sent East for grass-seed, which, with oats, were sown over and over again. Our referee on all agricultural questions assured us that the oats sprouted so soon, the oncoming blades of grass would be protected. He was so enthusiastically in earnest that he seemed to be studying the soil at all hours of the day to detect a verdant tinge.

One moonlight night we were attracted to the gallery by seeing him stalking slowly back and forth, waving his arms in apparent gesticulation of speech as he traversed the length of the parade-ground. Some said, in explanation, that the moon was at that stage when reason totters on her throne most readily; another declared that, having become tired of the career of a Mars, he had resumed his old rôle as a statesman, and was practising, addressing his imaginary constituents. All were wrong. The faithful promoter of the general good was sowing oats again, doubtless hoping that the witchery of the moonlight would be a potent spell to

induce their growth.   Even after such indefatigable
efforts, the soil refused to encourage the sprouting of
more than occasional patches of pallid green.

A portion of ground near the river was assigned the
companies for their gardens, and there were enough
soldiers looking forward to the result who counted it
no hardship to plant, dig, and weed.   All this tilling
of the soil inspired our energies, and a corner of our
own yard was prepared.   A high fence was put up so
that the stag-hounds, which make such incredible leaps,
could not scale the enclosure.   The household even
gathered about the general to see him drop the seed, so
full of interest were we all.   Long before it was time
to look for sprouting, we made daily pilgrimages to the
corner and peered through the fence.

The general, Colonel Tom, and I watered, weeded,
and watched the little bit of earth; the cook and
house-maid took our places and resumed our work
when we ceased.   Never was a patch of *terra firma*
so guarded and cared for!   At last Mary became impatient, and even turned the tiny sprouts upside down,
putting the plants back after examining the roots.   Her
watch was more vigilant than ours, and she actually
surprised the general one morning by putting beside
him a glass of radishes.   It was really a sensation in
our lives to have raised them ourselves, and we could
not help recalling the pitiful statement of a dear friend,
who also belonged to a mounted regiment, that she
had planted gardens for twelve successive springs, but
had never been stationed long enough in one place to
reap the benefit of a single attempt.   Of course, be-

ing naturally so sanguine as a family, we began in imagination almost to taste the oncoming beets, turnips,
etc. We reckoned too hastily, however, for a perfect
army of grasshoppers appeared one day. They came in
swarms, and when we looked up at the sun we seemed
to be gazing through clouded air. Absorbed in this
curious sight we forgot our precious garden; but Colonel Tom remembered, and insisted upon trying an ex-
periment recommended in print by a Minnesota farmer.
Seizing some tins from the kitchen, and followed by
the servants and their mistress, all armed in the same
manner, we adopted the advice of the newspaper paragraph, and beat the metal with perfectly deafening
noise around the small enclosure. Had grasshoppers
been sensitive to sound, it would have ended in our
triumph. As it was, they went on peacefully and stub-
bornly, eating every twig in our sight. Having finished everything, they soared away, carrying on their
departing wings our dreams of radishes and young
beets! The company gardens were demolished in the
same manner, and every one returned for another year
to the tiresome diet of canned vegetables.

I remember the look of amazement that came into
the face of a luxurious citizen when I told him that
we gave a dinner at once if we had the good-fortune
to get anything rare. "And, pray, what did you call
a rarity?" he responded. I was obliged to own that
over a plebeian cabbage we have had a real feast.
Once in a great while one was reluctantly sold us in
Bismarck for a dollar and a half.

We used condensed milk, and as for eggs, they were

the greatest of luxuries. In the autumn we brought from St. Paul several cases, but five hundred miles of jostling made great havoc with them.

The receipt-books were exasperating. They invariably called for cream and fresh eggs, and made the cook furious. It seemed to me that some officer's servant on the frontier must have given the receipt for waffles, for it bears the indefinite tone of the darky: "Eggs just as you haz 'em, honey; a sprinklin' of flour as you can hold in your hand; milk! well, 'cordin' to what you has."

The crystallized eggs, put up in cans and being airtight, kept a long time, and were of more use to us than any invention of the day. In drying the egg, the yolks and whites were mixed together, and nothing could be made of this preparation when the two parts were required to be used separately. It made very good batter-cakes, however, and at first it seemed that we could never get enough.

In the spring, when it was no longer safe to hunt, we had to return to beef, as we had no other kind of meat. My husband never seemed to tire of it, however, and suggested to one of our friends who had the hackneyed motto in his dining-room, that she change it to "Give us this day our daily beef."

Once only, in all those years of frontier life, I had strawberries. They were brought to me as a present from St. Paul. The day they came there were, as usual, a number of our friends on the piazza. I carefully counted noses first, and hastily went in before any one else should come, to divide the small supply into infinitesimal portions. I sent the tray out by the maid, and was delayed a moment before following her. My husband stepped inside, his face as pleased as a child over the surprise, but at the same time his eyes hastily scanning the buttery shelves for more berries. When I found that in that brief delay another officer had come upon the porch, and that the general had given him his dish, I was greatly disappointed. In vain my husband assured me, in response to my unanswerable appeal, asking him why he had not kept them himself, that it was hardly his idea of hospitality. I was only conscious of the fact that having been denied them all these years, he had, after all, lost his only strawberry feast.

This doubtless seems like a very trifling circumstance to chronicle, and much less to have grieved over, but there are those who, having ventured "eight miles from a lemon," have gained some faint idea what temporary deprivations are.

When such a life goes on year after year, and one forgets even the taste of fruit and fresh vegetables, it becomes an event when they *do* appear.

CHAPTER XIX.

GENERAL CUSTER'S LIBRARY.

THE order came early in the season to rebuild our burned quarters, and the suggestion was made that the general should plan the interior. He was wholly taken up with the arrangement of the rooms, in order that they might be suitable for the entertainment of the garrison. Though he did not enter into all the post gayety, he realized that ours would be the only house large enough for the accommodation of all the garrison, and that it should belong to every one. It was a pleasure to watch the progress of the building, and when the quartermaster gave the order for a bay-window, to please me, I was really grateful. The window not only broke the long line of the parlor wall, but varied the severe outlines of the usual type of army quarters.

On one side of the hall was the general's library, our room and dressing-room. The parlor was opposite, and was thirty-two feet in length. It opened with sliding-doors into the dining-room, and still beyond was the kitchen. Up-stairs there was a long room for the billiard-table, and we had sleeping-rooms and servant-rooms besides. To our delight, we could find a place for everybody. Space was about all we had, however; there was not a modern improvement. The walls were un-

papered, and not even tinted; the windows went up
with a struggle, and were held open by wooden props.
Each room had an old-fashioned box-stove, such as our
grandfathers gathered round in country school-houses.
We had no well or cistern, and not even a drain, while
the sun poured in, unchecked by a blind of even primitive shape. It was a palace, however, compared with
what we had been accustomed to in other stations, and
I know we were too contented to give much thought
to what the house lacked.

My husband was enchanted to have a room entirely
for his own use. Our quarters had heretofore been too
small for him to have any privacy in his work. He was
like a rook, in the sly manner in which he made raids on
the furniture scattered through the rooms, and carried off
the best of everything to enrich his corner of the house.
He filled it with the trophies of the chase. Over the
mantel a buffalo's head plunged, seemingly, out of the
wall. (Buffaloes were rare in Dakota, but this was one
the general had killed from the only herd he had seen
on the campaign.) The head of the first grisly that he
had shot, with its open jaws and great fang-like teeth,
looked fiercely down on the pretty, meek-faced jack-
rabbits on the mantel. (My husband greatly valued the
bear's head, and in writing to me of his hunting had said
of it: "I have reached the height of a hunter's fame—
I have killed a grisly.") Several antelope heads were
also on the walls. One had a mark in the throat where
the general had shot him at a distance of six hundred
yards. The head of a beautiful black-tailed deer was
another souvenir of a hunt the general had made with

Bloody Knife, the favorite Indian scout. When they sighted the deer they agreed to fire together, the Indian selecting the head, the general taking the heart. They fired simultaneously, and the deer fell, the bullets entering head and heart. The scout could not repress a grunt of approval, as the Indian considers the white man greatly his inferior as a hunter or a marksman. A sand-hill crane, which is very hard to bring down, stood on a pedestal by itself. A mountain eagle, a yellow fox, and a tiny fox with a brush—called out there a swift—were disposed of in different corners. Over his desk, claiming a perch by itself on a pair of deer-antlers, was a great white owl. On the floor before the fireplace, where he carried his love for building fires so far as to put on the logs himself, was spread the immense skin of a grisly bear. On a wide lounge at one side of the room my husband used to throw himself down on the cover of a Mexican blanket, often with a dog for his pillow. The camp-chairs had the skins of beavers and American lions thrown over them. A stand for arms in one corner held a collection of pistols, hunting-knives, Winchester and Springfield rifles, shot-guns and carbines, and even an old flint-lock musket as a variety. From antlers above hung sabres, spurs, riding-whips, gloves and caps, field-glasses, the map-case, and the great compass used on marches. One of the sabres was remarkably large, and when it was given to the general during the war it was accompanied by the remark that there was doubtless no other arm in the service that could wield it. (My husband was next to the strongest man while at West Point, and his life after that had only increased his power.) The sabre was a Damascus blade, and made of such finely-tempered steel that it could be bent nearly double. It had been captured during the war, and looked as if it might have been handed down from some Spanish ancestor. On the blade was engraved a motto in that high-flown language, which ran:

"Do not draw me without cause;
Do not sheathe me without honor."

Large photographs of the men my husband loved kept him company on the walls; they were of General McClellan, General Sheridan, and Mr. Lawrence Barrett. Over his desk was a picture of his wife in bridal dress. Comparatively modern art was represented by two of the Rogers statuettes that we had carried about with us for years. Transportation for necessary household articles was often so limited it was sometimes a question whether anything that was not absolutely needed for the preservation of life should be taken with us; but our attachment for those little figures, and the associations connected with them, made us study out a way always to carry them. At the end of each journey we unboxed them ourselves, and sifted the sawdust through our fingers carefully, for the figures were invariably dismembered. My husband's first occupation was to hang the few pictures and mend the statuettes. He glued on the broken portions and moulded putty in the crevices where the biscuit had crumbled. Sometimes he had to replace a bit that was lost, and, as he was very fond of modelling, I rather imagined that he was glad of an opportunity to practise on our broken statuettes.

My husband, like many other men who achieve success in the graver walks of life, could go on and accomplish his ends without being dependent on the immediate
voice of approval.   In all the smaller, more trifling acts
of daily life he asked for a prompt acknowledgment.
It amused me greatly, it was so like a woman, who can
scarcely exist without encouragement.   When he had
reset an arm or modelled a cap I could quite honestly
praise his work.

On one occasion we found the head of a figure entirely severed from the trunk.   Nothing daunted, he
fell to patching it up again.   I had not the conscience
to promise him the future of a Thorwaldsen this time.
The distorted throat, made of unwieldy putty, gave
the formerly erect, soldierly neck a decided appearance of goitre.   My laughter discouraged the impromptu artist, who for one moment felt that a "restora-
tion" is not quite equal to the original.   He declared
that he would put a coat of gray paint over all, so that
in a dim corner they might pass for new.   I insisted
that it should be a very dark corner!   Both of the statuettes represented scenes from the war.   One was called
"Wounded to the Rear," the other, "Letter Day."   The
latter was the figure of a soldier sitting in a cramped,
bent position, holding an inkstand in one hand and
scratching his head for thoughts, with the pen.   The in-
ane poise of his chin as he looked up into the uninspir-
ing air, and the hopeless expression of his eyes as he
searched for ideas, showed how unusual to him were all
efforts at composition.

We had a witty friend who had served with my husband during the war. Many an evening in front of our open fire they fought over their old battles together. He used to look at the statuette quizzically, as he seated himself near the hearth, and once told us that he never saw it without being reminded of his own struggles during the war to write to his wife. She was Southern in sympathies as well as in birth, but too absolutely devoted to her husband to remain at her Southern home. When he wrote to her at the North, where she was staying, it was quite to be understood that there was a limit to topics between them, as they kept strictly to subjects that were foreign to the vexed question. To the army in the field, the all-absorbing thought was of the actual occurrences of the day. The past was for the time blotted out; the future had no personal plans in the hearts of men who fought as our heroes did. And so it came to pass that the letters between the two, with such diversity of sentiment regarding the contest, were apt to be short and solely personal. How the eyes of that bright man twinkled when he said, "I used to look just like that man in the Rogers statuette, when I was racking my brains to fill up the sheet of paper. My orders carried me constantly through the country where my wife's kin lived. Why, Custer, old man, I could not write to her and say, 'I have cut the canal in the Shenandoah Valley and ruined your mother's plantation;' or, 'Yesterday I drove off all your brother's stock to feed our army.' Of course one can't talk sentiment on *every* line, and so I sometimes sent off a mighty short epistle."

We often lounged about my husband's room at dusk

without a lamp. The firelight reflected the large glittering eyes of the animals' heads, and except that we were such a jolly family, the surroundings would have suggested arenas and martyrs. I used to think that a man on the brink of *mania a potu*, thrust suddenly into such a place in the dim flickering light, would be hurried to his doom by fright. We loved the place dearly. The great difficulty was that the general would bury himself too much, in the delight of having a castle as securely barred as if the entrance were by a portcullis.

When he had worked too long and steadily I opened the doors, determined that his room should not resemble that of Walter Scott. An old engraving represents a room in which but one chair is significantly placed. In our plans for a home in our old age we included a den for my husband at the top of the house. We had read somewhere of one like that ascribed to Victor Hugo. The room was said not even to have a staircase, but was entered by a ladder which the owner could draw up the aperture after him.

CHAPTER XX.

THE SUMMER OF THE BLACK HILLS EXPEDITION.

I USED to be thankful that ours was a mounted regiment on one account: if we had belonged to the infantry, the regiment would have been sent out much sooner. The horses were too valuable to have their lives endangered by encountering a blizzard, while it was believed that an enlisted man had enough pluck and endurance to bring him out of a storm in one way or another. Tardy as the spring was up there, the grass began at last to be suitable for grazing, and preparations for an expedition to the Black Hills were being carried on. I had found accidentally that my husband was fitting up an ambulance for travelling, and as he never rode in one himself, nor arranged to take one for his own comfort, I decided at once that he was planning to take me with him. Mary and I had lived in such close quarters that she counted on going also, and went to the general to petition. To keep her from knowing that he intended to take us, he argued that we could not get along with so little room; that there was only to be allowed half a wagon for the camp outfit of the head-quarters mess. "You dun' know better'n that, giniral?" she replied; "me and Miss Libbie could keep house in a flour-barr'l."

At the very last, news came through Indian scouts that the summer might be full of danger, and my heart was almost broken at finding that the general did not dare to take me with him. Whatever peril might be awaiting me on the expedition, nothing could be equal to the suffering of suspense at home.

The black hour came again, and with it the terrible parting which seemed a foreshadowing of the most intense anguish that our Heavenly Father can send to his children. When I resumed my life, and tried to portion off the day with occupations, in order that the time should fly faster, I found that the one silver thread running through the dark woof of the dragging hours was the hope of the letters we were promised. Scouts were to be sent back four times during the absence of the regiment.

The infantry came to garrison our post. In the event of attack, my husband left a Gatling gun on the hills at the rear of the camp. It is a small cannon, which is discharged by turning a crank that scatters the shot in all directions, and is especially serviceable at short range. A detachment of soldiers was stationed on the bluff back of us, that commanded the most extended view of the country. The voice of the sentinel calling, at regular intervals during the night, "All's well," often closed our anxious eyes. Out there one slept lightly, and any unusual noise was attributed to an attack on our pickets, and caused us many a wakeful hour. With what relief we looked up daily to the little group of tents, when we finally realized that we were alone.

The officer who commanded this little station was an old bachelor who did not believe in marriage in the

army. Not knowing this, we told him, with some enthusiasm, how safe and thankful we felt in having him
for our defender. He quite checked our enthusiasm
by replying, briefly, "that in case of attack, *his duty*
was to protect Government *property;* the defence of
women came *last.*" This was the first instance I had
ever known of an officer who did not believe a woman
was God's best gift to man.

We were not effectually suppressed, for the only
safe place in which we could walk was along the beat
of the sentry, on the brow of the hill, near the tent
of this zoological specimen. Here we resorted every
evening at twilight to try and get cool, for the sun
burns fiercely during the short Northern summer. With
the hot weather the mosquito war began—Fort Lincoln
was celebrated as the worst place in the United States
for these pests. The inundations recurring each spring
opposite us, brought later in the year myriads of the
insects; those I had known on the Red River of the
South were nothing in comparison. If the wind was in
a certain direction, they tormented us all day long. I
can see now how we women looked, taking our evening
stroll: a little procession of fluttering females, with
scarfs and over-dresses drawn over our heads, whisking
handkerchiefs and beating the air with fans. It required constant activity to keep off the swarms of those
wretched little insects that annoyed us every moment
during our airing. In the evening we became almost
desperate. It seemed very hard, after our long winter's
imprisonment, to miss a single hour out-of-doors during
the short summer.

We had petitioned that in the rebuilding of our house the piazza around it should be made wide, like those we enjoyed in the South. On this delightful gallery we assembled every evening. We were obliged to make special toilets for our protection, and they were far from picturesque or becoming. Some one discovered that wrapping newspapers around our ankles and feet, and drawing the stocking over, would protect down to the slipper; then, after tucking our skirts closely around us, we fixed ourselves in a chair, not daring to move.

One night a strange officer came to see us, and taking his place among the group of huddled-up women, he tried not to smile. I discovered him taking in my *tout ensemble*, however, and realized myself what an incongruity I was on that lovely gallery and in the broad moonlight. I had adopted a head-net: they are little tarlatan bags, gathered at one end and just large enough to slip over the head; rattans are run round these to prevent their touching the face—they look like dolls' crinolines, and would make a seraph seem ugly. In desperation I had added a waterproof cloak, buckskin gauntlets, and forgot to hide under my gown the tips of the general's riding-boots! Tucked up like a mummy, I was something at which no one could resist laughing. The stranger beat off the mosquitoes until there lay on the floor before him a black semi-circle of those he had slain. He acknowledged later that all vanity regarding personal appearance would be apt to disappear before the attacks to which we were subjected. We fought in succession five varieties of mosquitoes; the last that came were the most vicious. They were so small they slid easily through the ordinary bar, and we had to put an inside layer of tarlatan on doors and windows. We did not venture to light a lamp in the evening, and at five o'clock the netting was let down over the beds, and doors and windows closed. When it came time to retire we removed our garments in another room, and grew skilful in making sudden sallies into the sleeping-room and quick plunges under the bar.

The cattle and horses suffered pitiably during the reign of the mosquitoes. They used to push their way into the underbrush to try if a thicket would afford them protection; if a fire were lighted for their relief, they huddled together on the side towards which the wind blew the smoke. As it was down by the river, they were worse off than ever. The cattle grew thin, for there were days when it was impossible for them to graze. We knew of their being driven mad and dying of exhaustion after a long season of torment. The poor dogs dug deep holes in the side of the hills, where they half smothered in their attempt to escape.

The Missouri River at the point where we had to cross sometimes represented a lifetime of terror to me. We were occasionally compelled to go to the town of Bismarck, four miles back on the other side. I could not escape the journey, for it was the termination of the railroad, and officers and their families coming from the East were often detained there; while waiting for the steamer to take them to their posts they were compelled to stay in the untidy, uncomfortable little hotel. If I sent for them they declined to come to us, fearing they might make extra trouble; if I went for them in

the post ambulance, I rarely made a fruitless errand.
Even when elated with the prospect of a little outing at
St. Paul, I so dreaded that terrible river that we must
cross going and coming, it almost destroyed my pleasure
for a time. The current was so swift that it was almost
impossible for the strongest swimmer to save himself
if once he fell in: the mud settled on him instantly,
clogged his movements, and bore him under. Some of
the soldiers had been drowned in attempting to cross,
in frail, insecure skiffs, to the drinking-huts opposite.
As I looked into this roaring torrent, whose current
rushes on at the rate of six miles an hour, I rarely failed
to picture to myself the upturned faces of these lost
men.

The river is very crooked, and full of sand-bars,
the channel changing every year. The banks are so
honeycombed by the force of the water that great portions are constantly caving in. They used to fall with
a loud thud into the river, seeming to unsettle the very
foundations of the earth. In consequence, it was hard
work for the ferry-boat to make a landing, and more
difficult to keep tied up, when once there.

The boat we were obliged to use was owned by some
citizens who had contracted with the Government to
do the work at that point. In honor of its new duty
they renamed it *The Union*. The Western word "ram-
shackly" described it. It was too large and unwieldy
for the purpose, and it had been condemned as unsafe
farther down the river, where citizens value life more
highly. The wheezing and groaning of the old ma-
chinery told plainly how great an effort it was to propel

the boat at all. The road down to the plank was so steep, cut deep into the bank as it was, that even with the brakes on, the ambulance seemed to be turning a somersault over the four mules. They kicked and struggled, and opposed going on the boat at all. We struck suddenly at the foot of the incline, with a thump that threw us off the seat of the ambulance. The "hi-yis" of the driver, the creak of the iron brake, and the expressive remarks of the boatman in malediction upon the mules, made it all seem like a descent into Hades, and the river Styx an enviable river in contrast. The ambulance was placed on deck, where we could see the patched boiler, and through the chinks and seams of the furnaces we watched the fire, expecting an explosion momentarily.

After we were once out in the channel the real trouble began. I never knew, when I started for Bismarck, whether we would not land at Yankton, five hundred miles below. The wheel often refused to revolve more than half-way, the boat would turn about, and we would shoot down the river at a mad rate. I used to receive elaborate nautical explanations from the confused old captain why that happened. My intellect was slow to take in any other thought than the terrifying one—that he had lost control of the boat. I never felt tranquil, even when the difficulty was righted, until I set my foot on the shore, though the ground itself was insecure from being honeycombed by the current. The captain doubtless heard my pæan of thanks when I turned my back on his old craft, for once afterwards I received from him a crumpled, soiled letter, with curious spelling and cramped hand, in which he addressed me as "highly honored lady," and in lofty-sounding terms proceeded to praise his boat, assuring me that if I would deign to confer on him the honor of my presence, he would prove it to be quite safe, and as "peert" a steamer as sailed. With a great flourish, he ended, " for *The Union* must and shall be preserved," and signed himself my most humble admirer.

We were told, when the expedition started, that we might expect our first letters in two weeks. The mail was delayed, unfortunately, and each day after the fortnight had expired seemed a month. In spite of all my efforts to be busy, there was little heart in any occupation. The women met together every day and read aloud in turn. Every one set to work to make a present for the absent ones with which to surprise them on their return. We played croquet. This was tame sport, however, for no one dared to vary the hum-drum diversion by a brisk little quarrel, which is the usual accompaniment of that game. We feared to disagree even over trifles, for if we did it might end in our losing our only companionship.

We knew that we could not expect, in that climate, that the freshness of summer would last for more than a short time after the sun had come to its supremest in the way of heat. The drouth was unbroken; the dews were hardly perceptible. That year even our brief enjoyment of the verdure was cut short. A sirocco came up suddenly. The sky became copper-colored, and the air murky and stifling; the slightest touch of metal, or even the door-handles, almost blistered the fingers. The strong wind that blew seemed to shrivel the skin as it touched us. The grass was burned down into the roots, and we had no more of it that season. This wind lasted for two hours, and we could not keep back apprehensions at the strange occurrence. After that, during the summer, as we walked over the little space allowed us, our shoes were cut by the crisp brown stubble, and the sod was dry and unyielding under our feet. As far as we could see, the scorched earth sent up over its surface floating waves of heated atmosphere. No green thing was left. The only flowers that had not been scorched out of existence were the soap plants, which have a sword-like stalk, out of which grow the thick, creamy petals of its flower. The roots that extend for many feet in all directions near the surface of the soil, enable it to secure moisture sufficient to keep it alive. The only other flower was the blue-bell, which dotted a hill where we were accustomed to climb in order to command a better view of the country in our efforts to discover the scouts with the mail. One can scarcely imagine how hungrily we gazed at those little blossoms. They swung lightly on their cunningly fashioned stems, that swayed and tossed the tiny azure cups, but withstood the strongest wind. I cannot see even a sketch of that flower now without thinking how grateful we were for them out there in that stripped and almost "God-forgotten" land. When we threw ourselves on the turf among them, the little bells almost seemed to us to ring out a tiny sound, as if they were saying, in flowery cadence, "The hand that made us is divine."

Some of our eyes seemed to be perpetually strained, watching the horizon for the longed-for scouts. At dawn one morning—which is at three o'clock in summer in Dakota—I was awakened by strange sounds at the door. When I drew the curtain, there were the Ree scouts, and on their ponies the mail-bag, marked by some facetious hand, "Black Hills Express." It took but a second to fling on a wrapper and fairly tumble down the steps. The Indians made the sign of long hair and called "Ouches," which is the word denoting that in their language. (The general had borne this name with them for some time.) I was too impatient to wait their tardy movements, and tried to loosen the mail bag. The Indian, always pompous and important if he carries despatches, wafted me away. I understood enough, to be sure, that no one would receive the mail but the officer in command. As the scouts slowly moved down the line towards his quarters, other impatient female figures with flying hair came dancing restlessly out on the porches. Every woman soon knew that news had come. Even the cooks, scantily attired, ran out to stand beside their mistresses and wave their fat arms to the Indians to hurry them on. Our faithful soldier, Keevan, whom my husband had left to care for us, hearing the commotion, came to ask what he could do. I sent him to bring back the letters. He, in his turn, thinking only to serve me, made an effort to open the mail-bag, but the watchful Indian suppressed him quickly. The old fellow's face beamed with delight when he placed the great official envelope, crowded with closely-written pages, in my hand. How soon they were devoured, though, and what a blank there seemed in the day when we knew that we had nothing more to expect!

Three times after that we had letters. They were most interesting, with descriptions of the charm of travelling over ground no white feet had ever before touched. My family could not avoid, even at that distance, studying up little plans to tease me. After describing their discovery and entrance into a large and almost hidden cave, my husband said that Colonel Tom and he had come upon the bones of a white man, doubtless the only one who had ever set foot in that portion of the world. Beside him lay a tin cup, some buttons from his coat, and a rusty, ancient flint-lock musket. All were marked with his initials. They were the same as those of one of the friends whom I had known when a little romping girl of seventeen. "This," they said, in the language of a dime novel, "explains the mysterious disappearance of your old love. Rather than meet such a fate as awaited him in marrying you, old lady, he has chosen to seek out solitude in a cavern, and there die." Of course I thought even the story of the finding of the cave a fabrication for my benefit. I enjoyed it hugely, and thought what ingenuity they had employed to invent such a tale. When they came back at the end of the summer, and brought the musket and other mementos, with the very initials rusting in the metal, and declared on honor that they had found the skeleton, I was compelled to believe them. Not that the remains of the unfortunate man were those of my early friend, who

was soon afterwards accounted for, but that some un-
happy man had actually wandered into that dismal
place and died a tragic death alone.

When the day of their return came, I was simply wild
with joy. I hid behind the door as the command rode
into garrison, ashamed to be seen crying and laughing
and dancing up and down with excitement. I tried to
remain there and receive the general, screened from the
eyes of outsiders. It was impossible. I was down the
steps and beside my husband without being conscious of
how I got there. I was recalled to my senses and overwhelmed with confusion by a great cheer from the soldiers, who, I had forgotten, were lookers-on. Regular
soldiers rarely cheer, and the unusual sound, together
with the embarrassment into which I had unconsciously
plunged myself, made the few steps back to the house
seem a mile.

When we could take time to look every one over,
they were all amusing enough. Some wives did not
know their husbands, and looked indignant enough when
caught in an embrace by an apparent stranger. Many,
like the general, had grown heavy beards. All were
sun-burnt, their hair faded, and their clothes so patched
that the original blue of the uniform was scarcely visible. Of course there had been nothing on the expedition save pieces of white canvas with which to rein-
force the riding-breeches, put new elbows on sleeves,
and replace the worn knees.

The boots were out at the toes, and the clothing of
some were so beyond repairing that the officers wanted
to escape observation by slipping, with their tattered

rags, into the kitchen-door. The instruments of the band were jammed and tarnished, but they still produced enough music for us to recognize the old tune of "Garryowen," to which the regiment always returned.

By-and-by the long wagon-train appeared. Many of the covers had elk horns strapped to them, until they looked like strange bristling animals as they drew near. Some of the antlers were brought to us as presents. Besides them we had skins, specimens of gold and mica, and petrified shells of iridescent colors, snake rattles, pressed flowers, and petrified wood. My husband brought me a keg of the most delicious water from a mountain-stream. It was almost my only look at clear water for years, as most of the streams west of the Missouri are muddy.

As soon as the column appeared in sight, the old soldier who had served me with such fidelity all summer went to Mary to tell her the news. He also said that as long as the general had put Mrs. Custer in his charge he knew how to behave. Now, being no longer on honor, he added, " I intend to celebrate their return by going on a tremendous 'bum.'" How any one could get drunk in so short a time was a mystery. The general had hardly removed his buckskin-coat before the old fellow stumbled up the steps and nearly fell in the door, with his arms full of puppies that had arrived during the summer. The rejoicing was too general for misdemeanors to be noticed. The man was thanked for his watchful care over me during the months past, and advised to find a place to go to sleep in as soon as possible.

CHAPTER XXI.

DOMESTIC TRIALS.

FROM the clouds and gloom of those summer days, I walked again into the broad blaze of sunshine which my husband's blithe spirit made. I did everything I could to put out of my mind the long, anxious, lonely months. It was still pleasant enough to ride, and occasionally we went out in parties large enough to be safe, and had a jack-rabbit or wolf chase. In the autumn we went into the States on a short leave of absence. Much to our regret we had to take our prized girl-friend home. Her family begged for her return. The last good-bye to us was an appeal from the young officers to bring back another; and we did so, for while we were East we had the good-fortune to persuade another father and mother to part with their daughter.

An incident of our journey was an amusing illustration of the vicissitudes of Western life. In passing through Fargo, on the Northern Pacific Railroad, an old townsman of ours always came to see us, but invariably after dark. He had taken a claim in the very heart of the town, which was disputed by an energetic widow. If he left his place in the daytime for a few hours, he invariably returned to find his cabin occupied by the goods and chattels of the widow, and his own effects reposing on the snow outside his door. Then ensued the ejection of the interloper by one of the town authorities, and our friend would re-establish himself. After these raids were repeated a few times, he learned to keep guard during the day and steal out after dark. In vain outsiders advised him to settle the difficulty by asking a clergyman to unite the claims. His eyes turned from the widow to a young girl in his native State, who now presides unmolested over the disputed domicile, while the widow has forsaken war for the peace of another hearthstone.

The question of servants was a very serious one to those living on the borders of civilization as we did. There was never a station equal to those frozen-up regions. Should servants go out there in the fall, they were almost certain to become engaged to the soldiers and marry after the trains were taken off and no new ones could reach us. It often happened that delicate ladies had to do all kinds of menial service for a time. Except for a kind-hearted soldier now and then, who was too devoted to the wife of his company officer to see her do everything, I hardly know how army ladies would have endured their occasional domestic trials. The soldiers were especially fond of children, and knew how to amuse them; indeed, a willing heart made them quick to learn all kinds of domestic work. I think they even regretted that they could not sew, when they saw an overtaxed lady wearily moving her needle. We had no trouble, fortunately. Our colored cook not only commanded us, and as much of the post as she could, but she tyrannized over her two sisters whom she had brought

from Kentucky for us. These were thought excellent
servants, but Mary, invested with a "little brief authority," ruled like a despot. The youngest having been
born after the emancipation proclamation, was looked
down upon by her elder sister, who had been a slave.
In her moments of rage the most deadly insult was to
call the younger one "you worthless free nigger, you!"
I think with deep gratitude of their devotion to us. As
they were colored people they had not even the excitement of beaux among the enlisted men. Sometimes
they sighed and longed for home. At such times Mary
used to say to me, "Miss Libbie, you has the giniral,
and you don' mind whar you is so long as you has him,
but you can't tell what it is for us to live in a country
wha' there's no festibuls, meetin'-houses, or dances."

When we reached St. Paul, on our return from leave
of absence, we were generally met with telegrams from
our friends at Fort Lincoln, imploring us to bring them
cooks. The railroad officials were good enough to give
us passes, so we could always take them without much
trouble. The first time after advertising, only the young
and pretty ones were selected from those who came to
us at the hotel. Their almost instantaneous capitula-
tion to the devotion of the soldiers taught us a lesson.
After that we only took the middle-aged and plain.
When we were fairly started on our journey, the general would look them over, chuckle to himself, and jog
my elbow for me to see the ancients as tourists. He
would add, under his breath, that evidently we had settled the question that time, for no soldier would look
at such antediluvians. He reckoned too soon. He hard-

ly took into consideration that after hundreds of soldiers had lived for months without seeing so much as
the distant flutter of a woman's drapery, they ceased to
be fastidious or critical. Without an exception these
antique, parchment-faced women, in a few weeks after
we had delivered them over to their mistresses, began
to metamorphose. They bought tawdry ornaments at
the sutler's store, and hurried after dinner to adorn
themselves to meet the enlisted men, who even under
adverse circumstances will "a-wooing go."

I remember well the disheartened eyes of one of our
pretty young friends when she told me it was of no
manner of use to try and keep a white servant. Even
the ugly old female that we had brought her, and that
cooked so well, was already beginning to primp and
powder. By this time our dearly loved neighbor had
become exhausted by the almost constant care of her
two children, and with only inefficient servants to help
her. Through our sympathy for the hard life she led
out in that wilderness we had fallen into the way of
calling her "poor Miss Annie," having known her as a
girl. In the States she would have been "rich Miss
Annie." With a brave, handsome husband, a distinguished father, an abundant income, and bright, health-
ful children, she *was* rich. It would not have been
strange if the clouds had obscured these blessings, living the taxing, wearying life she did on the frontier.
In vain the devoted husband sought to share her cares.
The very climax of her troubles seemed to have arrived
when she confided to me that she would soon need an
experienced nurse to care for her through her coming

peril. The trains had ceased running, so that one could not be sent on from St. Paul. There was no neighborly help to be expected even, for all of our ladies were young and inexperienced. There seemed to be no one to whom we could look for aid. Instead of rejoicing, as we would have done in the States over the sweet privilege of coming maternity, we cried and were almost disconsolate. There were no soft, dainty clothes to receive the little stranger, no one to take care of it when it did come; the young surgeon was wholly inexperienced in such duty, and the future looked gloomy enough. Fortunately, I remembered at last one of the camp women, who had long followed the regiment as laundress, and had led a quiet, orderly life. "Poor Miss Annie" shuddered when I spoke of her, for the woman was a Mexican, and like the rest of that hairy tribe she had so coarse and stubborn a beard that her chin had a blue look after shaving, in marked contrast to her swarthy face. She was tall, angular, awkward, and seemingly coarse, but I knew her to be tender-hearted. In days gone by I had found, when she told me her troubles, that they had softened her nature.

When she first came to our regiment she was married to a trooper, who, to all appearances, was good to her. My first knowledge of her was in Kentucky. She was our laundress, and when she brought the linen home, it was fluted and frilled so daintily that I considered her a treasure. She always came at night, and when I went out to pay her she was very shy, and kept a veil pinned about the lower part of her face. The cook told me one day that she was sick and in trouble, and I went to see her. It seemed the poor thing had accumulated several hundred dollars by washing, baking pies for the soldiers, and sewing the clothes for them that had been refitted by the tailor. Her husband had obtained possession of the money and had deserted. She told me that she had lived a rough life before coming to the 7th, even dressing as a man in order to support herself by driving the ox-teams over the plains to New Mexico. The railroads had replaced that mode of transporting freight, and she was thrown out of employment. Finding the life as a laundress easier, she had resumed her woman's dress and entered the army, and thinking to make her place more secure, had accepted the hand of the man whose desertion she was now mourning. It was not long after this, however, before " Old Nash " (for through everything she kept her first husband's name) consoled herself. Without going through the ceremony or expense of a divorce, she married another soldier, and had come with us out to Dakota. Of course her husband was obliged to march with his company. It was a hard life for her, camping out with the other laundresses, as they are limited for room, and several are obliged to share a tent together. In the daytime they ride in an army wagon, huddled in with children and baggage. After all the rough summer out-of-doors, it was a great boon to her to get a little cabin in Laundress Row, at our post. Another trouble came to her, however: her new husband succeeded in stealing her savings and deserting like the first. "Old Nash" mourned her money a short time, but soon found solace in going to

the soldiers' balls dressed in gauzy, low-necked gowns.
Notwithstanding her architectural build and massive
features, she had no sooner accumulated another bank
account than her hand was solicited for the third time.
Again ignoring the law, and thinking divorce a superfluous luxury, she captured the handsomest soldier in his
company. He was Colonel Tom's own man, and when
we were riding we often admired the admirably fitting
uniform his wife had made over, and which displayed
to advantage his well-proportioned figure. It was certainly a *mariage de convenance*. Fortunes are compar-
ative; a few hundred dollars out there was quite equal
to many thousands in New York. The trooper thought
he had done a very good thing for himself, for notwithstanding his wife was no longer young, and was unde-
niably homely, she could cook well and spared him from
eating with his company, and she was a good invest-
ment, for she earned so much by her industry. In addition to all these traits, she was already that most
desirable creature in all walks of life—"a woman of
means."

The bride and groom returned from the ceremony
performed by the Bismarck clergyman, and began house-
keeping in the little quarters "Old Nash" had refur-
bished for the occasion. When "Miss Annie" and I
went down to see her and make our petitions, we found
the little place shining. The bed was hung with pink
cambric, and on some shelves she showed us silk and
woollen stuffs for gowns; bits of carpet were on the
floor, and the dresser, improvised out of a packing-box,
shone with polished tins. Outside we were presented

to some chickens, which were riches indeed out there in that Nova Zemblian climate. She was very gentle with our friend when we told our errand, and gave her needful advice in her broken Mexican tongue. After listening to her tribute to the goodness of her husband, we made such pitiful entreaties that we at last prevailed on her to leave him. She insisted upon the promise that she might come home every evening and cook her "manny manny's supper." We learned from her that her own two children had died in Mexico, and that she had learned midwifery from her mother, and confirmed, what I had previously heard, that she had constant practice among the camp women. "Old Nash" appeared at the required hour, and was as skilful a physician as she was a nurse. My friend used to whisper to me that when she watched her moving about in the dim light of the sick-room, she thought with a shiver sometimes how like a man she seemed. Occasionally she came to the bed, and in her harsh voice asked, "Are you comph?" —meaning comfortable. The gentle, dexterous manner in which she lifted and cared for the little woman quieted her dread of this great giraffe. By degrees I was promoted to the duty of bathing and dressing the little new-comer, the young mother giving directions from the pillow. When "Old Nash" was no longer absolutely necessary she went back to her husband—a richer woman by much gratitude and a great deal of money.

Her past life of hardship and exposure told on her in time, and she became ailing and rheumatic. Finally, after we had left Dakota, we heard that when death approached, she made an appeal to the camp women who surrounded her and had nursed her through her illness; she implored them to put her in her coffin just as she was when she died and bury her at once. They, thinking such a course would not be paying proper attention to the dead, broke their promise. The mystery which the old creature had guarded for so many years, through a life always public and conspicuous, was revealed : "Old Nash," years before, becoming weary of the laborious life of a man, had assumed the disguise of a woman, and hoped to carry the secret into the grave. The surgeon's certificate, stating the sex of "Old Nash," together with the simple record of a laundress in the regiment for ten years, was all the brief history ever known. After enduring the gibes and scoffs of his comrades for a few days, life became unbearable to the handsome soldier who had played the part of husband in order to gain possession of his wife's savings and vary the plain fare of the soldier with good suppers; he went into one of the company's stables when no one was there and shot himself. When our friend, whom the old creature had so carefully nursed, read the newspaper paragraph describing the death, her only comment was a reference to the Mexican's oft-repeated question to her, "Poor old thing, I hope she is 'comph' at last."

CHAPTER XXII.

CAPTURE AND ESCAPE OF RAIN-IN-THE-FACE.

As the second winter progressed it bade fair to be a repetition of the first, until an event happened that excited us all very much.

I must preface my account of the occurrence by going back to the summer of the Yellowstone campaign. Two of the citizens attached to the expedition, one as the sutler, the other as the veterinary surgeon, were in the habit of riding by themselves a great deal. Not being enlisted men, much more liberty than soldiers have was allowed them. Many warnings were given, however, and an instance, fresh in the minds of the officers, of the killing by Indians of two of their comrades the year before was repeatedly told to them. One day their last hour of lingering came. While they stopped to water their horses, some Indians concealed in a gully shot them within sight of our regiment, who were then fighting on the hill, and did not find the bodies for some time afterwards. Both of the murdered men were favorites; both left families, and regret and sympathy were general throughout the command.

A year and a half afterwards information came to our post, Fort Lincoln, that an Indian was then at the Agency at Standing Rock, drawing his rations, blankets, and ammunition from the Government, and at the same time boasting of the murder of these two men. This intelligence created intense indignation in our garrison. A detachment was quickly prepared, and started out with sealed orders. The day was bitter, and not a still cold, for the wind blew, and cut like needle-points into the faces of the troopers. No one was aware even what direction they were to take. General Custer knew that it was absolutely necessary that caution and secrecy should be observed. At the next post, twenty miles below, there were scouts employed. They would not fail to send out a runner and warn the Standing Rock Indians of the coming of the command and its object, if they could learn what it was. When the runner carries important news he starts with an even gait in the morning and keeps it up all day, hardly stopping to drink at the streams he crosses. Such a courier would outstrip a command of cavalry in the ordinary time it makes on a march.

Accordingly, Fort Rice was left behind many miles before the orders were opened. They contained directions to capture and bring back an Uncapapa Indian, called Rain-in-the-face, the avowed murderer of the sutler and the veterinary surgeon. The command consisted of two officers and a hundred men. The general had selected his brother to assist in this delicate transaction, as he had been wont to do ever since they began their life of adventure together during the war. They arrived on the day that the Indians were drawing their rations of beef. There were five hundred at the Agency, armed with the latest long-range rifles. It was more and more clear that too much care could not be taken to prevent the object of the visit being known to the warriors.   An expedition had been sent down once before, but news of its intentions had reached the Agency in time for the culprit to escape.   He could not refrain, even after this warning, from openly vaunting his crime.

In order then to deceive as to the purport of their appearance at the Agency, the captain in command resorted to a ruse.   He sent fifty men to the camp ten miles away to make inquiries for three Indians who had murdered citizens on the Red River the year before. Colonel Custer was ordered to take five picked men and go to the trader's store, where the Indians resort constantly.   This required great coolness and extreme patience, for they had to lounge about, seemingly indifferent, until they could be certain the right man was discovered.   The cold made the Indians draw their blankets around them and over their heads.   There is never any individuality about their dress unless when arrayed for a council or a dance; it was therefore almost impossible to tell one from the other.

Colonel Tom had to wait for hours, only looking furtively when the sharp eyes of these wary creatures were off guard.   At last one of them loosened his blanket, and with the meagre description that had been given him, Colonel Tom identified him as Rain-in-the-face. Coming suddenly from behind, he threw his arms about him, and seized the Winchester rifle that the savage attempted to cock.   He was taken entirely by surprise. No fear showed itself, but from the characteristically

stolid face hate and revenge flashed out for an instant.
He drew himself up in an independent manner, to show
his brother warriors that he did not dread death.

Among them he had been considered brave beyond
precedent, because he had dared to enter the Agency
store at all, and so encounter the risk of arrest. The
soldiers tied his hands and mounted guard over him.
About thirty Indians surrounded them instantly, and
one old orator commenced an harangue to the others, in-
citing them to recapture their brother. Breathless excitement prevailed. At that moment the captain in
command appeared in their midst. With the same coolness he had shown in the war and during the six years
of his Indian campaigns, he spoke to them, through an
interpreter. With prudence and tact he explained that
they intended to give the prisoner exactly the treatment
a white man would receive under like circumstances;
that nothing would induce them to give him up; and
the better plan, to save bloodshed, would be for the
chiefs to withdraw and take with them their followers.
Seeing that they could accomplish nothing by intimi-
dation or by superior numbers, they had recourse to
parley and proposed to compromise. They offered as a
sacrifice two Indians of the tribe in exchange for Rain-
in-the-face.

It was generosity like that of Artemus Ward, who
offered his wife's relatives on the altar of his country,
for they took care not to offer for sacrifice any but
Indians of low rank. Rain-in-the-face was a very distinguished warrior among them, and belonged to a
family of six brothers, one of whom, Iron Horse, was

very influential.   The officers prevailed in the end, and the prisoner was taken to the cavalry camp.   During the time that the Indians were opposing his removal, the troopers had assembled around the entrance, ready for any emergency, and prepared to escort the murderer away.   The Indians instantly vanished; all went quickly and quietly to their camp, ten miles distant. Later in the day a party of fifty mounted warriors dashed through the Agency to the road beyond, which had to be taken by our troopers on the way home.   Of course our officers expected an attack from that party when they began their homeward march; to their surprise, they were unmolested.   We learned afterwards that the mounted Indians went to the camp of Two Bears to urge the young braves there to combine with them in the recapture of Rain-in-the-face.   Two Bears had long been friendly to the white man; he was too old to fight, and prevented his young men from joining in the contemplated rescue.

After the command had returned and the officers had reported, General Custer sent for Rain-in-the-face. He was tall, straight, and young.   His face was quite imperturbable.   In a subsequent interview the general locked himself in his room with him.   Through an interpreter, and with every clever question and infinite patience he spent hours trying to induce the Indian to acknowledge his crime.   The culprit's face finally lost its impervious look, and he showed some agitation. He gave a brief account of the murder, and the next day made a full confession before all the officers.   He said neither of the white men was armed when at-

tacked. He had shot the old man, but he did not die
instantly, riding a short distance before falling from
his horse. He then went to him and with his stone
mallet beat out the last breath left. Before leaving him
he shot his body full of arrows. The younger man
signalled to them from among the bushes, and they
knew that the manner in which he held up his hand
was an overture of peace. When he reached him the
white man gave him his hat as another and further
petition for mercy, but he shot him at once, first with
his gun and then with arrows. One of the latter entering his back, the dying man struggled to pull it
through. Neither man was scalped, as the elder was
bald and the younger had closely cropped hair.

This cruel story set the blood of the officers flowing hotly. They had already heard from one of the
white scouts a description of Rain-in-the-face at a sun-
dance, when he had betrayed himself as the murderer
of the veterinary surgeon, by describing in triumph his
beating out the brains of the old man with his mallet.
After all this, it is not to be wondered at that each
officer strode out of the room with blazing eyes.

Two Indians, one of them Iron Horse, had followed
the cavalry up from the Agency and asked to see their
comrade. The general sent again for Rain-in-the-face.
He came into the room with clanking chains and with
the guard at his heels. He was dressed in mourning.
His leggings were black, and his sable blanket was belted by a band of white beads. One black feather stood
erect on his head. Iron Horse supposed that he was
to be hung at once, and that this would be the final

interview. The elder brother, believing there was no hope, was very solemn. He removed his heavily-beaded and embroidered buffalo robe, and replaced it with the plain one that Rain-in-the-face wore. He exchanged pipes also, giving him his highly-ornamented one that he might afterwards present it to the general. These pipes are valuable, as the material of which the bowls are made has to be brought from Kansas. Then finding that there was a prospect of Rain-in-the-face having his trial in Washington, he took off the medal that had been given to his father by a former president, whose likeness was in the medallion, and placed it over the neck of his brother, that it might be a silent argument in his favor when he confronted the "Great Father."

It was an impressive and melancholy scene. Iron Horse charged his brother not to attempt to escape, saying, that if he did get back to the reservation he would surely be recaptured. He believed that he would be kindly treated while a captive, and perhaps the white chief would intercede for him to obtain his pardon. After asking him not to lose courage, they smoked again, and silently withdrew. In about ten days Iron Horse returned, bringing a portion of his tribe with him.

The valley of the Missouri is wide, and slopes gradually back to the bluffs. Beyond are the plains, rolling away for hundreds of miles to another river. There was a level stretch of three miles below our post down the river. From this direction we were accustomed to watch the approach of the bands of Indians coming from the reservation. We could see their arms glisten-

ing far down the valley long before we could dis-
tinguish who they were, except with a powerful field-
glass. As they came nearer, the sun caught a bit of
gaudy scarlet, or touched for a moment one of the
feathers in a war-bonnet.

A New York Charity Ball could bring out no more
antique heirlooms, nor take more time in preparations
than the costumes of Indians prepared for council.
The war-bonnets, shields, and necklaces of bear's claws
are all handed down from far-away grandfathers, and
only aired on grand occasions. Every available bit of
metal that could catch the light reflected and shone in
the morning sun. The belts were covered with brass
nails, shining with many an hour's polishing. They
had many weapons, all kept in a brilliant and glisten-
ing state. The tomahawk is one of the heirlooms of the
collection of arms. It is not like the ones I used to
see at Mackinac as a child. It looks more like a large
ice-pick. The knife, pistol, and Henry rifle are very
modern, and are always kept in the most perfect condition. Mrs. "Lo" is the Venus who prepares Mars
for war, and many a long weary hour she spends in
polishing the weapon and adorning the warrior.

The Indians with Iron Horse came directly to head-
quarters and asked for a council. As many as could get
into the general's room entered. There was time, while
they were preparing, to send for the ladies, and a few
of us were tucked away on the lounge, with injunctions
not to move or whisper, for my husband treated these
Indians with as much consideration as if they had been
crowned heads. The Indians turned a surprised, rather

scornful glance into the "ladies' gallery," for their
women are always kept in the background. In return
for this we did not hesitate to criticise their toilets.
They were gorgeous in full dress. Iron Horse wore an
elaborately beaded and painted buckskin shirt, with
masses of solid embroidery of porcupine quills. The
sleeves and shoulders were ornamented with a fringe
of scalp-locks; some of the hair, we saw with a shudder,
was light and waving. I could not but picture the little head, "sunning over with curls," from which it had
been taken, for all the Indian locks I have ever seen
were straight and black. The chief wore on his shoulders
a sort of cape, trimmed with a fringe of snowy ermine;
his leggings and moccasins were a mass of bead-work.
He wore a cap of otter, without a crown, though, for it
is their custom to leave the top of the head uncovered.
His hair was wound round and round with strips of
otter that hung down his back; the scalp-lock was also
tightly wound. Three eagle feathers, that denote the
number of warriors killed, were so fastened to the lock
that they stood erect. There were several perforations
in each ear from which depended bead ear-rings. He
had armlets of burnished brass; thrown around him
was a beaded blanket. The red clay pipe had the
wooden stem inlaid with silver, and was embellished
with the breast feathers of brilliantly plumaged birds.
The tobacco-bag, about two feet long, had not an inch
that was not decorated. The costume was simply
superb.

The next in rank had an immense buffalo robe as the
distinguishing feature of his dress. The inside was

tanned almost white, and his history was painted on the surface. Whoever ran might read, for it represented only two scenes, oft repeated—the killing and scalping of warriors and the capture of ponies.

The general's patience with Indians always surprised me. He was of such an active temperament and despatched his own work so rapidly that I have often wondered how he contained himself waiting an hour or more for them to get at the object of their visit. They took their places according to rank in a semicircle about the general. The pipe was filled and a match lighted by one of their number of inferior grade, and then handed to Iron Horse, who took a few leisurely whiffs. Though we were so shut in, the smoke was not oppressive. Their tobacco is killikinick, prepared by drying the bark of the ozier and mixing it with sumach. They inhale the smoke and exhale it from their nostrils. After all in the first circle had smoked a little, the general included, they observed the Indian etiquette and passed the pipe back through each warrior's hand to the chief. It was then relighted, and he began again. It seemed to us that it went back and forth an endless number of times. No matter how pressing the emergency, every council begins in this manner.

Iron Horse tired us out, but he was collecting himself and rehearsing his speech. We found afterwards that it was prepared in advance, for during its recital he forgot, and was prompted by one of the Indians in the outer circle.

When the pipe was finally put away, they asked to have Rain-in-the-face present. He came into the room, trying to hide his pleasure at seeing his friends and his grief at his imprisonment. In an instant the imperturbable expression settled down on his face like a curtain. The officers present could scarcely believe their eyes when they saw his brother approach and kiss him. Only once before, among all the tribes they had been with, had they seen such an occurrence. The Indian kiss is not demonstrative; the lips are laid softly on the cheek, and no sound is heard or motion made. It was only this grave occasion that induced the chief to show such feeling. Several of the ranking Indians followed his example; then an old man among them stepped in front of Rain-in-the-face, lifted his hands, and raising his eyes reverentially said a few words of prayer to the Great Spirit in behalf of their unfortunate brother. The prisoner dropped his head to hide the look in his eyes that he thought ill became a warrior as brave as he really was. The bitter, revengeful thoughts with which I had entered the room were for a moment forgotten, and I almost wished that he might be pardoned. The vision of the hearth-stones he had desolated came back to me directly, and I could not forget.

Iron Horse began his speech in the usual high-pitched, unchangeable key. He thanked the general for his care of his brother, and the whole tenor of the rest was repeated petitions to ask the Great Father in Washington to spare his life. He then slowly took off his elaborate buckskin shirt and presented it to my husband. He ended by making a singular request, which was worthy of Damon and Pythias: two shy young braves in the outer circle of the untitled asked permission through their chief to share the captivity of Rain-in-the-face. I could not help recalling what some one had told me in the East, that women sometimes go to the State prison at Sing Sing and importune to be allowed to share the imprisonment of their husbands or brothers; but no instance is found in the history of that great institution where a man has asked to divide with a friend or relative the sufferings of his sentence.

Consent was given to the comrades to return to the guard-house, but they were required to remain in confinement as he did until they were ready to return to the reservation. After all the ranking Indians had followed Iron Horse in speeches, with long, maundering, slowly-delivered sentences, each like the other, the pipe was again produced. When it was smoked, the whole band filed out to eat the presents of food the general had given them, and soon afterwards disappeared down the valley on their way home.

After his two friends had left him, Rain-in-the-face occupied a part of the guard-house with a citizen who had been caught stealing grain from the storehouse. For several months they had been chained together, and used to walk in front of the little prison for exercise and air. The guard-house was a poorly-built, insecure wooden building. After a time the sentinels became less vigilant, and the citizen, with help from his friends outside, who were working in the same way, cut a hole in the wall at night and escaped. He broke the chain attaching him to the Indian, who was left free to follow. We found afterwards that Rain-in-the-face did not dare to return to the reservation, but made his way to the hostile camp.   In the spring of 1874 he sent word from there by an Agency Indian that he had joined Sitting Bull, and was awaiting his revenge for his imprisonment.

As will be seen further on, the stained waters of the Little Big Horn, on June 25, 1876, told how deadly and fatal that was.   The vengeance of that incarnate fiend was concentrated on the man who had effected his capture.   It was found on the battle-field that he had cut out the brave heart of that gallant, loyal, and lovable man, our brother Tom.

CHAPTER XXIII.

GARRISON AMUSEMENTS.

THE second winter at Fort Lincoln was very much the same as the first. We had rented a piano at St. Paul in the autumn. It hardly had a respite from morning until late at night. Every day and evening the sound of happy voices went through the house. Old war-songs, college choruses, and negro melodies, that every one knew, were sung, and on Sunday our only church-service most of the time was to meet together and sing hymns. In our little circle of forty, many denominations were represented, but all knew the old-time hymns. The Moody and Sankey book had soon found its way out there, and incited every one that could raise a note to make the attempt. We had forgotten to bring a tuner for the piano, but the blacksmith made a very good one. One of the band, who had been in a piano-house before enlisting, kept the instrument in order. We had hard work to keep it in tune, for not only did the extreme cold affect the sound, but it had to endure the constant drumming of untaught fingers. Even my husband, who was not nervous, used sometimes to beg Colonel Tom to stop "feeling about for that tune!"

The general loved music, and had so correct an ear

that he often sang or whistled the airs of an opera after hearing them once. Music so charmed him that when we have been in the States, listening to an oratorio, the Thomas orchestra, or a recital of any kind, he has begged me not to be hurt if he did not speak during the rendering. There was a Swiss soldier in our regiment who had contrived to bring his zither with him. My husband would lie on the bear-skin rug in front of the fire and listen with delight as long as he ventured to tax the man. He played the native Tyrolese airs, which seemed to have caught in them the sound of the Alpine horn, the melody of the cascade, and the echo of the mountain passes. The general often regretted that he had not had the opportunity to learn music. It seemed to me that it was a great solace and diversion to officers if they knew some musical instrument well enough to enjoy practice. They certainly gave great pleasure to those around them.

If the ladies had any accomplishment that gave gratification to others, it was never allowed to grow rusty. Of course, where there was so little to interest, whatever they did was overrated. Some times we heard of one of the officers of the 7th matching the perfections of our ladies against those of another regiment which he might happen to be visiting. His *esprit de corps* carried him so far that he would insist that no women sang, played, danced, painted, or rode as we did! We could only hope that we would never see the people to whom he had boasted, and so awaken them from his overdrawn story to the reality.

I used to pity the officers from the bottom of my

heart because of the tameness and dead calm of their lives in winter. Each year's service with them made me wonder more and more how they could come through the test of so much unemployed time, the really fine men they were. Watts spoke lines that will do for all time, when he told us who it was that found mischief for idle hands. We had no good company libraries, like the infantry, because we had so long been without a place to call our own. Every officer coming from leave, brought what books he could, and they went the rounds until the worn leaves would hardly hold together. We women had many a simple occupation that interested us, but the men could not content themselves with trifles. If the young ladies and I stole away to try to take a nap or change our dress, we were almost invariably called back by the lonely men, who wished to be amused. They were certainly so grateful for the slightest kindness it was no tax. Besides, people cannot go up and down the face of the earth together for nine years of hardships, trials, and deprivation without being as nearly like one family as is possible.

I used to dread the arrival of the young officers who came to the regiment from West Point, fearing that the sameness and inactivity of the garrison life would be a test to which their character would succumb. When they came to pay the first ceremonious call in full uniform, we spoke of commonplace topics. I kept up a running line of comments to myself, usually on one subject: "I wonder if you are likely to go to the bad under temptation; I am sorry for your mother, having to give you up and be anxious for your habits at the same time;

I hope you don't drink; I pray that you may have stamina enough to resist evil." Our sister knew that I believed so in matrimony as a savior of young officers that she used to teasingly accuse me of greeting all of them when they arrived with the same welcome: "I am very glad to see you; I hope that you are engaged." I hardly remember being quite so abrupt as that in speaking, but I never failed to wish it to myself. Their frequent difficulty was that they desired to do everything that the old officers did. I have known them rub and try to mar their shining new uniforms to have them look as if they had seen service. One, especially youthful in appearance, wondered how I came to divine that the reason he wore his grandfather's fob and seal, and carried the gold-headed cane when off duty, was that he wished to look old and experienced. I could not help praising them when they went through the first few telling years of service and came off conquerors. I was sure that had I had the misfortune to be a man I could not have borne the tests to which I knew they were subjected.

I am sure that we could not have been so contented as we were under such circumstances had there not been such perfect health among us all. It was a pleasure to live among so many hundred people and scarcely see any one who was not perfectly well. Another relief in that life was that we never saw crippled or maimed people, and there were no suffering poor.

We found our new quarters admirable for the garrison gayety. On Friday nights we all gathered together to dance, or have private theatricals or games. During the early part of the winter, while the supply of eggs we had brought from St. Paul lasted, Mary used to give us cake, frozen custard, or some luxury of which these formed a part. This, in addition to the usual ham-sandwiches, coffee, and venison, made our refreshments. As winter advanced, and the supplies began to give out, we had to be content with crullers, coffee, and sandwiches. There was very little spirit of criticism, and in that climate one is always hungry.

Of course every one relied on cards as the unfailing amusement. Almost without exception they played well and with great enthusiasm. Every one struggled over me, and I really worked faithfully to become an adept. For though I did not enjoy it ever, it seemed very ungracious in me not to be able to take a hand when I was needed. There must have been something lacking in my mental organization, for I could not learn. I had one friend who was equally stupid. He certainly was a comfort to me. We became perfectly hardened to the gibes of our friends when they called to him, "Come, Smith, and try this new game; it is easy. Why, even Mrs. Custer learned it!" I labored on, until at the end of twelve years of effort I trumped my part-ner's ace, and was formally excused from ever trying again.

A fancy-dress party was always amusing out there, for it was necessary to exercise great ingenuity in get-ting up costumes. We were masked carefully, and often the dress was such a complete disguise that a husband and wife were kept in ignorance of each other until the signal for unmasking was given at supper.

It was impossible to conceal our eccentricities living

in such close daily association. As there was continual chaffing and innumerable practical jokes, it was difficult to know at what moment one's peculiarities were to be served up for the amusement of others. At all events, when one's personal traits and singularities were openly joked about, it was something of a consolation to know that the worst to be said was directed to the face and not behind the back, as is the general rule. There was one of our number towards whom we could not fire the shot and shell of ridicule. He was far older than any one at the post, and there was too much reverence for his hoary head to permit extreme raillery. I confess to laughing over some of his strange aberrations when his young lieutenant gave us an imitation of their company drill. The old officer, mounted on a horse as toned down as himself, stood in front of his troops and addressed them as he would have done his supporters in the old political days. They appreciated the stump eloquence, but more keenly the fact that while he talked they would escape the tedious evolutions of their work. Sometimes while going through the directions of the tactics, the captain lost his suavity and called a halt. Then, with all the inflections and emphasis placed as carefully as if he were flinging the Constitution at a crowd of citizens on the 4th of July, he harangued in slightly heated tones, "Men, do you suppose you are men? If so, act like men. If you are geese, act like geese." This would finish the self-control of even the oldest soldier, and a great guffaw would burst out. For nothing can be more ridiculous than a regular officer pausing to address his men in such a place. The drill is conducted usually without another word than a repetition of the exact language of the book of tactics. The young lieutenant in his position at the rear would nearly choke with laughter. He told us how he rode along the line, and prodded the soldiers in the back, without the captain seeing him, to try and make them more deferential. His short burlesque repetitions of the aphorisms, philosophy, and theories on all subjects, that the old captain delivered daily on the drill-ground, were convulsing. If the speeches themselves were half as funny as the imitations, the men would have been stolidity itself if they had not forgotten their discipline and laughed. My husband was truly attached to this officer, and spared him from hardships and trying campaigns when he could. In a measure he felt himself responsible for the incongruous position the elderly man occupied in a cavalry regiment full of young, active men. After the war, when the old officer was mustered out of the Volunteer service, he found that in his native State the waves had closed over him, and his place was lost in public life. The general went personally to the War Department, and solicited an appointment for him in the Regular Army. Some time after, he was surprised to find him assigned to his own regiment, doubtless because a personal application gave the impression that it would be a special favor to place him there. Had he only asked for an infantry appointment for the already tired out man, it would have been a far easier life for him, but it had not occurred to the general.

Many of us had been laughingly rechristened, and called a name that was in some way suggested by trifling incidents in our history. The names were absurd. One of the most delicate and refined of our women was a superb rider and had shot buffalo, so her intimates spoke of her, when trying to provoke repartee, as "Buffalo Ann." My sobriquet of "the old lady" dated back to the first days of my married life. When the general and his merry young staff returned from a raid in the Shenandoah Valley, they descried an old Dutchman, who did not care which side in the war succeeded, so long as he and his property were left alone. His house had been their head-quarters in a former raid, and they all rode up there to halt again. The old Hans stood on his steps as they approached and wafted them away, at the same time reiterating, by way of emphasis, "Gentlemens, I have no objections to your coming in, but the old lady she kicks agin it." After that I could not raise the mildest protest against any plan but that those mischievous brothers would exclaim pathetically, and in a most tormenting tone, "What a good time we might have if the old lady didn't kick agin it." Sometimes the mildest and quietest one of us all would be called by some appellation so suggestive of ruffianism and bloodshed that it was the extreme of the ridiculous to associate the person and the name together. For instance, the best regulated and least sensational one would find himself addressed as "Shacknasty Bill, or the Sinewy Slayer of the Ghostly Gulch." Another, always inclined to gloom, was given a rousing slap on the back as his good-morning, and a hearty "How are you, Old Skull and Cross-bones?" No one escaped. I used to think the joking was carried too far sometimes, but it was easy to go to extremes when the resources were so limited for a variety in our life. My own blood rose to lava heat when I found people twitting one another on unpleasant facts, and a smile of ridicule circulating. It was too great a triumph for the teaser to stir up wrath though, and the life was a lesson of constant self-control. Certainly it was excellent discipline, and calculated to keep one's self-confidence within bounds. It was the same sort of training that members of a large family have, and they profit by the friction, for they are rarely so selfish and exacting as only children usually are.

CHAPTER XXIV.

AN INDIAN COUNCIL.

THE Indians came several times from the reservations for counsel, but the occasion that made the greatest impression upon me was towards the spring. They came to implore the general for food. In the fall the steamer bringing them supplies was detained in starting. It had hardly accomplished half the required distance before the ice impeded its progress, and it lay out in the channel, frozen in, all winter. The suffering among the Indians was very great. They were compelled to eat their dogs and ponies to keep from starving. Believing a personal appeal would be effectual, they asked to come to our post for a council.

The Indian band brought their great orator Running Antelope. He was intensely dignified and fine-looking. His face when he spoke was expressive and animated, contrary to all the precedents of Indian oratory we had become familiar with. As he stood among them all in the general's room, he made an indelible impression on my memory. The Indians' feet are usually small; sometimes their vanity induces them to put on women's shoes. The hands are slender and marvellously soft considering their life of exposure. Their speech is full of gesture, and the flexible wrist makes their movements expressive. A distinguished scholar, speaking of the aid the hand is to an orator, calls it the "second face." It certainly was so with Running Antelope. He described the distressing condition of the tribe with real eloquence. While he spoke, lifting his graceful hands towards Heaven in appeal, one of my husband's birds that was uncaged floated down and alighted on the venerable warrior's head. It had been so petted, no ordinary movement startled the little thing. It maintained its poise, spreading its wings to keep its balance, as the Indian moved his head in gesture. The orator saw that the faces of the Indians showed signs of humor, but he was ignorant of what amused them. His inquiring eyes saw no solution in the general's, for, fearing to disconcert him, General Custer controlled every muscle in his face. Finally the bird whirled up to his favorite resting-place on the horn of the buffalo head, and the warrior understood the unusual sight of a smile from his people.

His whole appeal was most impressive, and touched the quick sympathies of my husband. He was a sincere friend of the reservation Indian. The storehouses at our post were filled with supplies, and he promised to telegraph to the Great Father for permission to give them rations until spring. Meantime, he promised them all they could eat while they awaited at the post the answer to the despatch. Not content with a complaint of their present wrongs, Running Antelope went off into an earnest denunciation of the agents, calling them dishonest.

One of the Indians, during the previous summer, with fox-like cunning had lain out on the dock all day apparently sleeping, while he watched the steamer unloading supplies intended for them. A mental estimate was carefully made of what came off the boat, and compared as carefully afterwards with what was distributed. There was an undeniable deficit. A portion that should have been theirs was detained, and they accused the agent of keeping it. The general interrupted, and asked the interpreter to say that the Great Father selected the agents from among good men before sending them out from Washington. Running Antelope quickly responded, "They may be good men when they leave the Great Father, but they get to be desperate cheats by the time they reach us." I shall have to ask whoever reads, to substitute another more forcible adjective, such as an angry man would use, in place of "desperate." The Indian language is not deficient in abusive terms and epithets.

When the council was ended and the Indians were preparing to leave, my husband asked me to have Mary put everything we had ready to eat on the dining-room table. The manner in which Running Antelope folded his robe around him and strode in a stately way down the long parlor was worthy of a Roman emperor.

I had been so impressed by his oratory and lordly mien that I could hardly believe my eyes when I saw him at table, and descend from the lofty state of mind into which he had taken me to realize what he was doing. After gorging himself, he emptied the plates and swept all the remains from before the places of the other chiefs into the capacious folds of his robe. This he re-belted at the waist, so that it formed a very good temporary haversack. With an air signifying to "the victor belong the spoils," he swept majestically out of the house.

The answer came next day from the Secretary of War that the Department of the Interior which had the Indians in charge refused to allow any army supplies to be distributed. They gave as a reason that it would involve complexities in their relations with other departments. It was a very difficult thing for the general to explain to the Indians. They knew that both army and Indians were fed from the same source, and they could not comprehend what difference it could make when a question of starvation was pending. They could not be told, what we all knew, that had the War Department made good the deficiencies it would have reflected discredit on the management of the Department of the Interior. The chiefs were compelled to return to their reservations, where long ago all the game had been shot and their famishing tribe were many of them driven to join the hostiles. We were not surprised that the warriors were discouraged and desperate, and that the depredations of Sitting Bull on the settlements increased with the new accessions to his numbers.

CHAPTER XXV.

BREAKING UP OF THE MISSOURI.

The day of the final breaking up of the ice in the Missouri was one of great excitement to us. The roar and crash of the ice-fields could be heard a great distance. The sound of the tremendous report was the signal for the whole garrison to go out on the hill near the infantry post and watch the grand sight. Just above us was a bend in the river, and around this curve great floes of ice rushed, heaping up in huge masses as they swept down the furious current. All the lowlands that lay between Bismarck and the river were inundated, and the shore far in covered with blocks of ice that the force of the water had thrown there. Just across the river from us was a wretched little collection of huts, occupied by outlaws, into which the soldiers were decoyed to drink and gamble. The law forbidding liquor to be sold on the reservation was so strict that whiskey venders did not dare set foot on the Government land. The reservation was too large to permit them to place themselves on its other boundaries; they would have been at such a distance from the post that it would not have been worth while. Just on the water's edge opposite, these human fiends had perched to watch and entice the enlisted men. Over their rude cabins they had painted elaborate and romantically expressed signs. In the midst of bleak surroundings rose an untidy canvas-covered cabin, called "My Lady's Bower," or over the door of a rough log-hut was a sign of the "Dew Drop Inn" (Do drop in).

These shanties were placed on a little rise of ground, with a precautionary thought of the usual spring floods. The day of the first ice-breaking we saw the water rise to such a height that cabin after cabin was abandoned. The occupants dragged their property as best they could to the little rise where one or two, more cautious than the rest, had built. On this narrow neck of land huddled together the whole of the group, in desperate peril. No one on our side of the river could help them, for the water was the maddest of whirlpools, while on the other side the overflow had made a great lake, cutting them off from Bismarck. As we watched them scrambling on the little knoll, like drowning men clinging to the upturned keel of a boat, we suffered real distress at our powerlessness to help them. The company commanders, remembering how they had been the cause of the demoralization of some of their best soldiers, openly avowed at first their relief that the whole wretched lot were about to drown; but as the peril increased, not one of the officers' hearts remained unsoftened. They forgot what an utterly abandoned, lawless company it was, and wished that some means might be found by which they could be saved.

We women had discovered through the field-glasses a few of our own sex among them, and were alarmed at their danger; for no matter what they were, the helplessness of women at such a time makes one forget everything, save that their lives hang in the balance. At last one of them stepped into the only small boat they had been able to retain, and standing bravely at the side of the one man at the bow, they were swept down the river out of sight among the gorge of ice-blocks and never again heard from. It was too exhausting watching these imperilled beings, knowing how incapable we were of helping them, and we went back to our quarters to spend hours of suspense. We could not set ourselves about doing anything while the lives of human beings so near us were in jeopardy. As day began to close, word came for our relief that the water was subsiding; not, alas, until some of them had been borne to their last home. Those that were left waded back to their huts, and, unheeding the warning of that fearful day, began again their same miserable existence.

Of all our happy days, the happiest had now come to us at Fort Lincoln. I never knew more united married people than those of our regiment. It will be easily understood that in the close companionship involved in the intimate relationships of that life, either uncontrollable hatred or increasing affection must ensue. If a desperate attack of incompatibility set in out there, the climate, fine as it was, simply had to disagree with the wife, for it was next to madness for both of them if they did not escape from a life where almost every hour is spent with each other. The wife had the privilege of becoming the comrade of her husband in that isolated existence, and the officers seemed to feel that every amusement was heightened if shared by the other sex. That perpetual intimacy was a crucial test of the genuineness of the affection. My husband used to quote a line or two from one of Mrs. Stowe's books that we had read together. The new husband is asked why he knows that he loves his wife: "Because she never tires me; she never makes me nervous." He believed that if husbands and wives bore that proof successfully as time advanced, they might count on a happy future.

Life grew more enjoyable every day as we realized the blessings of our home. When the winter was finally gone there was not an hour that we would not have recalled. I have seen my husband with all the abandon of a boy throw himself on a rug in front of the fire and enumerate his blessings with real gratitude. Speaking of his regiment first, his district (for he then had five posts under his command), the hunting, his dogs and horses, and his own room, which was an unceasing delight, he used to declare to me that he would not exchange places with any one—not even a friend in civil life who stood at the head of his profession as a journalist, who had wealth and youth, and who lived in almost princely luxury. My husband used to tell me that he believed he was the happiest man on earth, and I cannot help thinking that he was. For with all the vicissitudes of those twelve eventful years, I never knew him to have an hour's depression. The presence of so many of his family about him was an unceasing pleasure. There was an abiding fondness between his brother, Colonel Tom, and himself. This brother was scarcely more than a lad when he joined us. The general said to some Eastern friends when he was in the States the last time, "To prove to you how I value and admire my brother as a soldier, I think that he should be the general and I the captain."

Colonel Tom always lived with us, and the brothers played incessant jokes on each other. Both of them honored and liked women extremely. Colonel Tom used to pay visits of an unconscionable length to ladies of the garrison, and no amount of teasing on his brother's part would induce him to shorten them. He never knew, when he started to go home from these visits, but that he would find on the young lady's door-mat his trunk, portmanteau, and satchel — this as a little hint from the general that he was overtaxing the lady's patience. I used to think my husband too severe with his brother, for in his anxiety not to show favoritism he noticed the smallest misdemeanor. If, in visiting with the young ladies in our parlor, he overstayed the hour he was due at the stables or drill, the general's eye noticed it, and perhaps overlooked others in the room who were erring in the same manner. I knew that a reprimand would be sent from the adjutant's office in the morning if I did not invent some way to warn the offender, so I learned the bugle-call for stables, and hovering around Colonel Tom, hummed it in his ear, which the voice of the charmer had dulled to the trumpet-call. When the sound penetrated, he would make a plunge for his hat and belt, and tear out of the house, thus escaping reproof.

When spring came again, it is impossible to express the joy I felt that there was to be no summer campaign;

and for the first time in many years I saw the grass grow without a shudder. The general began the improvement of the post with fresh energy, and from the drill-ground came the click of the horses' hoofs and the note of the bugles repeating the commands of the officers. As soon as it was warm enough, several charming girls came out from the States to our garrison to visit us. They gave every one pleasure, and effectually turned the heads of the young officers.

We had supposed that when travelling from the Gulf of Mexico almost to the border of the British possessions, we could safely call ourselves "West;" but we found that there was a post fifteen hundred miles beyond us, on the Missouri River. The steamers were constantly taking officers and their families from Bismarck into Montana. Sometimes the delay of the boats in starting gave us the privilege of entertaining them. I remember going down to bid good-bye to a family who had gone on board a steamer at our landing. The officer was returning from an infantry recruiting detail in the States. He had eight children and a dog. These, with a lieutenant's pay, constituted his riches. He disappeared into a state-room and brought out the new baby, exhibiting it with as much pride as if it had been the first-born! They told me afterwards that during all that slow, wearisome journey of fifteen hundred miles, on a boat that needs be seen to be appreciated, the mother was placid and happy. There were no guards around the deck, so she tied the children separately to the different articles of stationary furniture, and let them play out to the limits of their tethers.

Almost our only exercise on summer evenings was walking on the outskirts of the garrison surrounded by the dogs. It was dangerous to go far, but we could walk with safety in the direction of the huts of the Indian scouts. Their life always interested us, and by degrees they became so accustomed to our presence that they went on with all their occupations without heeding us.

There was a variety of articles among the litter tossed down in front of these Indian quarters; lariates, saddles, and worn-out robes were heaped about an arrangement for conveying their property from place to place. The construction was simple, and rendered wheels unnecessary. About midway on two long saplings, placed a short distance apart, is a foundation of leather thongs. Upon this the effects belonging to an Indian family are lashed. Two pole ends are attached to either side of a rude harness on the pony, while the other two drag on the ground. In following an Indian trail, the indentation made by the poles, as they are pulled over the ground, traces the course of travel unmistakably.

Some of their boats lay upturned about the door. They were perfectly round, like a great bowl, and composed of a wicker frame over which buffalo hide was tightly drawn. The primitive shape and construction dates back to the ancient Egyptians, and these boats were called coracles in olden times. They seemed barely large enough to hold two Indians, who were obliged to crouch down as they paddled their way with short, awkward oars through the rapid current of the Missouri.

Bloody Knife was naturally mournful; his face still looked sad when he put on the presents given him. He was a perfect child about gifts, and the general studied to bring him something from the East that no other Indian had.

He had proved himself such an invaluable scout to the general that they often had long interviews. Seated on the grass, the dogs lying about them, they talked over portions of the country that the general had never seen, the scout drawing excellent maps in the sand with a pointed stick. He was sometimes petulant, often moody, and it required the utmost patience on my husband's part to submit to his humors; but his fidelity and cleverness made it worth while to yield to his tempers.

I was always interested in the one pretty squaw among them, called Et-nah-wah-ruchta, which means Medicine Mother. Her husband was young, and she was devoted to him. I have seen him lounging on the floor of the hut while she made his toilet, combing and plaiting his hair, cutting and oiling the bangs which were trimmed to cover his forehead, and plucking the few scattered hairs from his chin—for they do not consider it an honor to have a suspicion of a beard. She strapped on his leggings, buckled his belt, and finally lighted his pipe. Once the war bonnet of her lord had to be rearranged. He deigned to put it on her head, readjusted the eagle feathers, and then gave it to her to fasten them in securely. The faithful slave even used to accompany him to his bath. Indians do bathe—at long intervals. I was not ambitious to know if she actually performed the ablutions. However, I have seen him, at a distance, running along the river bank on his return, his wife waving a blanket behind him to keep off the mosquitoes!

If the Indians kill any game, they return home, order the squaws to take the ponies and bring back what they have killed, and then throw themselves down to sleep among the sprawling Indian babies, tailless dogs, and general filth. The squaws do all the labor, and every skin is tanned by their busy fingers. I never knew but one Indian who worked. He was an object of interest to me, though he kept himself within the gloom of the cabin, and skulked around the fire when he cooked. This was the occupation forced upon him by the others. He had lacked the courage to endure the torture of the sun-dance; for when strips of flexible wood had been drawn through the gashes in his back, and he was hung up by these, the poor creature had fainted. On reviving he begged to be cut down, and ever after was an object of scorn. He was condemned to wear squaw's clothing from that time on. They mocked and taunted him, and he led as separate an existence as if he were in a desert alone. The squaws disdained to notice him, except to heap work upon his already burdened shoulders.

Once my husband and I, in walking, came suddenly upon a queer little mound, that we concluded we would observe at a distance. An Indian was seen carrying buckets and creeping with difficulty into the small aperture. It was about six feet in diameter, and proved to be a kind of steam-bath, which they consider great medicine. A hole is first dug in the ground and filled with stones; a fire is kindled upon them long before, and they are heated red-hot. The round framework of saplings over these is covered with layer upon layer of blankets and robes, so that no air can penetrate. The Indians, almost stripped of their clothing, crouch round them, while the one acting as servant brings water to pour on the heated rocks. The steam has no escape, and the Indians are thoroughly roasted. While we were looking at this curious bath-house a small Indian boy crept out from under the edges of the blankets, and ashamed to have given in before the rest, drew his almost parboiled little body into a hiding-place. Ever ambitious, like small boys of all nationalities, he had at first believed experience better than hearsay.

We went one day into a tepee that was placed by itself to see an Indian who was only slightly ill. His father and friends were talking to him of his death as a certainty, and making all the plans in advance. They even took his measure for a coffin, assuring him that they would honor him by putting him in a box in imitation of the white man. The general used to listen wonderingly when they referred to their dead in the speeches in council. It was always in some roundabout way, never directly.

The Indians all seemed a melancholy people. They sometimes ask embarrassing questions. Perhaps, when some young girl accompanied us, they spoke to my husband in the sign language, in which he was versed. Once they inquired if the young lady was his other wife. The blush of the girl so amused us that our laugh rang out among them, and seemed to be a sound they knew nothing of. They sat on the ground for hours, gambling for iron, brass and silver rings, but always glum and taciturn. The tallest Indian of them all, Long Soldier, grew to be very cunning when he learned what a curiosity he was. He would crouch down at our approach, and only at the sight of a coin as a "tip" would he draw up his seven feet of height.

The Ree scouts entertained their chief, Star-of-the-North, during the summer. We were all asked to the feast, and all formally presented to the distinguished stranger, who could not comprehend why he was expected to shake hands with women. After going through what he found was courtesy among the whites, he offered us a place around the circle. Taking a bone from the meat broiling before the fire he offered it to the general. My husband, after getting some salt, had the courage to eat it. It was want of tact on my part to decline, but my heart failed me when I recognized the master of ceremonies for the evening. As he proffered me some meat, I found him to be the ferocious-looking savage who had killed his enemy from another tribe and eaten his heart warm.

CHAPTER XXVI.

CURIOUS CHARACTERS AND EXCURSIONISTS AMONG US.

I WISH that I could recall more about the curious characters among us. Most of them had some strange history in the States that had been the cause of their seeking the wild life of the frontier. The one whose past we would have liked best to know was a man most valued by my husband. All the important scoutings and most difficult missions where secrecy was required were intrusted to him. We had no certain knowledge whether or not he had any family or friends elsewhere, for he never spoke of them. He acknowledged once, in a brief moment of confidence, that he was a gentleman by birth. Startled, perhaps, by the look of curiosity that even a friend's face showed, he turned the conversation, and said, " Oh, but what's the use to refer to it now ?" We did not even know whether Charley Reynolds was his real name or one that he had assumed. Soon after we reached Dakota the general began to employ him as a scout. He remained with him much of the time, until he fell in the battle of the Little Big Horn. My husband had such genuine admiration for him that I soon learned to listen to everything pertaining to his life with marked interest. He was so shy that he hardly raised his eyes when I extended my hand at

the general's introduction. He did not assume the picturesque dress, long hair, and belt full of weapons that
are characteristic of the scout.   His manner was perfectly simple and straightforward, and he could not be induced to talk of himself.   He had large, dark-blue eyes,
and a frank face.   Year after year he braved the awful
winters of Dakota alone.   I have known him start out
from Fort Lincoln when even our officers, accustomed as
they were to hardships, were forbidden to go.   He had
been the best shot and most successful hunter in the territory for fifteen years.   When I watched the scouts
starting off on their missions, I invariably thanked Heav-
en that I was born a woman, and consequently no deed
of valor would ever be expected from me.   I felt,
though, that were I compelled to be brave, I would far
rather go into battle with the inspiration of the trumpet-
call and the clash of arms, than go off alone and take
my life in my hands as did the scouts.

The year that the regiment explored the Black Hills,
Charley Reynolds undertook to carry despatches through
to Fort Laramie, over one hundred and fifty miles distant.
He had only his compass to guide him, for there was not
even a trail.   The country was infested with Indians,
and he could only travel at night.   During the day he
hid his horse as well as he could in the underbrush, and
lay down in the long grass.   In spite of these precautions
he was sometimes so exposed that he could hear the
voices of Indians passing near.   He often crossed Indian trails on his journey.   The last nights of his march
he was compelled to walk, as his horse was exhausted,
and he found no water for hours.   The frontiersmen

frequently dig in the beds of dried-up streams and find water, but this resource failed. His lips became so parched and his throat so swollen that he could not close his mouth. In this condition he reached Fort Laramie and delivered his despatches. It was from the people of that post that the general heard of his narrow escape. He came quietly back to his post at Fort Lincoln, and only confessed to his dangers when closely questioned by the general long afterwards. When I think how gloriously he fell, fighting for his country, with all the valor and fidelity of one of her officers, my eyes fill with tears; for he lies there on that battle-field, unwept, un- honored, and unsung. Had he worn all the insignia of the high rank and the decorations of an adoring coun- try, he could not have led a braver life or died a more heroic death; and yet he is chronicled as " only a scout."

We were inundated with excursionists during the summer. In order to induce immigration the railroads had reduced the rates. One of the incidents of the trip was to cross from Bismarck to Fort Lincoln. Some- times I had assistance in entertaining, but oftener I was left to perform this duty alone. I have been sitting with the general and four of his family, when we would see the post-ambulance unloading at the door. In an instant I would find myself standing alone in the room, the vanishing forms of all the family disappearing through the doors, and even out of the windows open- ing upon the piazza. In vain I entreated them to re- turn; a smothered laugh at my indignation was all the response.

It was sometimes tiresome to receive large groups of

people, who wanted to know impossible things about the
country, and if it was a good soil for wheat. I only
remember one party who taxed my patience to the ut-
termost. They cared nothing about Dakota as an agricultural territory, but had come on purpose to see the
general. To satisfy them, I sent the servants and orderly to find him, but all returned with the same answer—
he was nowhere to be seen. I walked about the garrison with them, explaining our post as best I could; the
band came to play for them; and finally, as a last resort,
I opened the general's room to show them his hunting
mementos. It was all of no avail. One very decided
woman said, "This is all very interesting, but we *came*
to see General Custer, and we do not intend to leave
until we do." Finally I said, in desperation, he is much
interested in improvements for the post, and spends
much time out-of-doors. "Very well," said the chief
spokesman, "we will go all around the garrison and try
to find him." As soon as I had bowed them away, I ran
out to Mary to ask where the general really was. I had
known from the first, by a twinkle in her eye, that she
was helping him to escape. "Law, Miss Libbie, the
giniral most got sunstroke hidin' in the chicken-coop."
The coop was still unroofed, and my husband had been
superintending the building of a double wall to keep
out the cold in winter; and there I found him, really ill,
having beaten his hasty retreat without a hat, and remained in the broiling sun rather than submit to the
odious ordeal of being on exhibition.

Our house was so full of company, and we had so
little time for each other, that in order to visit together

we were obliged to take our horses, and ride up and down the valley as far as it was safe to go. Even then my husband's eyes scanned the horizon so searchingly, hardly turning his face away from where the Indians were wont to dash, that it intimidated me to see such watchfulness. If we went even a few paces beyond our usual beat, which was bounded by the grazing stock and the guard, and the busy chatter at his side ceased, my husband would look quickly to see the cause of the un- usual silence. My lip quivered with fear, and I was wont to wink busily and swallow to keep back a tear of terror, of which I was always ashamed, and against which I made constant battle. The moment our horses' heads were turned towards home the endless flow of laughter and talk began again. When we could not ride, we went out on the bluffs, just on the edge of the garrison, for an uninterrupted hour. We were often out for hours, my husband shooting at a mark, while I was equally busy taking accurate aim at the ever-present mosquito, our constant companion in all our good times.

As the soldiers and citizens all knew the general's love of pets, we had constant presents. Many of them I would have gladly declined, but notwithstanding a badger, porcupine, raccoon, prairie-dog, and wild-turkey, all served their brief time as members of our family. They were comparatively harmless, and I had only the inconvenience to encounter. When a ferocious wild- cat was brought in, with a triumphant air, by the donor, and presented with a great flourish, I was inclined to mutiny. My husband made allowance for my dread of the untamed creature, and decided to send him into the

States, as a present to one of the zoological gardens; for in its way it was a treasure. While it remained with us it was kept in the cellar. Mary used to make many retreats, tumbling up the stairs, when the cat flew at her the length of its chain. She was startled so often that at last she joined with me in requesting its removal as soon as convenient. The general regretted giving it up, but Keevan was called to chloroform and box it for the journey. Colonel Tom printed some facetious words on the slats of the cover—something like "Do not fondle." They were somewhat superfluous, for no one could approach the box, after the effects of the chloroform had passed away, without encountering the fiery-red eyes, and such scratchings and spittings and mad plunges as suggested the propriety of keeping one's distance. Some detention kept the freight-train at a station over Sunday; the box with the wild-cat was put in the baggage-room. The violence of the animal as it leaped and tore at the cover loosened the slats, and it escaped into the room. The freight agent spent a wretched day! Chloroform was again resorted to, and it was deemed a good riddance when the animal was sent off. When we received a letter of thanks from the Scientific Board for so splendid a specimen, I was relieved to know that the wild-cat was at last where it could no longer create a reign of terror.

At one time the general tamed a tiny field-mouse, and kept it in a large, empty inkstand on his desk. It grew very fond of him, and ran over his head and shoulders, and even through his hair. Women are not responsible for their fear of mice; they are born so. I had fortunately only to keep away from the desk when the little creature was free, for it was contented to consider that its domain. The general, thinking at last that it was cruel to detain the little thing in-doors when it belonged by nature to the fields, took it out and left it on the plain. The kindness was of no earthly use; like the oft-quoted prisoner of the Bastile, it was back again at the steps in no time, and preferred captivity to freedom.

CHAPTER XXVII.

RELIGIOUS SERVICES.—LEAVE OF ABSENCE.

WE had clergymen and missionaries of different denominations as our guests during the summer months. Among them was a man from the East, who was full of zeal and indifferent to the opinion of others as long as he felt that he was right. He began to brave public opinion on his way to Fort Lincoln. The cars had stopped for some time at a station where there was a town; the missionary, wishing to improve every opportunity for doing good, went out on the platform and began a sermon. Before long he had a crowd of people around him, listening with curiosity. There were laughter and sneers when the quavering voice of the old man started a hymn that was familiar throughout the length and breadth of the land. No one joined. Our brother Tom and a friend, sitting in the car, but knowing nothing of the mission of the man, realized his unsupported position, and quickly went to him. Standing on either side of him, they joined their fresh young voices in the hymn. Before long one after the other of the crowd joined in the music, inspired by the independence of the example. The missionary returned then with the officers, and came to our house, where my husband asked him to remain indefinitely. We found him almost a monomaniac on the subject of converting the Indians, and had not the general prevented him from risking his life, he would have gone out alone among the war-like tribes.

While he was waiting for an opportunity to go farther west, he begged to begin meetings among the soldiers, and said that in order to do more good and get at the hearts of those he would help, he must live among them. For this purpose he left us, and went down to share the rations of the enlisted men. The general had a room in a vacant barrack put in order, and there the old man began his work. Every night the garrison echoed with the voices of hundreds of soldiers singing hymns. The simple, unaffected goodness of the missionary caused them to believe in him, and he found his way to many a heart that beat under the army blue. My husband felt thankful to have some work go on among the enlisted men. We often talked of their condition, and he felt that some of the energies of good people in behalf of foreign missions might well be expended upon our army on the frontier. Among his plans was the building of an assembly-room at the post, especially for the soldiers: a place where they could have their own entertainments, and where the papers, magazines, and general library might be kept. He regretted constantly that there was no regular place where there could be services for the men when the itinerant clergyman came. The service was usually held in our parlor, but it was only large enough for the officers and their families. In the following letter he touches upon the subject of bettering the condition of the enlisted men, and bears tribute to the good man who forgot himself in his love for mankind.

"FORT LINCOLN, DAKOTA, *September* 17, 1875.
" Dr. Newman:

"DEAR SIR,—I take the liberty of addressing you a few lines in regard to the Christian work in which Mr. Matchett has been engaged at this post. He came here under the auspices of the Indian Bureau, intending to labor among the tribes of the Upper Missouri River, but owing to some obstacles encountered at points above this on the river, he returned here some weeks ago to await further instructions from those under whom he is acting.

"In the mean time he has devoted himself to missionary work among the soldiers — a class, by-the-way, whose moral welfare, at least on the frontier, is as sadly neglected as that of any of our aboriginal tribes. Mr. Matchett enters into his work with great earnestness and zeal. He has impressed all with whom he has been associated with his unselfishness, his honesty of purpose, and his great desire to do good.

"It is but due to him and the holy cause he represents, and a pleasure to me, to testify to the success which has crowned his labors, particularly among the soldiers of this command. If our large posts on the remote frontier, which are situated far from church and Church influences, had chaplains who were as faithful Christians as I believe Mr. Matchett to be, and who, like him, are willing to labor faithfully among the enlisted men, the moral standard, now necessarily so low among that neglected class, would be elevated far above its present level, and great results would follow.

"Hoping you will receive these lines in the spirit which prompts me to send them, I am truly yours,

"G. A. CUSTER, Brevet Major-General U. S. A."

In the autumn we went into the States, and spent most of the winter delightfully in New York. We went out a great deal. Of course we were compelled to dress very plainly, and my husband made great sport of his only citizen overcoat—an ulster. He declared that it belonged so to the past that he was the only man beside the car-drivers that wore one. It did not disturb him in the least; neither did going in the horse-cars to receptions and dinners. He used laughingly to say, "Our coachman wears our livery, Libbie," when the car-driver had on an army overcoat. No one so perfectly independent as he was could fail to enjoy everything.

Colonel Tom and one of the oldest friends we had in the 7th were with us part of the time, and we had many enjoyable hours together. The theatre was our unfailing delight. They were all desirous that I should see the military play of "Ours," which was then so admirably put on the stage at Wallack's, but dreaded the effect it would have on me. At last one of them said that it was too finely represented for me to miss, and I heard them say to each other, "We must take 'the old lady,' though it will break her heart and she will cry." It ended in my going. When we reached the part in the play where the farewell comes, and the sword is buckled on the warrior by the trembling hands of the wife, I could not endure it. Too often had the reality of such suffering been my own. The three men were crying like children, and only too willing to take me out into the fresh air.

My husband spent many hours with Mr. Barrett in his dressing-room at the theatre, during the long wait of *Cassius* in the play of "Julius Cæsar." There were forty nights that these friends sat side by side, until the call-boy summoned the actor to the footlights. The general listened every evening with unflagging interest to the acting of his friend.

Every one seemed to vie with every one else in show-ing appreciation of my husband during that winter. He dined often with men who learned to draw him out in talk of his Plains life. While in the midst of some story, the butler would pass him a dish that he especially liked. The host at once directed the man to pass on, and told my husband that he could not spare time for him to take a second helping while they were impatient for the rest of the tale. After going hungry once or twice, the general learned to dine with me before he left the hotel, so that he might be free to give himself up to others.

He repeated a story to me about Ole Bull, who was asked to dinner and requested to bring his violin. He accepted for himself, but sent word that his violin did not dine. My husband made a personal application of the story, and threatened, playfully, to send word that his Indian stories did not dine, hoping thereby to secure to himself the privilege of satisfying his hunger unmo-lested. At the Century Club he received from distin-guished men the most cordial congratulations on his essay into the literary field. They urged him with many an encouraging word to continue the work. Some of the authors he met there were double his age, and he received each word they said with deep gratitude. My husband knew how I valued every expression of appre-ciation of him, and he used to awaken me, when he re-turned, to tell me what was said. He never failed to preface every such hesitating and reluctant repetition by exacting promises of secrecy. He feared that in my wifely pride I might repeat what he told me, and it would look like conceit on his part. I knew that he did not tell me the half, for when the tears of delight dropped from my eyes at the acknowledgment and commendation of others his voice ceased. I felt that nine years was a long time out of a young life to live in the wilderness, away from the sound of approving voices, and the association of men whose very presence incites to new effort. In February we had to say good-bye to all this pleasurable life. Our friends asked us why we went so soon. In army life it is perfectly natural to speak of one's financial condition, and it did not occur to us that civilians do not do the same. I do not wonder now that they opened their eyes with well-bred astonishment when we said we were obliged to go because we had used all the money we had saved for leave of absence.

CHAPTER XXVIII.

A WINTER'S JOURNEY ACROSS THE PLAINS.

WHEN we reached St. Paul the prospect before us was dismal, as the trains were not to begin running until April, at the soonest. The railroad officials, mindful of what the general had done for them in protecting their advance workers in the building of the road, came and offered to open the route. Sending us through on a special train was a great undertaking, and we had to wait some time for the preparations to be completed. One of the officers of the road took an engine out some distance to investigate, and it looked discouraging enough when he sprang down from the cab on his return in a complete coating of ice.

The train on which we finally started was an immense one, and certainly a curiosity. There were two snow-ploughs and three enormous engines; freight-cars with coal supplies and baggage; several cattle-cars, with stock belonging to the Black Hills miners who filled the passenger-coaches. There was an eating-house, looming up above everything, built on a flat car. In this car the forty employés of the road, who were taken to shovel snow, etc., were fed. There were several day-coaches, with army recruits and a few passengers, and last of all the paymaster's car, which my husband and

I occupied. This had a kitchen and a sitting-room. At first everything went smoothly. The cook on our car gave us excellent things to eat, and we slept soundly. It was intensely cold, but the little stove in the sitting-room was kept filled constantly. Sometimes we came to drifts, and the train would stop with a violent jerk, start again, and once more come to a stand-still, with such force that the dishes would fall from the table. The train-men were ordered out, and after energetic work by the stalwart arms the track was again clear and we went on. One day we seemed to be creeping; the engines whistled, and we shot on finely. The speed was checked so suddenly that the little stove fairly danced, and our belongings flew through the car from end to end. After this there was an exodus from the cars; every one went to inquire as to the ominous stop. Before our train there seemed to be a perfect wall of ice; we had come to a gully which was almost filled with drifts. The cars were all backed down some distance and detached; the snow-ploughs and engines having thus full sweep, all the steam possible was put on, and they began what they called "bucking the drifts." This did a little good at first, and we made some progress through the gully. After one tremendous dash, however, the ploughs and one engine were so deeply embedded that they could not be withdrawn. The employés dug and shovelled until they were exhausted. The Black Hills miners relieved them as long as they could endure it; then the officers and recruits worked until they could do no more. The impenetrable bank of snow was the accumulation of the whole winter, first

snowing, then freezing, until there were successive layers of ice and snow.   It was the most dispiriting and
forlorn situation.

Night was descending, and my husband, after restlessly going in and out to the next car, showed me that
he had some perplexity on his mind.   He described to
me the discomfort of the officers and Bismarck citizens
in the other coach in not having any place to sleep.
His meaning penetrated at last, and I said, "You are
waiting for me to invite them all to room with us?"
His "exactly" assured me it was precisely what he intended me to do.   So he hurried out to give them my
compliments and the invitation.   The officers are generally prepared for emergencies, and they brought in
their blankets; the citizens left themselves to the general's planning.   In order to make the car-blankets go
further, he made two of the folding-beds into one
broad one.   Two little berths on each side, and rolls
of bedding on the floor, left only room for the stove,
always heated to the last degree.   I was invited to
take the farthest place towards the wall, in the large
bed; then came my husband.   After that I burrowed
my head in my pillow, and the servant blew out some
of the candles and brought in our guests.   It is unnecessary for me to say that I did not see the order
in which they appeared.   The audible sleeping in our
bed, however, through the long nights that followed,
convinced me that the general had assigned those places
to the oldest, fattest, and ranking civilians.   Every
morning I awoke to find the room empty and all the
beds folded away.   The general brought me a tin basin

with ice-water, and helped me to make a quick toilet; our eleven visitors waited in the other coach, to return to breakfast with us in the same room. Every one made the best of the situation, and my husband was as rollicking as ever. Though I tried to conceal it, I soon lost heart entirely, and it cost me great effort to join with the rest in conversation.

The days seemed to stretch on endlessly; the snow was heaped up about us and falling steadily. All we could see was the trackless waste of white on every side. The wind whistled and moaned around the cars, and great gusts rocked our frail little refuge from side to side. The snow that had begun to fall with a few scattered flakes now came down more thickly. I made the best effort I could to be brave, and deceived them as to my real terrors—I had no other idea than that we must die there. We tried to be merry at our meals, and made light of the deficiencies that occurred each time we sat down. The increase at the table quickly diminished our stores, and I knew by the careful manner in which the wood was husbanded that it was nearly exhausted. The general, always cool and never daunted by anything, was even more blithe, to keep me from knowing that there was anything alarming in the situation. If I could have worked as the men did, even though it was at the hopeless snow-drifts, the time would not have seemed so long. Of course I had needle-work, but at such a time any industry that admits of thinking is of little use as a distraction. During those anxious days it used to seem strange to hear a dinner-bell through the air, muffled with snow. For an instant I was deluded into the thought that by some strange necromancy we had been spirited on to a station, and that this was the clang of the eating-house bell.   It was only the call from the car where the employés were fed.   The lowing of the cattle and howling of our dogs in the forward cars were the only other sounds we heard.   Finally the situation became desperate, and with all their efforts the officers could no longer conceal from me their concern for our safety.

Search was made throughout all the train to find if there was a man who understood anything about telegraphy, for among the fittings stowed away in the car a tiny battery had been found, with a pocket-relay.   A man was finally discovered who knew something of operating, and it was decided to cut the main wire.   Then the wires of the pocket-relay were carried out of our car and fastened to either end of the cut wire outside, so making an unbroken circuit between us and our Lincoln friends, besides uniting us with Fargo station.   In a little while the general had an answer from Colonel Tom, most characteristic: "Shall I come out for you? You say nothing about the old lady; is she with you?" The "old lady" begged the privilege of framing the reply.   I regretted that the telegram could not be underscored—a woman's only way of emphasizing—for I emphatically forbade him to come.   On this occasion I dared to assume a show of authority.   The stories of the risk and suffering of our mail-carriers during the two previous winters were too fresh in my memory for me to consent that Colonel Tom should encounter so much for our sake.

After that we kept the wires busy, talking with our friends and devising plans for our relief. We only succeeded in suppressing our headlong brother temporarily. Against our direct refusal he made all his preparations, and only telegraphed, when it was too late to receive an answer, that he was leaving garrison. Then our situation was forgotten in our solicitude about him. The time seemed to move on leaden wings, and yet it was in reality not long. He went to Bismarck, and looked up the best stage-driver in all the territory, and hired him. This driver was cool, intrepid, and inured to every peril. At an old stage-station along the route he found relays of mules that belonged to the mail-sleigh.

At last a great whoop and yell, such as was peculiar to the Custers, was answered by the general, and made me aware for the first time that Colonel Tom was outside. I scolded him for coming before I thanked him, but he made light of the danger and hurried us to get ready, fearing a coming blizzard. His arms were full of wraps, and his pockets crowded with mufflers and wraps the ladies had sent out to me. We did ourselves up in everything we had, while the three hounds were being placed in the sleigh. The drifts were too deep to drive near the cars, so my husband carried me over the snow and deposited me in the straw with the dogs. They were such strangers they growled at being crowded. Then the two brothers followed, and thus packed in we began that terrible ride, amid the cheers of those we were leaving. It was understood that we were to send back help to those we left.

The suspense and alarm in the car had been great,

but that journey through the drifts was simply terrible. I tried to be courageous, and did manage to keep still; but every time we plunged into what appeared to be a bottomless white abyss, I believed that we were to be buried there. And so we would have been, I firmly believe, had it not been for the experience and tenacity of will shown by the old driver. He had a peculiar yell that he reserved for supreme moments, and that always incited the floundering mules to new efforts. The sleigh was covered, but I could look out in front and see the plucky creatures scrambling up a bank after they had extricated us from the great drift at the bottom of the gully. If there had been a tree to guide us, or had it been daytime, it would not have seemed so hopeless a journey. The moon was waning, and the clouds obscured it entirely from time to time. There was nothing to serve as guide-posts except the telegraph-poles. Sometimes we had to leave them to find a road where the sleigh could be pulled through, and I believed we never would reach them again. Divide after divide stretched before us, like the illimitable waves of a great white sea. The snow never ceased falling, and I knew too much of the Dakota blizzard not to fear hourly that it would settle into that driving, blinding, whirling atmosphere through which no eyes can penetrate and no foot progress. It is fortunate that such hours of suspense come to an end before one is driven distracted.

When at last I saw the light shining out of our door at Fort Lincoln I could not speak for joy and gratitude at our release from such peril. Our friends gathered about us around the great log-fire in the general's room.

No light ever seemed so bright, no haven ever so blessed, as our own fireside. The train remained in the spot where we had left it until the sun of the next spring melted down the great ice banks and set free the buried engines. All the help that Bismarck could give was sent out at once, and even the few cattle that survived were at last driven over that long distance, and shelter found for them in the town.

Hardly had we arrived before a despatch came recalling the general to the East. I had no thought but that I would be allowed to accompany him, and went at once to repack my things. My husband found me thus employed, and took my breath away by telling me he could not endure the anxiety of having me go through such peril again. In vain I pleaded, and asked him to remember that I had summoned sufficient self-control not to utter a word about my fears; I promised more courage the next time. It was of no avail, I had to submit.

Not the shadow of an anxiety, nor the faintest sign of dread of the coming journey over the snow again came into his face. He left me with the same words with which he always comforted me: "Be sure, Libbie, it's all for the best; you know we always find it so in the end." With these farewell words he stepped into the sleigh—which he knew well might be his tomb.

It is not possible for me to speak in detail of the days that followed. Life seemed insupportable until I received a despatch saying that my husband had again passed safely over that two hundred and fifty miles of country where every hour life is in jeopardy.

CHAPTER XXIX.

OUR LIFE'S LAST CHAPTER.

OUR women's hearts fell when the fiat went forth that there was to be a summer campaign, with probably actual fighting with Indians.

Sitting Bull refused to make a treaty with the Government, and would not come in to live on a reservation. Besides his constant attacks on the white settlers, driving back even the most adventurous, he was incessantly invading and stealing from the land assigned to the peaceable Crows. They appealed for help to the Government that had promised to shield them.

The preparations for the expedition were completed before my husband returned from the East, whither he had been ordered. The troops had been sent out of barracks into a camp that was established a short distance down the valley. As soon as the general returned we left home and went into camp.

The morning for the start came only too soon. My husband was to take Sister Margaret and me out for the first day's march, so I rode beside him out of camp. The column that followed seemed unending. The grass was not then suitable for grazing, and as the route of travel was through a barren country, immense quantities of forage had to be transported. The wagons themselves seemed to stretch out interminably. There were pack-mules, the ponies already laden, and cavalry, artillery, and infantry followed, the cavalry being in advance of all. The number of men, citizens, employés, Indian scouts, and soldiers was about twelve hundred. There were nearly seventeen hundred animals in all.

As we rode at the head of the column, we were the first to enter the confines of the garrison. About the Indian quarters, which we were obliged to pass, stood the squaws, the old men, and the children singing, or rather moaning, a minor tune that has been uttered on the going out of Indian warriors since time immemorial. Some of the squaws crouched on the ground, too burdened with their trouble to hold up their heads; others restrained the restless children who, discerning their fathers, sought to follow them.

The Indian scouts themselves beat their drums and kept up their peculiar monotonous tune, which is weird and melancholy beyond description. Their war-song is misnamed when called music. It is more of a lament or a dirge than an inspiration to activity. This intoning they kept up for miles along the road. After we had passed the Indian quarters we came near Laundress Row, and there my heart entirely failed me. The wives and children of the soldiers lined the road. Mothers, with streaming eyes, held their little ones out at arm's-length for one last look at the departing father. The toddlers among the children, unnoticed by their elders, had made a mimic column of their own. With their handkerchiefs tied to sticks in lieu of flags, and beating old tin pans for drums, they strode lustily back and forth in imitation of the advancing soldiers. They were fortunately too young to realize why the mothers wailed out their farewells.

Unfettered by conventional restrictions, and indifferent to the opinion of others, the grief of these women was audible, and was accompanied by desponding gestures, dictated by their bursting hearts and expressions of their abandoned grief.

It was a relief to escape from them and enter the garrison, and yet, when our band struck up "The Girl I Left Behind Me," the most despairing hour seemed to have come. All the sad-faced wives of the officers who had forced themselves to their doors to try and wave a courageous farewell, and smile bravely to keep the ones they loved from knowing the anguish of their breaking hearts, gave up the struggle at the sound of the music. The first notes made them disappear to fight out alone their trouble, and seek to place their hands in that of their Heavenly Father, who, at such supreme hours, was their never-failing solace.

From the hour of breaking camp, before the sun was up, a mist had enveloped everything. Soon the bright sun began to penetrate this veil and dispel the haze, and a scene of wonder and beauty appeared. The cavalry and infantry in the order named, the scouts, pack-mules, and artillery, and behind all the long line of white-covered wagons, made a column altogether some two miles in length. As the sun broke through the mist a mirage appeared, which took up about half of the line of cavalry, and thenceforth for a little distance it marched, equally plain to the sight on the earth and in the sky.

The future of the heroic band, whose days were even

then numbered, seemed to be revealed, and already there seemed a premonition in the supernatural translation as their forms were reflected from the opaque mist of the early dawn.

The sun, mounting higher and higher as we advanced, took every little bit of burnished steel on the arms and equipments along the line of horsemen, and turned them into glittering flashes of radiating light. The yellow, indicative of cavalry, outlined the accoutrements, the trappings of the saddle, and sometimes a narrow thread of that effective tint followed the outlines even up to the head-stall of the bridle. At every bend of the road, as the column wound its way round and round the low hills, my husband glanced back to admire his men, and could not refrain from constantly calling my attention to their grand appearance.

The soldiers, inured to many years of hardship, were the perfection of physical manhood. Their brawny limbs and lithe, well-poised bodies gave proof of the training their out-door life had given. Their resolute faces, brave and confident, inspired one with a feeling that they were going out aware of the momentous hours awaiting them, but inwardly assured of their capability to meet them.

The general could scarcely restrain his recurring joy at being again with his regiment, from which he had feared he might be separated by being detained on other duty. His buoyant spirits at the prospect of the activity and field-life that he so loved made him like a boy. He had made every plan to have me join him later on, when they should have reached the Yellowstone.

The steamers with supplies would be obliged to leave our post and follow the Missouri up to the mouth of the Yellowstone, and from thence on to the point on that river where the regiment was to make its first halt to renew the rations and forage. He was sanguine that but a few weeks would elapse before we would be reunited, and used this argument to animate me with courage to meet our separation.

As usual we rode a little in advance and selected camp, and watched the approach of the regiment with real pride. They were so accustomed to the march the line hardly diverged from the trail. There was a unity of movement about them that made the column at a distance seem like a broad dark ribbon stretched smoothly over the plains.

We made our camp the first night on a small river a few miles beyond the post. There the paymaster made his disbursements, in order that the debts of the soldiers might be liquidated with the sutler.

In the morning the farewell was said, and the paymaster took sister and me back to the post.

With my husband's departure my last happy days in garrison were ended, as a premonition of disaster that I had never known before weighed me down. I could not shake off the baleful influence of depressing thoughts. This presentiment and suspense, such as I had never known, made me selfish, and I shut into my heart the most uncontrollable anxiety, and could lighten no one else's burden. The occupations of other summers could not even give temporary interest.

We heard constantly at the Fort of the disaffection of

the young Indians of the reservation, and of their joining the hostiles. We knew, for we had seen for ourselves, how admirably they were equipped. We even
saw on a steamer touching at our landing its freight of
Springfield rifles piled up on the docks *en route* for the
Indians up the river. There was unquestionable proof
that they came into the trading-posts far above us and
bought them, while our own brave 7th Cavalry troopers
were sent out with only the short-range carbines that
grew foul after the second firing.

While we waited in untold suspense for some hopeful
news, the garrison was suddenly thrown into a state of
excitement by important despatches that were sent from
Division Headquarters in the East. We women knew
that eventful news had come, and could hardly restrain
our curiosity, for it was of vital import to us. Indian
scouts were fitted out at the Fort with the greatest despatch, and given instructions to make the utmost speed
they could in reaching the expedition on the Yellowstone. After their departure, when there was no longer
any need for secrecy, we were told that the expedition
which had started from the Department of the Platte,
and encountered the hostile Indians on the head-waters
of the Rosebud, had been compelled to retreat.

All those victorious Indians had gone to join Sitting
Bull, and it was to warn our regiment that this news
was sent to our post, which was the extreme telegraphic
communication in the North-west, and the orders given
to transmit the information, that precautions might be
taken against encountering so large a number of the
enemy. The news of the failure of the campaign in the

other department was a death-knell to our hopes. We felt that we had nothing to expect but that our troops would be overwhelmed with numbers, for it seemed to us an impossibility, as it really proved to be, that our Indian scouts should cross that vast extent of country in time to make the warning of use.

The first steamer that returned from the Yellowstone brought letters from my husband, with the permission, for which I had longed unutterably, to join him by the next boat. The Indians had fired into the steamer when it had passed under the high bluffs in the gorges of the river. I counted the hours until the second steamer was ready. They were obliged, after loading, to cover the pilot-house and other vulnerable portions of the upper deck with sheet-iron to repel attacks. Then sand-bags were placed around the guards as protection, and other precautions taken for the safety of those on board. All these delays and preparations made me inexpressibly impatient, and it seemed as if the time would never come for the steamer to depart.

Meanwhile our own post was constantly surrounded by hostiles, and the outer pickets were continually subjected to attacks. It was no unusual sound to hear the long-roll calling out the infantry before dawn to defend the garrison. We saw the faces of the officers blanch, brave as they were, when the savages grew so bold as to make a day-time sortie upon our outer guards.

A picture of one day of our life in those disconsolate times is fixed indelibly in my memory.

On Sunday afternoon, the 25th of June, our little group of saddened women, borne down with one com-

mon weight of anxiety, sought solace in gathering together in our house. We tried to find some slight sur-
cease from trouble in the old hymns: some of them
dated back to our childhood's days, when our mothers
rocked us to sleep to their soothing strains. I remember
the grief with which one fair young wife threw herself
on the carpet and pillowed her head in the lap of a
tender friend. Another sat dejected at the piano, and
struck soft chords that melted into the notes of the
voices. All were absorbed in the same thoughts, and
their eyes were filled with far-away visions and long-
ings. Indescribable yearning for the absent, and untold terror for their safety, engrossed each heart. The
words of the hymn,

> "E'en though a cross it be,
> Nearer, my God, to Thee,"

came forth with almost a sob from every throat.

At that very hour the fears that our tortured minds
had portrayed in imagination were realities, and the souls
of those we thought upon were ascending to meet their
Maker.

On the 5th of July — for it took that time for the
news to come — the sun rose on a beautiful world, but
with its earliest beams came the first knell of disaster.
A steamer came down the river bearing the wounded
from the battle of the Little Big Horn, of Sunday, June
25th. This battle wrecked the lives of twenty-six women
at Fort Lincoln, and orphaned children of officers and
soldiers joined their cry to that of their bereaved
mothers.

From that time the life went out of the hearts of the "women who weep," and God asked them to walk on alone and in the shadow.

Mrs. Custer very naturally ends her work with the coming of the news that put so many women's lives in shadow. She has attempted no account of the Little Big Horn expedition, and none seems necessary here; but it is deemed best to add the following very brief outline by way of explanation to any reader whose memory may need refreshing:

The expedition during the summer of 1876, which ended so fatally with the battle of the Little Big Horn, was under General Terry, the ranking officer. General Custer commanded under him the 7th Cavalry. As it marched, the force struck a fresh Indian trail, and scouts were sent to follow it up and ascertain the number of warriors in the band. This can be done with great accuracy. The number of Indians can be estimated by following the trail far enough to get its average width and the size of the circle grazed over at night by the ponies on which the warriors ride. In this case the scouts followed the trail far enough to ascertain that twelve hundred Indians were in the band, but did not learn the location of the village where they were encamped. Upon their return General Terry and General Custer consulted together. It was well known to them that the vigilance of the Indian keeps outposts and signal-fires on every hill-top, thus making it an impossibility to approach one of their villages unobserved. Neither could it be kept from their quick eyes what the strength of the approaching force was. To await an attack or to advance with superior numbers was to give the Indians a chance to escape, and their wariness was known to all. Accordingly it was determined that General Custer should take such force as he thought the Indians, seeing him approach, would stand against awaiting its attack. He was convinced that the 7th Cavalry was as large a body as could be taken with safety, and was a match for twelve hundred Indians. He knew his men, and knew what he was doing. It was suggested that he should take a piece of artillery, but the scouts had described the bad lands over which they must march, and General Custer knew that artillery would hamper his movements besides increasing the apparent size of the command. He started with only his regiment, and the rest of the expedition halted to await the result. The officers and men went out feeling certain that a fight awaited them. If there had been but twelve hundred warriors, as there was every reason to suppose, the affair would have ended well; but Indian reinforcements, covering a trail half a mile wide (as was learned after the battle), had come from the North, and in an opposite direction to that in which the Indians were going. Instead, therefore, of a thousand, the gallant 7th Cavalry encountered about five thousand Indians, who were emboldened by success in their battle in another department, and made even more venturesome by their increase of numbers.

General Custer called a halt as he approached the village, and summoning his officers, explained to them his plan of attack, which was the same that had proved so successful in the battle of the Washita, in the previous history of the regiment. He offered the lead to that officer who should first report his company ready for battle. In a few seconds one of the highest in rank received this desired honor. Dividing the command into three detachments, General Custer led the body of his regiment in that final charge, in which afterwards the line of battle of a portion could be traced by the dead men and horses as they fell at the post of duty, and from which no man escaped.

APPENDIX.

THE YELLOWSTONE EXPEDITION OF 1873.

Extracts from Letters written by General Custer to his Wife during the Expedition to the Yellowstone in 1873.

[Many of the letters from which the following extracts are taken are very long, but so much of them is of a personal nature that I have sought here to give only those portions that convey an idea of the camp-life and daily experiences of a campaign on the frontier.

I regret that I have not the letters giving an account of the Indian fights. I have substituted a copy of General Custer's official report to complete the story of the summer of 1873.—E. B. C.]

Camp on Heart River, D. T., June 26, 1873.

WHEN I may have an opportunity to send this, or when it may reach you, I cannot tell; but I will have it ready, and when the first courier leaves he shall carry these tidings to you.

This is our sixth day out from Fort Rice. We reached this river yesterday about noon, and are remaining in camp to-day as it is somewhere in this locality that we expect to find the railroad engineers, and Lieut. D—— and four companies of infantry that left Fort Rice before you did.

Our march has been perfectly delightful thus far. We have encountered no Indians, although yesterday we saw the fresh tracks of about fifteen ponies, showing that they are in our vicinity.

I never saw such fine hunting as we have constantly had since we left Fort Rice. I have done some of the best shooting I ever did, and as you are always so interested I want to tell you about it. I take twenty-five picked men with me, and generally have several

officers in the party besides.   It is not necessary to go out of sight
of the column, as the game is so abundant we can even eclipse your
story about antelope running into the men's arms!   They actually
ran through our wagon-train, and one was run over by a wagon and
caught!   Tom* immediately remarked, "Well, by George, we can
beat Libbie's story now!"

The first day out the dogs caught an antelope and I shot one,
since when I have brought in from two to four daily.   Day before
yesterday the members of our mess killed eight antelope.   But I
must tell you of some of my recent shots with my new Springfield
rifle.

Three days ago F—— and I with a party were out in sight of the
column, when an antelope started up fully two hundred yards distant, and ran rapidly parallel to us.   I fired five times at it while
running, at this distance.   It then stopped, and I got about twenty-
five paces nearer when I fired off-hand, aiming directly at the head.
It fell, and I measured the distance, which proved to be one hundred
and seventy yards, and the antelope was found to be shot through
the head.   Of the five shots which I had fired at it while running at
a distance of two hundred yards, four had struck the antelope, one
breaking its thigh and two going through its body.

Yesterday a fine large buck came bounding over the hill across
our path.   He was so far that no one seemed to think it worth while
to aim at him, but I thought I would try.   Jumping off my thorough-
bred, Vic, in an instant I had my rifle at my shoulder and levelled at
the buck, which was running at full speed.   I pressed the trigger,
and waiting an instant to give the bullet time to reach its mark, the
buck was seen to fall lifeless in the grass.   To be accurate in the distance I requested F—— to measure it.   He did so, and found it to
be two hundred and eighty yards.   Galloping to where the antelope
had fallen, I found him shot directly through the centre of the neck,
about one foot from the head, the neck being broken by the shot.
I put him entire on the orderly trumpeter's horse and sent him to
the wagons to be carried to camp, where I butchered him.   He was
the fattest antelope I ever saw.

I sent H—— and M——'s messes each a quarter.   I have not

---

* The general's brother.

only been fortunate enough to keep our own mess supplied with game every meal since we left Fort Rice, but have had quantities to send to the infantry officers, to the band, and to many of our own officers.

Poor Fred and Tom! They have accompanied me frequently— Fred always along—and yet neither of them has been able thus far to kill a single antelope. I tease them a great deal, for they use the Winchester rifle. It is remarkably accurate up to one hundred yards, and not so beyond that distance.

You know when Tom takes a notion to get anything of mine how very persistent he is. Well, his latest dodge is to obtain possession of my Springfield rifle, which I allow my orderly, Tuttle, to carry. Night before last he carried it off to his tent without saying anything about it; but Tuttle slipped down while Tom was at breakfast and recaptured the rifle!

I wish you could have seen one of our hunting-parties coming into camp a few days ago, after a hunt of not more than four hours, in sight of the column all the time. My orderlies and I had four antelope strapped to our saddles; then came Captain F——, with a fine, large buck strapped behind him and a saddle in his front, while his orderly was similarly loaded; then McD—— and his orderly, each with a splendid antelope on his saddle, while others of the men who had accompanied me were well provided with game— except poor H——. He and the four men of his company who went with us had equal chances with the rest, but they had nothing. The officers give H—— no rest now on the subject of antelope; the last advice given him was that his only chance now is to spread his fish-net (which the officers ridicule him for bringing into such a country as this) and catch the antelope in that way! Tuttle killed two antelope at one shot with my Springfield at pretty long range.

Yesterday Fred and I had an exciting time with an elk that swam the river twice near us, but we only succeeded in wounding him before he got away to the bluffs beyond sight of the command, where we did not deem it prudent to follow him.

I am glad that I posted myself with regard to taxidermy; for yesterday, after reaching camp, I devoted all the afternoon to preparing the head of the antelope I killed for preservation. The antlers the officers think the finest they ever saw. I have prepared the entire head, and the skin of about one foot of the neck. I also have a beautiful set of elk antlers that I hope to get through safely. I carry them strapped on top of the ambulance of Mary, our cook.

I do not think we are going to have any serious difficulty with the Indians—at least this is General Rosser's opinion. He thinks this expedition is too large and unwieldy to perform the desired work promptly, and I agree with him.

There is an officer temporarily detailed with the command who inspires my respect because he regards the wishes of his mother so highly. He has some fine rifles at home, but did not bring any with him, merely to please his mother, who feared that if he brought his guns along he would be tempted to wander off alone hunting.

It is four days since I began this letter, but we have been moving in the mean while, so that but little opportunity for writing has been allowed.

With the ten companies of the 7th I started to join the engineers, leaving the infantry and train to follow us. I marched thirty miles over a bad country, besides building a bridge over a stream thirty feet wide and ten feet deep. I superintended and planned it, and about one hundred and eighty men worked to complete it. About twenty men had to cross the stream before the bridge could be begun. An officer must go with them, so I detailed McD—— and twenty of his men. They had to strip off and swim across. You ought to have heard the young officers on the bank hooting at McD—— when he was preparing to lead the "light brigade" across the water! I built a bridge in about two hours, over which the whole command and wagon-train passed.

The officers have a good joke on Lieut. H——. Nearly all of them have killed antelope, so Mr. H—— concluded he must kill his. He went out yesterday near the column and soon espied an antelope quietly lying in the grass about one hundred yards distant. Quickly dismounting from his horse, he crawled on the ground until near enough, as he thought, to kill it. Taking deliberate aim he fired, but the ball fell short a few feet; yet the antelope was not disturbed. This is not unusual. Again he took aim this time with great care, fired, and to his joy he saw the fur fly from the antelope. Never doubting but that he had given him a mortal wound, Mr. H—— leaped into his saddle and galloped up to the antelope to cut its throat. Imagine his disgust to find that the antelope had been dead several days, and had already been taken possession of by the flies! The officers will never let him hear the last of it.

Well, I have joined the engineers, and am having such pleasant visits with General Rosser. We talk over our West Point times and discuss the battles of the war. I stretch the buffalo-robe under the fly of the tent, and there in the moonlight he and I, lying at full length, listen to each other's accounts of battles in which both had borne a part. It seemed like the time when we were cadets together, huddled on one blanket and discussing dreams of the future. Rosser said the worst whipping he had during the war was the one I gave him the 9th of October, when I captured everything he had, including the uniform now at home in Monroe. He said that on the morning of that fight, just as the battle was commencing he was on a hill on our front, which I well remember, watching us advance. He was looking at us through his field-glass, and saw and recognized me as plainly as if I had been by his side. I was at the head of my troops—all of which I remember—and advancing to the attack.

Rosser said as soon as he recognized me he sent for his brigade commanders and pointed me out to them, saying, "Do you see that man in front with long hair? Well, that's Custer, and we must bust him up to-day."

"And so," General Rosser continued, "we would have done had you attacked us as we thought you intended to; but instead of that you slipped another column away around us, and my men soon began calling out, 'We're flanked! we're flanked!' then broke and ran, and nothing could stop them."

Rosser wanted to meet you at the crossing, but failed, and wrote to his wife to try and see you in St. Paul, but you had already gone through.

He too asked if you did not accompany me almost everywhere; so you see what an extended reputation for campaigning you have. And, do you know, he tells me he thinks I am anxious to get back to you. But I did not tell him that I was already counting the days.

I killed another antelope yesterday, two the day before, and two the day before that. Mary made us a delicious pot-pie out of two curlew I shot. Whenever the subject of pot-pies comes up, Mr. Calhoun, Tom, and I at once begin talking of the place where we got the best pot-pies we ever tasted. One will say, "I'll tell you where you can get the very nicest pot-pie you ever put in your mouth," and before he can go any further the other two will call out, "At mother's."

I saw the most beautiful red-deer yesterday I ever have seen. It was a new species to me; of the deepest red, as red as the reddest cow you ever saw. I was too far away to get a shot.

All the officers were up at my tent last night at twilight, sitting under the awning in front, all jolly, all good-humored, full of their jokes, and prouder than ever of the 7th, as they *modestly* compared the regiment with the infantry.

This letter of forty-four closely-written pages would make a *Galaxy* article so far as its length goes ; suppose you send me a check for it as the *Galaxy* people do for theirs ?

You must read a good deal of it to mother, or tell her of its contents, and say that this time this letter must do for the family. I hope your going home will be a comfort to her and improve her health.

Tell D—— if she is going to come into the Custer family she must be prepared to receive little billet-doux something the size of this volume !

Tom says, "Tell Libbie I intended writing, but when I saw the length of this letter I knew that there was nothing left to tell her !"

Yellowstone River, July 19, 1873.

Well, here we are, encamped on the banks of the far-famed and to you far distant Yellowstone ! How I have longed to have you see, during our progress, what seems to me almost like another world. Truly can this interesting region be termed the " Wonder-land !"

When the command arrived at what was supposed to be a distance of about fifteen miles from the river, it became necessary and important to ascertain where the steamboat with supplies that had come by river was located. I volunteered to go on a steamboat hunt, as I had hunted almost every other species of game ; so taking two troops and leaving our tents and wagons, I started on a search for the *Key West*. Several of the officers applied to go, and General Rosser, who is always ready for a trip of this kind, accepted my invitation to accompany us.

No artist—not even a Church or a Bierstadt—could fairly represent the wonderful country we passed over, while each step of our progress was like each successive shifting of the kaleidoscope, presenting to our wondering gaze views which almost appalled us by their sublimity.

We passed over a region so full of cañons and precipices. Much of our journey was necessarily made on foot, our horses being led in single file, except my own noble "Dandy." He seemed to realize the difficulties of the route, and although permitted to run untethered, he followed me as closely and carefully as a well-trained dog.

Sometimes we found ourselves on the summit of a high peak, to ascend which we had to risk both life and limb, and particularly imperil the safety of our horses. Once we came to a steep declivity which neither man nor horse could descend. It was impossible to retrace our steps, as the sides of the peak were so steep our horses could not turn about without great danger of tumbling hundreds of feet. Asking the rest to wait a moment, I looked about and discovered a possible way out to our left, provided a huge rock which lay in the path could be removed. Bidding Tuttle "Look out," and uttering a few words of caution to Dandy, who seemed to comprehend our situation and say, "All right, don't mind me," I left him clinging to the soft and yielding soil of the mountain. I succeeded in dislodging the rock after some work, and sent it leaping down the rocky side leading to the valley, sometimes taking hundreds of feet at one plunge. The way being clear, a simple "Come on, Dandy," and we took the advance, followed by the rest. We were well repaid for our risk and trouble by the grandeur of the scenery that lay spread out beneath us.

I am making a rare collection of the fossils that the country is rich in—vegetable and mineral specimens. I hope you will approve of my plan of disposal of them : I intend to give them to the college at Ann Arbor. What would you think to pass through thousands of acres of petrified trees, some of which are twelve feet in diameter, with trunks and branches perfect! The fallen trunks of some as they lie on the ground are so natural in grain and color, the officers are sometimes deceived and sit down, thinking them but lately felled.

To return to my search for the steamboat. After struggling through the beds of deep cañons and climbing almost inaccessible peaks, we finally emerged into the valley of the Yellowstone. We were still obliged in crossing swales to struggle on by walking, leading, climbing, and stumbling, and after a ride of ten miles we came to where the boat was moored.

Every one is congratulating F—— on getting the place I applied to Rosser for, as a member of the party of engineers. He will get $60 a month, and a prospect later of advancement and higher salary. It is such a pleasure when I can help young men who evince a disposition to help themselves. I never forget those who gave me my first encouragement in life. How I have wished that some of our home boys, who possess talent and education, but lack means and opportunity, would cast themselves loose from home and try their fortunes in this great enterprising western country, where the virtues of real manhood come quickly to the surface, and their possessor finds himself transformed from a mere boy to a full-fledged man almost before he realizes his quick advancement. It is such a comfort to me to feel independent. Much as I dote on my profession, and earnestly as I am devoted to it, yet should accident cast me adrift and I be thrown upon my own resources, I have not a fear but that energy and a willingness to put my shoulder to the wheel would carry me through and with reasonable success.

In this country, no man, particularly if moderately educated, need fail in life if determined to succeed, so many and varied are the avenues to honorable employment which open on all hands before him.

The climate is perfect out here; not five men are sick out of the whole ten troops, and one poor fellow who was about to be discharged before we left for disability, as he was thought to be in consumption, is now well and does not desire his discharge. Though it is July we sleep under blankets constantly.

Regarding the dogs, I find myself more warmly attached to Tuck than to any other I have ever owned. Did I tell you of her catching a full-grown antelope-buck, and pulling him down after a run of over a mile, in which she left the other dogs far behind? She comes to me almost every evening when I am sitting in my large camp-chair, listening to the band or joining with the officers in conversation. First she lays her head on my knee, as if to ask if I am too much engaged to notice her. A pat of encouragement and her fore-feet are thrown lightly across my lap ; a few moments in this post-ure and she lifts her hind-feet from the ground, and, great, over-grown dog that she is, quietly and gently disposes of herself on my lap, and at times will cuddle down and sleep there for an hour at a time, until I become so tired of my charge that I am compelled to transfer her to mother earth; and even then she resembles a well-cared for and half-spoiled child, who can never be induced to retire until it has been fondled to sleep in its mother's arms.

Tuck will sleep so soundly in my lap that I can transfer her gently to the ground and she will continue her slumber, like a little baby carefully deposited in its crib. As I write she is lying at my feet. She makes up with no other person.

I have just told Tom if he expects letters from you, he must write first. He answers that he would like to know what he can find to write "after she receives that *book* from you." And one might think that the eighty pages of this letter had exhausted every subject, but there is much I must leave untold.

I am prouder and prouder of the 7th, Libbie; not an officer or man of my command has been seen intoxicated since the expedition left Fort Rice. H—— and I have our periodical official tussles, as usual, but I see a great deal of him and like him better than ever.

We have just parted with a member of the expedition who is not a loss to us, for he is a gossip but not viciously inclined—rather the contrary. He peddles tiresome tales without meaning harm. Every-body in the 7th Cavalry camp is content to attend to his own busi-ness and not meddle with other people's affairs.

You will scarcely credit what I am about to tell you, but it is an undeniable fact: here we have been encamped for several days with pickets and guards surrounding our camp for its protection.

Our march here was over a stretch of wild, almost unknown country, supposed to be infested with hostile Indians. Small parties were not deemed safe beyond sight of our column, and yet to-day imagine our surprise to see a plain white covered spring-wagon, drawn by two mules and accompanied by a single individual, ap-proach our camp from the direction we came more than one week ago. It proved to be the travelling-conveyance of an humble priest, who, leaving Fort Rice seven days ago, traversed alone and unguided, ex-cept by our trail, through more than two hundred miles of hostile and dangerous country, fording rivers winding through deep and almost impassable cañons, toiling over mountains, at each step liable to be massacred by hostile Indians. The country was entirely new to him, he never having been west of Fort Rice before. He came believing he could be of spiritual benefit to many who would otherwise be wholly deprived of such comfort. He carried no arms, adopted no special precautions for his safety, but with a simple and unpretentious cross reverently erected and borne above his travelling-wagon, he took his life in his hand and boldly plunged into the wilds of this almost unknown region, evidently relying upon Him who ruleth over all, to guide and protect him in his perilous journey. This to me is an act of Christian heroism and physical courage which entitles this humble priest to immeasurable honor and praise.

Yellowstone River, above Powder River, July 31, 1873.

. . . The *Josephine* is unloading her cargo about one mile below here, and leaves for Bismarck within an hour. We expected to have an opportunity to write letters to-day, but as the boat receives five hundred dollars a day it is important to discharge her as soon as practicable.

The command is not in camp yet. I took a squadron and started ahead to find a road. You have no idea what difficulty we have, looking out a route through this country over which it is possible to move a train. Yesterday I took two companies and travelled about forty miles. To-day we reached the Yellowstone at 9.30.

We have been sleeping since (and it is now 4 P.M.) under the large trees standing on the river bank. I have just received one letter from you, and I think it is the first instalment only, for I hear there are seven sacks of mail on board the boat. I am sorry I am compelled to write under such hurried circumstances. I am lying on the ground, using my horse-blanket for a desk.

Official Report of the Engagements with Indians on the 4th and 11th ultimo.

Copy.

Head-quarters Battalion 7th Cavalry,
Pompey's Pillar, Yellowstone River, Montana, Aug. 15, 1873.

Acting Assistant Adjutant-general Yellowstone Expedition :

SIR,—Acting under the instructions of the Brevet-major-general commanding, I proceeded at five o'clock, on the morning of the 4th instant, with one squadron of my command, numbering about ninety men, to explore a route over which the main column could move. Having reached a point on the Yellowstone River, near the mouth of Tongue River, and several miles in advance, and while waiting the arrival of the forces of the expedition, six mounted Sioux dashed boldly into the skirt of timber within which my command had halted and unsaddled, and attempted to stampede our horses. Fortunately our vedettes discovered the approach of the Indians in time to give the alarm. A few well-directed shots soon drove the Indians to a safe distance, where they kept up a series of yells, occasionally firing a few shots. As soon as the squadron could mount, I directed Captain Moylan to move out in pursuit, at the same time I moved with the troops in advance, commanded by First Lieutenant T. W. Custer. Following the Indians at a brisk gait, my suspicions became excited by the confident bearing exhibited by the six Sioux in our front, whose course seemed to lead us near a heavy growth of timber which stood along the river bank above us. When almost within rifle range of this timber, I directed the squadron to halt, while I with two orderlies, all being well mounted, continued after the Sioux in order to develop their intentions. Proceeding a few hundred yards in advance of the squadron, and keeping a watchful eye on the timber to my left, I halted. The six Indians in my front also halted, as if to tempt further pursuit. Finding all efforts in this direction unavailing, their plans and intentions were quickly made evident, as no sooner was it seen that we intended to advance no farther, than with their characteristic howls and yells over three hundred well-mounted warriors dashed in perfect line from the edge of the timber, and charged down upon Captain Moylan's squadron, at the same time endeavoring to intercept the small party with me. As soon as the speed of the thorough-bred on which I was mounted brought me within hailing distance of Lieutenant Custer's troop, I directed that officer to quickly throw forward a dismounted line of troopers, and endeavor to empty a few Indian saddles. The order was obeyed with the greatest alacrity, and as the Sioux came dashing forward, expecting to ride down the squadron, a line of dismounted cavalrymen rose from the grass and delivered almost in the faces of the warriors a volley of carbine bullets which broke and scattered their ranks in all directions, and sent more than one Sioux reeling from his saddle. This check gave us time to make our dispositions to resist the succeeding attacks, which we knew our enemies would soon make upon us. The great superiority of our enemies in numbers, the long distance separating us from the main command, and the belief, afterwards verified, that the woods above us still concealed a portion of the savage forces, induced me to confine my movements, at first, strictly to the defensive. The entire squadron (except the horse-holders) was dismounted and ordered to fight on foot. The Indians outnumbering us almost five to one were enabled to envelop us completely between their lines, formed in a semicircle, and the river which flowed at our backs. The little belt of timber in which we had been first attacked formed a very good cover for our led-horses, while the crest of a second table-land, conveniently located from the timber, gave us an excellent line of defence. The length of our line and the numbers of the enemy prevented us from having any force in reserve; every available officer and man was on the skirmish-line, which was in reality our line of battle, even the number of men holding horses had to be reduced, so that each horse-holder held eight horses. Until the Indians were made to taste quite freely of our lead they displayed unusual boldness, frequently charging up to our line and firing with great deliberation and accuracy. Captain Moylan exercised command along the entire line; Lieutenant Custer commanded the centre; my adjutant, Lieutenant James Calhoun, commanded the right; and Lieutenant Charles A. Varnum, the left. The first Indian killed was shot from his pony by "Bloody Knife," the Crow who acted as my guide and scout. Soon after Private Charles P. Miller, of "A" troop 7th Cavalry, succeeded in sending a carbine bullet directly through the body of a chief who had been conspicuous throughout the engagement. At the same time it was known that our firing had disabled many of their ponies, while owing to our sheltered position the only damage thus far inflicted upon us was one man and two horses wounded, one of the latter shot in three places.

Finding their efforts to force back our line unavailing, the Indians now resorted to another expedient. By an evidently preconcerted plan they set fire in several places to the tall grass which covered the ground in our front, hoping by this means to force us back to the rear, and thus finish us at their pleasure. Fortunately for us there was no wind prevailing at the time, while the grass was scarcely dry enough to burn rapidly. Taking advantage of the dense curtain of smoke which rose from the burning grass, the Indians, by following the course of the flame, could often contrive to obtain a shot at us at comparatively close range; but my men, observing that there was no danger to be apprehended from the slowly advancing flames, could frequently catch an opportunity to send a shot through a break in the curtain of smoke, and in this way surprised the Indian by the adoption of his own device.

The fight began at 11.30 A.M., and was waged without cessation until near three o'clock, all efforts of the Indians to dislodge us proving unsuccessful. The Indians had become extremely weary, and had almost discontinued their offensive movements, when my ammunition ran low. I decided to mount the squadron and charge the Indians, with the intention of driving them from the field.

Captain Moylan promptly had his men in the saddle, and throwing forward twenty mounted skirmishers, under Lieutenant Varnum, the entire squadron moved forward at a trot. No sooner did the Indians discern our intentions than, despite their superiority in numbers, they cowardly prepared for flight, in which preparation they were greatly hastened when Captain Moylan's squadron charged them and drove them "pell-mell" for three miles.

Five ponies killed or badly wounded were left on the battle-ground or along the line of their flight. So rapidly were they forced to flee that they abandoned and threw away breech-loading arms, saddle equipments, clothing, robes, lariats, and other articles comprised in an Indian outfit.

Among the Indians who fought us on this occasion were some of the identical warriors who committed the massacre at Fort Phil. Kearney, and they no doubt intended a similar programme when they sent the six warriors to dash up and attempt to decoy us into a pursuit past the timber in which the savages hoped to ambush us. Had we pursued the six warriors half a mile farther, instead of halting, the entire band of warriors would have been in our rear, and all the advantage of position and numbers would have been with them.

So far as the troops attacked were concerned, the Indians, to offset their own heavy losses, had been able to do us no damage except to wound one man and two horses; but unfortunately two non-combatants, Veterinary Surgeon John Honsinger, 7th Cavalry, and Mr. Baliran, of Memphis, Tenn., in endeavoring to come from the main column to join the squadron in advance, were discovered by the Indians during the attack, and being unarmed were overtaken and killed almost within view of the battle-ground. Fortunately the Indians were so pressed as not to be able to scalp or otherwise mutilate the remains.

On the 8th instant we discovered the trail of a large village, evidently that to which the party that attacked us on the 4th belonged. The course of the trail led up the Yellowstone, and apparently was not more than two days old. Acting under the authority of the Brevet-major-general commanding, I ordered my command, consisting of four squadrons of the 7th Cavalry, in readiness to begin the pursuit that night. The Brevet-major-general also directed the detachment of guides and Indian scouts under Lieutenant Daniel H. Brush, 17th Infantry, to report to me for temporary service. Leaving all tents and wagons behind, and taking with us rations for seven days, we started in pursuit at ten o'clock on the night of the 8th instant, having waited until that hour until the moon should enable us to follow the trail. Following the trail as rapidly as the rough character of the country would permit, daylight next morning found us nearly thirty miles from our starting-point. Concealing horses and men in a ravine, a halt of three hours was ordered to enable the horses to graze and the men to obtain refreshments. Renewing the march at eight o'clock, the pursuit was continued without halting until noon, when, to avoid discovery, as well as to obtain needed rest for men and animals, it was decided to conceal ourselves in the timber, and await the cover of night to continue the pursuit.

Starting out at 6.30 P.M., the trail was followed rapidly for six miles, when, to our disappointment, we discovered that the Indians had taken to the river, and crossed to the east side. In following their trail to this point it was evident that the movement of the Indians was one of precipitate flight, the result of the engagement on the 4th. All along their trail and in their camping-places were to be found large quantities of what constitutes an Indian's equipments, such as lodge-poles, robes, saddle equipments, arms, and cooking utensils. In a hastily abandoned camp-ground nearly two hundred axes, besides a great many camp-kettles and cups, were found.

My entire command was disappointed when the trail showed that the Indians had crossed to the other side, particularly as our rapid marching had carried us to the point of crossing, the evening of the day on which the last of the Indians had crossed over, so that one more march would have enabled us to overhaul them. Bivouacking in a belt of timber on the river bank, we waited until daylight to begin an attempt to cross the command over the river, which at this point is about six hundred yards wide. At early dawn the entire command forded the river to an island located about the middle of the channel; but our difficulties in the way of crossing here began, as the volume of water and the entire force of the current were to be encountered between the island and the opposite bank—the current here rushes by at a velocity of about seven miles an hour, while the depth of the water was such that a horse attempting to cross would be forced to swim several hundred yards. Still, as we knew the Indians had not discovered our pursuit, and were probably located within easy striking distance of the river, it was most desirable that a crossing should be effected, To accomplish this, Lieutenant Weston, 7th Cavalry, with three accomplished swimmers from the command, attempted to cross on a log-raft, carrying with them a cable made of lariats. The current was so strong that Lieutenant Weston's party were unable to effect a landing, but were swept down the river nearly two miles, and then forced to abandon the raft and swim to shore.

Lieutenant Weston, with characteristic perseverance and energy, made repeated attempts afterwards to carry the cable over, but although succeeding in reaching the opposite bank in person was unable to connect the cable with the shore. Almost the entire day was spent in these unsuccessful efforts, until finally a crossing in this manner had to be abandoned. I then caused some cattle to be killed, and by stretching the hides over a kind of basket-frame prepared by the Crow guide, made what are known among the Indians as bull-boats; with these I hoped to be able to connect a cable with the opposite bank at daylight next morning, but just at sunset a small party of Indians were seen to ride down to the bank opposite us and water their ponies. They discovered our presence, and at once hastened away. Of course it was useless now to attempt a surprise, and the intention to cross the river the following morning was abandoned.

At early dawn the next day (the 11th instant), the Indians appeared in strong force on the river bank opposite us, and opened a brisk fire upon us from their rifles. No attention was paid to them until encouraged by this they had collected at several points in full view, and within range of our rifles, when about thirty of our best marksmen, having posted themselves along the bank, opened a well-directed fire upon the Indians and drove them back to cover.

In the mean time strong parties of Indians were reported by our pickets to be crossing the river below and above us, their ponies and themselves being so accustomed to the river as to render this operation quite practicable for them. Captain French, commanding the right wing, was directed to watch the parties crossing below, while Colonel Hart, commanding the left wing, posted a force to discharge this duty with regard to parties crossing above. It would have been possible, perhaps, for us to have prevented the Indians from effecting a crossing, at least when they did, but I was not only willing but anxious that as many of them should come over as were so disposed. They were soon reported as moving to the bluffs immediately in rear of us from the river. Lieutenant Brush was directed to employ his scouts in watching and reporting their movements—a duty which they discharged in a thorough manner.

While this was transpiring I had mounted my command and formed it in line close under the bluffs facing from the river, where we quietly waited the attack of the Indians in our front. The sharp-shooting across the river still continued, the Indians having collected some of their best shots—apparently armed with long-range rifles—and were attempting to drive our men back from the water's edge. It was at this time that my standing orderly, Private Tuttle, of "E" troop, 7th Cavalry, one of the best marksmen in my command, took a sporting Springfield rifle and posted himself, with two other men, behind cover on the river bank, and began picking off the Indians as they exposed themselves on the opposite bank. He had obtained the range of the enemy's position early in the morning, and was able to place his shots wherever desired. It was while so engaged that he observed an Indian in full view near the river. Calling the attention of his comrade to the fact, he asked him "to watch him drop that Indian," a feat which he succeeded in performing. Several other Indians rushed to the assistance of their fallen comrade, when Private Tuttle, by a skilful and rapid use of his breech-loading Springfield, succeeded in killing two other warriors. The Indians, enraged no doubt at this rough handling, directed their aim at Private Tuttle, who fell pierced through the head by a rifle-bullet. He was one of the most useful and daring soldiers who ever served under my command.

About this time Captain French, who was engaged with the Indians who were attacking us from below, succeeded in shooting a warrior from his saddle, while several ponies were known to be wounded or disabled. The Indians now began to display a strong force in our front on the bluffs. Colonel Hart was ordered to push a line of dismounted men to the crest, and prevent the further advance of the enemy towards the river. This duty was handsomely performed by a portion of Captain Yates's squadron. Colonel Hart had posted Lieutenant Charles Braden and twenty men on a small knoll which commanded our left. Against this party the Indians made their first onslaught. A mounted party of warriors, numbering nearly two hundred, rode boldly to within thirty yards of Lieutenant Braden's position, when the latter and his command delivered such a well-directed fire that the Indians were driven rapidly from that part of the field, after having evidently suffered considerable loss.

Unfortunately Lieutenant Braden received a rifle-ball through the upper part of the thigh, passing directly through the bone, but he maintained his position with great gallantry and coolness until he had repulsed the enemy. Hundreds of Indians were now to be seen galloping up and down along our front, each moment becoming bolder, owing to the smallness of our force which was then visible.

Believing the proper time had arrived to assume the offensive, orders to this effect were accordingly sent to Colonel Hart and Captain French, the two wing commanders. Lieutenant Weston was directed to move his troop " L " up a deep ravine on our left, which would convey him to the enemy's position, and as soon as an opportunity occurred he was to charge them, and pursue the Indians with all the vigor practicable. Immediately after, Captain Owen Hale was directed to move his squadron, consisting of " E " and " K "

troops, in conjunction with "L" troop, and the three to charge simultaneously. Similar dispositions were ordered in the centre and
right. Lieutenant Custer, commanding "B" troop, was ordered to
advance and charge the Indians in front of our centre, while Cap-
tains Yates and Moylan moved rapidly forward in the same direction. Before this movement began, it became necessary to dislodge
a large party of Indians posted in a ravine and behind rocks in our
front, who were engaged in keeping up a heavy fire upon our troops
while the latter were forming. It was at this point that the horse
of Lieutenant Hiram H. Ketchum, Acting-assistant-adjutant-general
of the expedition, was shot under him. My own horse was also
shot under me within a few paces of the latter.

The duty of driving the Indians engaged in sharp-shooting was
intrusted to Lieutenant Charles A. Varnum, 7th Cavalry, with a detachment of "A" troop, 7th Cavalry, who soon forced the Indians
back from their cover.

Everything being in readiness for a general advance, the charge
was ordered, and the squadrons took the gallop to the tune of "Garryowen," the band being posted immediately in rear of the skirmish
line. The Indians had evidently come out prepared to do their best,
and with no misgivings as to their success, as the mounds and high
bluffs beyond the river were covered with groups of old men,
squaws, and children, who had collected there to witness our de-
struction. In this instance the proverbial power of music to soothe
the savage breast utterly failed, for no sooner did the band strike
up the cheery notes of "Garryowen," and the squadrons advance
to the charge, than the Indians exhibited unmistakable signs of
commotion, and their resistance became more feeble, until finally
satisfied of the earnestness of our attack they turned their ponies'
heads and began a disorderly flight. The cavalry put spurs to their
horses and dashed forward in pursuit, the various troop and squadron commanders vying with one another as to who should head the
advance. The appearance of the main command in sight, down the
valley at this moment, enabled me to relieve Captain French's command below us, and he was ordered to join in the pursuit. Lieutenant McIntosh, commanding "G" troop, moved his command up
the valley at a gallop, and prevented many of the Indians from crossing. The chase was continued with the utmost vigor until the In-

dians were completely dispersed, and driven a distance of nine miles from where the engagement took place, and they were here forced back across the Yellowstone, the last pony killed in the fight being shot fully eight miles from the point of attack.

The number of Indians opposed to us has been estimated by the various officers engaged as from eight hundred to a thousand. My command numbered four hundred and fifty, including officers and men. The Indians were made up of different bands of Sioux, principally Uncpapas, the whole under command of "Sitting Bull," who participated in the second day's fight, and who for once has been taught a lesson he will not soon forget.

A large number of Indians who fought us were fresh from their reservations on the Missouri River. Many of the warriors engaged in the fight on both days were dressed in complete suits of the clothes issued at the agencies to Indians. The arms with which they fought us (several of which were captured in the fight) were of the latest improved patterns of breech-loading repeating rifles, and their supply of metallic rifle-cartridges seemed unlimited, as they were anything but sparing in their use. So amply have they been supplied with breech-loading rifles and ammunition that neither bows nor arrows were employed against us. As an evidence that these Indians, at least many of them, were recently from the Missouri River agencies, we found provisions, such as coffee, in their abandoned camps, and cooking and other domestic utensils, such as only reservation Indians are supplied with. Besides, our scouts conversed with them across the river for nearly an hour before the fight became general, and satisfied themselves as to the identity of their foes. I only regret that it was impossible for my command to effect a crossing of the river before our presence was discovered, and while the hostile village was located near at hand, as I am confident that we could have largely reduced the necessity for appropriation for Indian supplies the coming winter. . . .

The losses of the Indians in ponies were particularly heavy, while we know their losses in killed and wounded were beyond all proportion to that which they were enabled to inflict upon us, our losses being one officer badly wounded, four men killed, and three wounded; four horses killed and four wounded.

Careful investigation justifies the statement that including both days' battles, the Indians' losses will number forty warriors, while their wounded on the opposite bank of the river may increase this number. Respectfully submitted.

(Signed)   G. A. CUSTER,
Lieutenant-colonel 7th Cavalry,
Brevet-major-general, U. S. A., commanding.

"Stockade" on the Yellowstone, September 6, 1873.

. . . I know you will rejoice when your eyes fall upon the date and heading of this letter, and you learn that we are thus far on our homeward journey, all safe and well. This letter is to be a SHORT one (after having finished the letter I underscore the word), as it has only been decided a few hours ago to despatch three of our Indian scouts from here to Fort Buford—one hundred and twenty miles distant by river, only eighty by land—with mail, and to bring back what awaits us in return. As there are many official matters for me to attend to between now and to-morrow morning—the time of the departure of the scouts—I do not hope to give you but the main points of a letter, the details to be filled up by word of mouth.

I am here with six companies of cavalry, having separated from the main expedition several days ago on the Mussel Shell River, and marched to this point direct, a distance of about one hundred and fifty miles. The mules of the large trains began giving out; forage was almost exhausted, the horses being allowed only about three pounds per day, fourteen pounds being regular allowance. The country was entirely unknown; no guides knew anything of the route before us. General —— did not think it wise to venture into the unknown and uninviting region with his command. But I did not feel inclined to yield to obstacles, and made an application to take the main portion of the cavalry and strike through for the stockade direct instead of turning back. I asked that the railroad engineers be allowed to continue with me. Consent was given and we started.

At head-quarters it was not believed that I would get through. So strong was this impression, that in the official order issued for my movement there was a clause authorizing me to burn or abandon all my wagons or other public property, if, in my opinion, such steps were necessary to preserve life. I could not help but smile to myself as I read that portion of the order. I had no idea of burning or abandoning a wagon. After we had separated from the main column, the chief of the engineers remarked to the officers, "How positively sanguine the general is that he will make this trip successfully." And so I was. I assured him from the first, and from day to day, that the 7th Cavalry would bring them through all right. We had the good-luck to strike across and encounter, instead of serious obstacles, the most favorable country yet met by us for marching. Hitherto we had made about fifteen miles per day; when we started on this trip we marched twenty-two miles one day and thirty-five the next, and so on, and brought in every wagon with which we started, reaching here about seven o'clock the morning of the sixth day from our separation.

The main command headed back towards the Yellowstone, and expects to be twelve or thirteen days in making the trip. I am going to send an officer with his squadron in charge of fourteen wagons loaded with forage to the relief of the rest of the command.

Our location for next winter is settled. We shall be at Fort Lincoln, and the decision is satisfactory to me. I presume you wish you were here to give the lieutenant-colonel of the battalion* a little advice as to what companies shall be designated for each station. So far as this reason alone is concerned, I am glad that you are not here, as I not only would not wish you to attempt to influence such a decision, but that no person or persons might have just ground for imagining that you had done so. The officers are hinting strongly in the endeavor to ascertain "Who goes where?" but thus far none are any the wiser, for the simple reason that I have not decided the matter yet in the case of a single troop.

It is a delicate, and in some respects an undesirable task, as all, so far as I know, desire to go to Fort Lincoln. If no accident occurs, we shall reach there before October 1st—less than a month from this date, and probably less than ten days from the time you receive this, so that all your anxiety about me will be at an end. I do not

* This reference is to himself.

intend to relax my caution on the march between here and Lincoln, as I do not forget that the two officers killed last year met their deaths near the close of the expedition.

I think I told you in my letter of eighty pages about my chasing elk four miles and killing three. Since then I have had the good-fortune to kill a fine large buck-elk taller than "Dandy,"* weighing, cleaned, eight hundred pounds, and with the handsomest pair of antlers I ever saw, and such a beautiful coat. I killed him only a mile and a half from camp, sent for a wagon, and carried him entire back with us, when the officers and men, and even those belonging to the scientific party, flocked to the grassy plot in front of my tent to see him.

The photographer who accompanied the scientists hitched up his photograph-wagon and drove over to take a picture of what they called the "King of the Forest." All the officers and the photographer insisted that not only the game but the hunter should appear in the picture. So I sat down, dressed as I was in my buckskins, resting one hand on an antler, and you may judge of the immense size of the elk when I tell you that as I sat there my head only reached to about half the height of the antlers. The picture is to form one of the series now being collected on the expedition under the auspices of the Smithsonian Institute.

Since the expedition started I have become acquainted with the gentlemen of the scientific corps, particularly with the zoologist and the taxidermist. The latter has been kind enough to make me a pupil of his, and I can now preserve animals for all practical purposes. I have been able to supply the gentlemen referred to with many specimens of animals, and, in return, they have not only taught me but supplied me with all the means necessary to preserve prepared animals.

You should see how very devoted I am to this, to me, very pleasant and interesting pastime. Often, after marching all day, a light may be seen in my tent long after the entire camp is asleep, and a looker-on might see me, with sleeves rolled above the elbow, busily engaged preparing the head of some animal killed in the chase. Assisting me might be seen the orderly and Hughes, both, from their

---

* His favorite hunting-horse.

sleepy looks, seeming to say, "How much longer are we to be kept out of our beds?"

I have succeeded so well in taxidermy that I can take the head and neck of an antelope, fresh from the body, and in two hours have it fully ready for preservation. I have prepared a most beautiful buck-antelope head and neck for Tom. He intends it for his sweetheart, and will send it by express from Bismarck.

I have just finished heads for two officers, which they intend as presents for their wives, and one I shall give to the Audubon Club. Then I have the heads of two black-tailed deer, of a buck and doe antelope for *us*, and the head and skin with claws of a grisly-bear. The latter is not thoroughly cured, owing to our constant marching and the immense amount of fat contained in the neck and hide. The *ne plus ultra* of all is the "King of the Forest." I have succeeded in preserving him entire—antlers, head, neck, body, legs, and hoofs—in fine condition, so that he can be mounted and look *exactly as in life*. To prevent the hair being rubbed, I have caused the head to be well covered with grain-sacks, and this, with the entire skin, to be sewed up securely in canvas.

The scientists informed me that there were but few specimens on this continent of elk preserved entire, and none so fine as mine. When I first began work on it I only intended to save the head, neck, and antlers, but finding that I was able to save the whole, I decided upon the latter course. Had I kept the head and neck only, it was intended for you; but having it complete alters my intention, as it would require a room to contain it. So I have concluded, with your approval, to present it to the Audubon Club in Detroit.*

I have a fine buffalo head for you, beautifully haired and with symmetrical horns. A pair of sage-chickens, a pair of curlew, and a jack-rabbit complete my present collection. . . .

One day I shot three antelope without changing my position, the nearest of the three being three hundred and twenty yards from me.

Our mess continues to be successful. Nearly every day we have something nice to send to Lieutenant Braden.† Only think of him,

---

* It is now in Detroit.

† Lieutenant Braden was wounded in the battle described in the official report which accompanies this letter.

with his shattered thigh, having to trail over a rough country for three hundred miles! He is not transported in an ambulance, but a long stretcher arranged on wheels about thirty feet apart, pulled and pushed by men on foot. They carry him much more steadily than would horses or mules. It requires a full company of men each day to transport Mr. Braden in this way. He is with the main command, but was doing well when we left. The day the command divided I had the band take a position near the route where the rest of the expedition would pass, and when he and his escort approached they struck up "Garryowen." He acknowledged the attention as well as he could.

Upon our arrival here what was our joy to find quite a large mail awaiting us! It had been forwarded from Rice and Lincoln to Fort Buford, and from there came here by scouts. I received four letters from you. . . . Do you know, on the 4th of August—the very day you were writing me one of the letters I received—I was fighting, probably at the same time. . . . After I received my four letters I threw myself down on the bed to read them. When any one poked his head inside my large and comfortable tent, and ventured a question, you can probably imagine the brevity and abruptness of a certain man's replies. My communication was strictly Biblical, being either "Yea, yea, or Nay, nay."

East Bank of the Yellowstone, September 10th.

. . . When I began my letter, a few days ago, announcing our safe return to the stockade, I said you must only expect a few lines; but those few lines stretched out until they covered five sheets of letter-paper. I could now cover five times five and then only have begun my letter, but where the time is to be found I cannot tell.

We are just taking the men across the river on the *Josephine*, which arrived yesterday. My head-quarters and about half the troops are over, the rest will have followed by night. As Sheldon & Co., publishers of the *Galaxy*, say, I am going to "boil down" this letter to as many brief allusions as possible.

Instead of waiting here for the rest of the command to move, to-morrow will find us on our way to Lincoln. I take six troops of the 7th, two companies of infantry, and with the engineers set out on our return. We rely confidently on reaching Lincoln before

October 1st. The reports brought by those who came on the boat place everything in a bright light regarding our new quarters at Lincoln.

I think we will have a charming garrison this winter. I wish we had some one competent to give us lessons in private theatricals. I learn by the boat that Department Head-quarters have telegraphed to Lincoln that it is possible I may wish to take a long leave. They almost take it for granted I will go, but I shall not. Do you remember, on my return from the Washita campaign, I was offered a leave in a similar manner? I have no desire to be absent from my post now. . . .

I have enjoyed a few very great luxuries to-day. At dinner, on the *Josephine*, for the first time this season (September 10th) I tasted new potatoes and cucumbers; but these were not the greatest. What do you imagine was a greater luxury? RAW ONIONS!!!!* Even at this great distance I almost tremble when I inform you that I not only had onions for dinner, but the captain of the boat gave me a whole bushel of fine large ones. I supped on RAW ONIONS; I will probably breakfast, lunch, and dine on them to-morrow, and the next day, and the day after *ad libitum ad infinitum*, until—not time, but onions—shall be no more. As one by one I dispose of each goodly-sized fragment of a huge onion, I remark, *sotto voce*, "Go it, old fellow! Make the most of your liberties! You are on the home-stretch now, and school soon commences;" in other words, "If you intend to eat raw onions, now is your only time, for 'missus is comin'.'"

I would be glad to have every one of the officers now with me stationed at my post. My relations with them, personal and official, are extremely agreeable. They are all counting on going to Lincoln, but I know some of them will have to be disappointed. . . .

The steamer *Josephine* will probably leave for Lincoln to-morrow or next day, and should reach there in four or five days, so that you should receive this letter in about one week. . . . The steamer brought me two splendid letters from you, one dated the 18th, another the 25th of August. I received them on the 9th, which is pretty quick, considering. . . .

---

* I have copied the words as he printed them.

My collection of geological specimens for the Michigan University is growing satisfactorily. The Indian battles hindered the work of collecting, while in that immediate region it was unsafe to go far from the command. . . .

P.S.—Good-morning! . . . I am sitting in my large, comfortable tent, writing before breakfast. And now I must refer to a matter which thrusts itself upon my attention almost daily, yes, hourly, and that is the great degree of comfort which I have enjoyed throughout this long and ever-changing march; and it is all due to your thoughtfulness and foresight, and the manner in which you fitted me up surpasses all my comrades. No mess has compared with mine in its appointments and outfit. I have the best cook, and certainly no bed can equal mine. Whenever I look around me I see the evidences of your handiwork and care for my welfare. . . .

You never knew people more enthusiastic over the 7th than the engineers connected with the railroad party. . . . Well, I must terminate this letter, as I see no likelihood of my being able to tell you one-tenth of what I have to say. However, we will have all winter in our "brand, spankin'" new house to talk it over and over. . . .

Here I have reached my thirty-second page of this large paper. I only thought of writing three or four, and have "boiled down" as hard as I could. . . .

Fort Lincoln, September 23, 1873.

. . . Where are the numerous bridges now which you have been crossing and recrossing in regard to our return being delayed until late in October, perhaps until the first of November? Well, here we are, not only "as good as new," but, if anything, heartier, healthier, and more robust than ever.

I have not drawn a single unhealthy breath since we started on the expedition, and if ever a lot of hardy, strong, and athletic young fellows were assembled in one party, it is to be seen in a group of the officers of the 7th. What a history and reputation this 7th Cavalry has achieved for itself! Although a new and young regiment, it has left all the older fellows in the lurch, until to-day it is the best and most widely known of any in the service.

I am provoked to think I wrote you a long letter on the Yellowstone, also a telegram, and intrusted them to an officer who was to take passage in the steamer *Josephine*, and leave about the time we did. It should have reached here several days before we arrived, but I took six troops of cavalry and the engineers, crossed the Yellowstone to this side, and reached Fort Lincoln in eight days.

We took everybody by surprise, and beat the steamer here, so that your letter and telegram are still on the boat somewhere between this point and the stockade. You may rely upon it that no grass grew under our feet on our return march. I knew that my family —consisting of one—was in advance somewhere, and, as the saying is, I just "lit out." * I am so comfortably fixed in my large, heavy canvas railroad tent that was given me on the expedition, I am sure that you and I could live comfortably in it all winter.

I am much pleased with the appearance of the citizens who have come across the river from Bismarck to pay their respects and offer congratulations on the summer's campaign. Some of the Yankton gentlemen are here attending court, and they also came over to see me.

I have just had a telegram from General Sheridan: "Welcome home."

Fort Lincoln, September 28, 1873.

. . . When you find that I have just sent the 7th Cavalry band to serenade —— on his departure, you will say to yourself, "He has been too forgiving again." Well, perhaps I have. I often think of the beautiful expression uttered by President Lincoln at the consecration of the Gettysburg monument, and feel how nearly it expresses my belief, " With malice toward none, with charity for all!" and I hope this will ever be mine to say.†

---

* Here follows a description of Fort Lincoln. His sanguine temperament made it seem little short of an earthly paradise. He did not seem to realize that the prosaic and plain Government buildings were placed on a treeless and barren plain. In a carefully prepared plan of our house which he had drawn, he gave the dimensions and description of each room, and over the door of his library a triple underlining of his words, "MY ROOM," and the motto, "Who enters here leaves hope behind." He thus began, before we had even occupied the house, playfully to threaten any one who disturbed his writing or studies.

† The officer to whom reference is made had been a persistent and exasperating enemy of my husband during the summer, and I could not forget or forgive,

Adopting your wise and deserved suggestion, I have at last written my long delayed letter to Mr. Ford, and among other things told him I would send him per express the skins of two young elk that I killed, to have them tanned, and a pair of shoes made for each of us. So, you see, I did as I generally do, obeyed my " other half," who nine times out of ten is right, and generally the *tenth time, too.*

During a halt of two days, just before we started for home, I wrote a long *Galaxy* article, and shall mail it with this.   Not only did I do that instead of resting, because of the appeals of the magazine editors, but it behooved me to get off my contributions with some regularity; for if I stop now, those who attribute them to you would say all the more it was because you were not along to do the work for me.   If people only knew the amusement they have afforded us by laying the responsibility of these articles on your shoulders.

I must not forget to tell you that during the expedition I killed with my rifle and brought into camp forty-one antelope, four buffalo, four elk, seven deer (four of them black-tails), two white wolves, and one red fox.

Geese, ducks, prairie-chickens, and sage-hens without number completed my summer's record.

No one assisted me in killing the antelope, deer, or elk, except one of the latter.

One porcupine and a wildcat I brought in alive.   Both of these amiable creatures I intend to send to Central Park. . . .

LETTERS FROM THE BLACK HILLS, 1874.

The following Extracts are taken from Letters sent from the Expedition to the Black Hills, referred to in Chapter XX.

Thirteen Miles from Fort Lincoln, July 3, 1874.

. . . . Yesterday was a hard day on the trains.   The recent rains had so softened the ground that the heavily-loaded wagons sunk to the hubs, and instead of getting in camp by noon as we expected, one battalion did not get in until after dark.   But we had a good

---

even after apologies were offered, especially as they were not offered in the presence of others.

dinner, and every one is feeling well this morning. I am making a late start in order to give the mules a chance to graze.

I send you by bearer a young curlew, as a playmate to the wild-goose. Should it live, its wings had better be clipped. Grasshoppers are its principal diet.

Our mess is a great success. Last night, notwithstanding the late hour at which we reached camp, Johnson, our new colored cook, had hot biscuit, and this morning hot cakes and biscuit. We will not be over twenty or twenty-five miles from the post to-night. The men are standing around waiting to take down the tents, so I must say good-bye.

Prospect Valley, Dakota,
Twelve miles from the Montana line, July 15th.

. . . We are making a halt of one day at this charming spot, in order to rest the animals and give the men an opportunity to wash their clothes. I will begin by saying everything is and has been perfectly satisfactory. Every one—officers, men, and citizens—are in the best of health and spirits.

We have marched through an exceedingly interesting country. We are now in the most beautiful valley we have seen thus far, and encamped on a small tributary of the Little Missouri, and about five miles from the latter. So beautiful did this place seem to us when we first came in sight of it, I directed the engineer-officer, who is making a map of the country, to call it Prospect Valley.

Three days ago we reached the cave referred to, before we started, by the Indian called "Goose." It was found to be about four hundred feet long, and just as he described, the walls and top covered with inscriptions and drawings. The prints of hands and feet are also in the rocks. I think this was all the work of Indians at an early day, although I cannot satisfactorily account for the drawings of ships found there.

"Bos,"* though this is his first expedition, takes to life on the plains as naturally as if bred to it. One of the officers says he thinks it must "run in the blood." He has to go through the usual experience that falls to all "plebs." Every one practises jokes on him, but he has such a good disposition it does not even *ruffle him.* I

---

* Our younger brother.

know that you would espouse his cause against us if you had seen him take some bits of rocks out of his pocket every night after we had reached camp, and put them to soak in his wash-basin. They were given to him by Tom, who assured him that they were sponge stone—a variety that softened by keeping them in water for a certain length of time. After a few nights of faithful practice it dawned upon him that he was again the victim of a practical joke, and he quietly dropped them by the way without saying a word. You need not trouble yourself to take up arms in his defence, for he gets even with us in the long-run.

He has been so pleased with his mule from the first, and has praised him to me repeatedly. He *is* a good animal, for a *mule*, but endurance, in his constitution, rather triumphs over speed. I could not resist taking advantage of the country to play a trick on "Bos" one day.

The land was undulating, and you know how it always seems as if one could surely see for miles beyond when the top of each divide is reached, and how one can go on all day over the constant rise and fall of the earth, thinking the next divide will reveal a vast stretch of country. "Bos" rode beside me, and I invented an excuse to go in advance; I made "Vic" gallop slowly over the divide, and when out of sight on the other side I put spurs to him and dashed through the low ground. When "Bos" came in sight I was slowly ambling up the next divide and calling to him to come on. He spurred his mule, shouted to him, and waved his arms and legs to incite him to a faster gait. When he neared me I disappeared over another divide, and giving "Vic" the rein only slackened speed when it became time for "Bos" to appear. Then, when I had brought my horse down to a walk I called out, "Why on earth don't you come on?" Believing that the gait he saw me take had been unvarying, he could not understand why I lengthened the distance between us so rapidly. I kept this up until he discovered my joke, and I was obliged to ride back to join him and suit "Vic's" steps to those of his exhausted mule. . . .

No Indians or signs of Indians were seen from the time we left Lincoln until the day before yesterday, when about twenty were discovered near the column. They scampered off as soon as observed. Yesterday we came where they had slept. The officer on rear-guard duty saw about twenty-five following our trail.

Signal smokes were sent up all around us yesterday afternoon by the Indians, and some were seen watching us after we reached camp, but no hostile demonstrations have been made. Our Indian guides say the signals may be intended to let the village know where we are, so that they may keep out of our way. . . .

We expect to reach the base of the Black Hills in about three days. Professor Winchell and Mr. Grinnell discovered yesterday the fossil remains of an animal belonging to some extinct race which in life exceeded in size the largest elephant. . . .

I am gradually forming my annual menagerie. I have one live rattlesnake—for Agnes*—two jack-rabbits, half grown, one eagle, and four owls. I had also two fine badgers, full grown, but they were accidentally smothered. . . .

These are the first lines I have written since my last letter to you, nearly a fortnight since, and you cannot imagine how tired my hand and arm have become already. I have made no attempt to write on the march; the short time I have after reaching camp every day is devoted to rest and sleep. . . .

General "Sandy" is delighted with the 7th Cavalry; he says no regiment compares with it except perhaps the 4th. There has not been a single card-party nor a drunken officer since we left Lincoln. . . .

Our mess is a decided and gratifying success. Johnson is not only an excellent cook but very prompt. We breakfast at four o'clock every morning. Every day I invite some officer to dine with us.

I remember your wishes and ride at the head of the column, keeping inside our lines all the time, although it is a great deprivation to me not to go outside and hunt. I feel exactly like some young lady extremely fond of dancing, who, having a cold, has been forbidden by her anxious mamma to do more than look on at some elegant party. I received my orders from my commanding officer before starting, and I am going to try and render strict obedience.†

---

* This was our young visitor, whose horror of snakes General Custer well knew.

† This reference to commanding officer meant his wife, whose authority only extended to precautionary instructions as to his safety and health. The reiterated petition was that he should never leave the column alone.

. . . In looking for a road I sometimes get a mile or perhaps two ahead of the command, but I always have seventy or eighty men with me, and after to-day I mean to take in addition two more companies. I have no intention of getting beyond sight and hearing of the main column. There is an advance-guard always, and the Indian scouts at the front and on the flanks. . . .

I have killed six antelope at the head of the command. . . . Only think! one-fifth of the time expired day before yesterday, and by the time this reaches you one-third of our time of separation will have passed.

We will not be delayed in our return later than I expected when we left Fort Lincoln. . . .

As I write, the dogs surround me: "Cardigan" is sleeping on the edge of my bed, "Tuck" at the head, and "Blücher" near by. . . . I am not certain whether I will be able to send back more scouts or not. This mail is to be carried by two Rees, Bull Bear and Skunk's Head. Bloody Knife is doing splendidly on this trip.

There is not a single man on the sick-report in this entire command—a fact which the medical officer regards as unprecedented. . . . We will move into the valley of the Little Missouri to-morrow, and probably follow that stream to the Black Hills. You may judge of the fine country we have passed over by the fact that our mules and beef - herd have actually improved since we left Lincoln. We have travelled two hundred and twenty-seven and a half miles, and in a straight line we are one hundred and seventy miles from Lincoln. I must stop now, and write my official report.

                         Camp near Harney's Peak, August 2, 1874.

I wish you could see me at this moment as I am prepared to write to you. First I must tell you that I cannot send a very long letter —not that I have not volumes to say to you, but for reasons which I will briefly explain. In the evening, after reaching camp, I am too much occupied and have too much hard work to find time to write. After dinner I usually take an escort and search out a few miles of road for the following day. When I return I am ready to hasten to my comfortable bed.*

---

* Nothing but excessive fatigue and a determination to make the best of everything could have prompted him to describe it as comfortable. On the first day's

We have *reveille* regularly at a quarter before three, so that it behooves one to get to bed as early as possible. . . . To-day has been letter-day. Charlie Reynolds leaves in the morning with the mail for Fort Laramie. I am going to explore some twenty-five or thirty miles in that direction, and Reynolds will go with me. I take five companies. Two others started off in another direction this morning to be absent three days; so you see they are kept moving. I will be gone three days; the next day after that we turn our faces northward and begin our homeward march. I must not forget to explain the other reason why I cannot send you a letter of thirty pages or so this time—one of those that Tom calls my "little notes" to you. I was busy with the office duties until ten to-day, and then I began my official report. I had so many interruptions I was at last driven to print "Engaged" on a placard and pin it on the front of my tent; I tied up the flaps, shutting myself in until the twenty-two pages of my report were written.

It is now a quarter to one. Breakfast is at four, and "Boots and Saddles" will sound at five. I wish I could go more into detail in describing the expedition, which has exceeded all previous ones, and in success has surpassed my most sanguine expectations.

I did not hope to have my wagon-train with me, and here it has followed me everywhere. We have discovered a rich and beautiful country. We have had no Indian fights and will have none. We have discovered gold without a doubt, and probably other valuable metals. All are well, and have been the entire trip.

My report, which you will see, will contain much that I would have sent you in a letter. . . .

August 3d.

P.S.— . . . We have marched forty-five miles to-day, in a southerly direction from Harney's Peak, and are now encamped on the south fork of the Cheyenne River, about ninety miles from Fort Laramie. Reynolds* leaves us here. We are now all seated or lying around a camp-fire, writing the closing words to our letters. . . .

---

march out from garrison a careless soldier forgot the three boards that were intended to keep the bedding from absorbing the dampness in case of rain. During the entire summer, owing to this piece of forgetfulness, the mattress was laid down every night on ground that was always uneven and sometimes wet.

* The scout mentioned in Chapter XXVI. It was on this trip to Fort Laramie, carrying the despatches and mail, that he suffered such hardships and peril.

I must say good-bye. A few days more and we shall be at home, for we start north at five o'clock in the morning. . . .

Bear Butte, Dakota, August 15th.

Though we shall so soon be at home, I must send a few lines by the scout who takes the official despatches. I cannot tell you how busy I have been, and how hard and constantly I have worked to try and make the expedition successful. I have attempted to be several other things besides commanding-officer—particularly guide—since the expedition started.

Now that we have been in and through the Black Hills, I have the satisfaction of knowing that the whole undertaking has proved a success, exceeding the expectations of the most sanguine. I think that my superior officers will be surprised and gratified at the extent and thoroughness of our explorations. . . .

The photographer who accompanied us has obtained a complete set of magnificent stereoscopic views of Black Hills scenery, so I will not attempt to allude to this lovely country until I can review it with you by aid of the photographs. I send you one that will show you that at last I have killed a grisly after a most exciting hunt and contest. . . . Colonel Ludlow, Bloody Knife, and Private Noonan are with me in the group, as we constituted the hunting-party. The bear measured eight feet. I have his claws.

The scouts are on their ponies waiting for the mail, and I must hasten. . . .

It would have been such a treat to have had you see all that we have seen this summer, and shared the enjoyment of this beautiful land. But, never mind, you shall come next summer, for we all hope to return again. . . .

No Indians have been seen lately, but I intend to be careful until the end of the trip. . . . _____

LETTERS FROM THE YELLOWSTONE, 1876.

Extracts from Letters written on the Second Expedition to the Yellowstone, during the Summer of 1876.

Forty-six Miles from Fort Lincoln,
May 20th, 1876—9.15 P.M.

. . . It has just been decided to send scouts back to Lincoln. They leave here at daylight, and will remain there thirty-six hours, returning to us with despatches and mail. We are having the "parrot's time" with the expedition.

It is raining now, and has been since we started. The roads are fearfully bad. Here we are on the Little Muddy, after marching four days, and only forty-six miles from home. Everybody is more or less disgusted except me, and I feel the relief of not having to bear the responsibility of the delays.

The elements seem against us, but a wet season and bad roads can be looked for always in this region in the months of May and June.

We have not seen any signs of Indians thus far, and hardly look for any for a few days yet. I have been extremely prudent—sufficiently so to satisfy you. I go nowhere without taking an escort with me. I act as if Indians were near all the time. The mess prospers well. Tom and I have fried onions at breakfast and dinner, and raw onions for lunch!"* The scouts that were left at Lincoln joined us yesterday about 10 A.M. with the mail. I wish that you knew how good it was to get the letters. You must send me more by the scouts we send out to-morrow. . . . Since beginning this letter it is decided that they go at once, for I know it is best to get them out of camp at night; so they have been directed to saddle-up immediately, and I must therefore cut this letter short.

I said this evening that if I was sure this expedition would go no farther the next four days than it has those just past, I would be glad to take despatches to Lincoln and return, just for the sake of getting home again for a few hours. . . .

On Little Missouri, May 30th—10 P.M.

. . . I am determined to sit up, even though it is ten o'clock, and write to you, notwithstanding I have had a tremendous day's work. I breakfasted at four o'clock, was in the saddle at five, and between that hour and 6 P.M. I rode fifty miles over a rough country, unknown to everybody, and only myself for a guide.

We had halted here for one day in order to determine the truth of the many rumors which you and all of us have heard so long and

---

* They both took advantage of their first absence from home to partake of their favorite vegetable. Onions were permitted at our table, but after indulging in them they found themselves severely let alone, and that they did not enjoy.

often, to the effect that the hostile Indians were gathered on the Little Missouri River, with the intention of fighting us here.

I suggested to General Terry to send out a strong scouting-party up the river to find out all that could be ascertained. He left the matter to me, and I took four companies of cavalry and a part of the scouts, and at five o'clock we were off. The valley of the river averages about one mile in width, hemmed in on both sides by impassable Bad Lands. The river is crooked beyond description.

To shorten the story, we marched the fifty miles and got back before dark, having settled the question beyond a doubt that all stories about large bodies of Indians being here are the merest bosh. None have been here for six months, not even a small hunting-party.

We took pack-mules with us to carry feed for the horses. When we lunched, all the officers got together and we had a jolly time.

Only think, we found the Little Missouri River so crooked and the Bad Lands so impassable that in marching fifty miles to-day we forded the river thirty-four (34) times. The bottom is quicksand. Many of the horses went down, frequently tumbling their riders into the water; but all were in good spirits, and every one laughed at every one else's mishaps.

General Terry just left my tent a few moments since, and when I asked him not to be in a hurry he said, " Oh, I'll leave you, for you must be tired and want to go to bed." I did not tell him that I was going to write to you before I slept.

Bloody Knife looks on in wonder at me because I never get tired, and says no other man could ride all night and never sleep. I know I shall sleep soundly when I do lie down; but, actually, I feel no more fatigued now than I did before mounting my horse this morning. . . .

What I am going to tell you is for you alone. But —— came to me the other day, and asked me to arrange that he should be stationed at our post next winter. He says he wants to be in a garrison where the duty is strict, and, above all, he desires to prove that he is, and desires to be, a man, and he believes that he could do much better than he has if he could serve under me. He says the very atmosphere of his post seems filled with evil for him. I have a scheme by which I think I can accomplish his coming, and I believe that you will approve.*

The scouts reached here in good time, and glad was I to get my letters. . . .

In Camp, about Ten Miles West of the Little Missouri,
May 31st.

. . . We left camp about eight o'clock. After marching a few miles, Tom, "Bos," and I, taking some men, started on a near route across the country, knowing that we would intercept the column later on. This is the second time I have left the main command, and both times they have lost their way; so you see my "bump of locality" is of some use out here. We reached this camp about three-quarters of an hour from the time we left the column, but the latter strayed off, and while we were here by 9 A.M., the rest did not reach here until two o'clock. When they found they were lost, the officers all assembled at the head of the column to consult together and try and find the right way.

To-day, while out with Tom and "Bos," we were riding through a part of the country filled with small *buttes*, in which it was easy to lose one's self. "Bos" stopped a few moments as we were riding through a ravine, and dismounted to take a pebble from his pony's shoe. I observed it, and said to Tom, "Let's slip round the hill behind 'Bos,' where he can't find us, and when he starts we'll fire in the air near him." The moment we passed out of sight our entire party galloped around the hill behind him and concealed ourselves. Tom and I crawled to the top of the hill and peeped through the grass without being seen. Sure enough, "Bos" thought he was lost, as we could nowhere be seen in the direction he expected to find us.

Tom and I were watching him, and just as he seemed in a quandary as to where we were, I fired my rifle so that the bullet whizzed over his head. I popped out of sight for a moment, and when I looked again "Bos" was heading his pony towards the command, miles away. I fired another shot in his direction, and so did Tom, and away "Bos" flew across the plains, thinking, no doubt, the Sioux

---

* We had been extremely anxious about the officer to whom my husband refers, and longed to save him from himself. Since he is gone, I think that I am not betraying confidence in quoting from this letter.

were after him. Tom and I mounted our horses and soon over-hauled him. He will not hear the last of it for some time.

Charlie Reynolds killed two big-horn sheep to-day and gave me the finest of the two heads. I have it in my tent now and hope to preserve it, although I came away without my preservative powders.

Nearly all my amusement is with "Bos" and Tom. We lunch together every day. . . . I have about made up my mind that when I go on expeditions like this you are to go too. You could have endured this as well as not. . . .

Powder River, about Twenty Miles above its Mouth,
June 9, 1876.

. . . We are now in a country heretofore unvisited by white men. Reynolds, who had been guiding the command, lost his way the other day, and General Terry did not know what to do about find-ing a road from O'Fallon's Creek across to Powder River. I told him I thought I could guide the column. He assented; so Tom, "Bos," and I started ahead, with company D and the scouts as escort, and brought the command to this point, over what seems to be the only practicable route for miles on either side, through the worst kind of Bad Lands. The general did not believe it possible to find a road through. When, after a hard day's work, we arrived at this river by a good, easy road, making thirty-two miles in one day, he was delighted and came to congratulate me.

Yesterday I finished a *Galaxy* article, which will go in the next mail; so, you see, I am not entirely idle. Day before yesterday I rode nearly fifty miles, arose yesterday morning, and went to work at my article, determined to finish it before night, which I did, amidst constant interruptions. It is now nearly midnight, and I must go to my bed, for *reveille* comes at three.

As a slight evidence that I am not very conceited regarding my personal appearance, I have not looked in a mirror or seen the reflec-tion of my beautiful (?) countenance, including the fine growth of *auburn* whiskers, since I looked in the glass at Lincoln.*

---

* This reference to the color of his beard, which he only allowed to grow on campaigns, was a reminder of the fact upon which we had long since agreed: that though Titian might have found beauty in that tint, we did not.

On Yellowstone, at Mouth of Powder River,
June 11th—10.30 P.M.

. . . This morning we left our camp on Powder River, I acting again as guide. The expedition started to make its way through unknown Bad Lands to the mouth of the river. General Terry felt great anxiety in regard to the trip, as he feared that we could not get through with the wagons. He had been down the river to its mouth with cavalry, and he and those with him said that wagons could not make the march in a month, and the Bad Lands looked still more impracticable. He came to my tent before daylight, and asked me if I would try to find the road. He seems to think I have a gift in that way, and he hoped that we might get within ten miles of the river's mouth to-day. What rendered our condition more embarrassing was that the men had only rations for one day left.

I started with one company and the scouts, and in we "plunged boldly." One company had been sent out the previous day to look for a road, and their failure to return the same day increased the anxiety. I thought likely they had lost their way and had slept in the Bad Lands. Sure enough we found them about 10 A.M.

After passing through some perfectly terrible country I finally struck a beautiful road along a high plateau, and instead of guiding the command within ten miles of here we have all arrived and the wagon-train beside.

If you will look on the map near my desk you will find the mouth of Powder River and our present location on the Yellowstone, almost due west from Lincoln. Follow up the Yellowstone a short distance, and the first stream you come to is the Tongue River, to which point we will move after resting three or four days. We will there be joined by the six companies of the regiment now absent on a scout, and I shall then select the nine companies to go with me. . . .

The steamer *Far West* leaves for Fort Buford to-morrow. . . . As I was up at three this morning, and have had a hard day's march, and as it is now going on to twelve, I must hie to bed to get a little rest and slumber. . . .

Monday, June 12th—before Breakfast.

. . . I rose early this morning, without waiting to be called to breakfast, in order that I might write my letter. The Yellowstone is very high; steamers loaded to their utmost capacity can go up some distance above the mouth of the Big Horn. I wanted to send you a letter that I wished you to read and afterwards re-mail, had I not thought you might have found an opportunity to come up the river in the *Josephine*. The new supplies for our mess—of onions, potatoes, and dried apples—have just come from the boat.

"Tuck"* regularly comes when I am writing, and lays her head on the desk, rooting up my hand with her long nose until I consent to stop and notice her. She and Swift, Lady and Kaiser sleep in my tent.

You need not be anxious about my leaving the column with small escorts; I scarcely hunt any more.† . . .

Mouth of Tongue River, June 17th.

. . . I fear that my last letter, written from the mouth of Powder River, was not received in very good condition by you. The mail was sent in a row-boat from the stockade to Buford, under charge of a sergeant and three or four men of the 6th Infantry. Just as they were pushing off from the *Far West* the boat capsized, and mail and soldiers were thrown into the rapid current; the sergeant sank and was never seen again. The mail was recovered, after being submerged for five or ten minutes. Captain Marsh and several others sat up all night and dried it by the stove. I was told that my letter to you went off all right, also my *Galaxy* article. The latter was recognized by a young newspaper reporter and telegraph operator who came up on the train with us from St. Paul, and he took special pains in drying it.

With six companies of the 7th, the Gatling battery, the scouts, and the pack-mules, I left the mouth of Powder River Thursday morning, leaving all our wagons behind, and directing our march for this point, less than forty miles distant. General Terry and staff followed by steamer. We marched here in about one and a quarter days. The boat arrived yesterday evening. . . . The officers were ordered to leave their tents behind. They are now lying under tent-flies or in shelter-tents. When we leave here I shall only take a tent-fly. We are living delightfully. This morning we had a splendid

---

* She was my husband's favorite dog.

 † This letter was scorched and defaced, but fortunately I could read it all, thanks to those who sat up all night to dry the mail.

dish of fried fish, which Tom, "Bos," and I caught a few steps from my tent last evening.

The other day, on our march from Powder River, I shot an antelope. That night, while sitting round the camp - fire, and while Hughes was making our coffee, I roasted some of the ribs Indian fashion, and I must say they were delicious. We all slept in the open air around the fire, Tom and I under a fly, "Bos" and Autie Reed on the opposite side. Tom pelted "Bos" with sticks and clods of earth after we had retired. I don't know what we would do without "Bos" to tease. . . .

Yesterday Tom and I saw a wild - goose flying over-head quite high in the air. We were in the bushes and could not see each other. Neither knew that the other intended to fire. Both fired simultaneously, and down came the goose, killed. Don't you think that pretty good shooting for rifles?

On our march here we passed through some very extensive Indian villages—rather the remains of villages occupied by them last winter. I was at the head of the column as we rode through one, and suddenly came upon a human skull lying under the remains of an extinct fire. I halted to examine it, and lying near by I found the uniform of a soldier. Evidently it was a cavalry uniform, as the buttons on the overcoat had "C" on them, and the dress-coat had the yellow cord of the cavalry uniform running through it. The skull was weather-beaten, and had evidently been there several months. All the circumstances went to show that the skull was that of some poor mortal who had been a prisoner in the hands of the savages, and who doubtless had been tortured to death, probably burned. . . .

We are expecting the *Josephine* to arrive in a day or two. I hope that it will bring me a good long letter from you, otherwise I do not feel particularly interested in her arrival—unless, by good-luck, you should be on board; you might just as well be here as not. . . . I hope to begin another *Galaxy* article, if the spirit is favorable. . . .

Mouth of Rosebud, June 21, 1876.

. . . Look on my map and you will find our present location on the Yellowstone, about midway between Tongue River and the Big Horn.

The scouting-party has returned. They saw the trail and deserted camp of a village of three hundred and eighty (380) lodges. The trail was about one week old. The scouts reported that they could have overtaken the village in one day and a half. I am now going to take up the trail where the scouting-party turned back. I fear their failure to follow up the Indians has imperilled our plans by giving the village an intimation of our presence. Think of the valuable time lost! But I feel hopeful of accomplishing great results. I will move directly up the valley of the Rosebud. General Gibbon's command and General Terry, with steamer, will proceed up the Big Horn as far as the boat can go. . . . I like campaigning with pack-mules much better than with wagons, leaving out the question of luxuries. We take no tents, and desire none.

I now have some Crow scouts with me, as they are familiar with the country. They are magnificent-looking men, so much handsomer and more Indian-like than any we have ever seen, and so jolly and sportive; nothing of the gloomy, silent red-man about them. They have formally given themselves to me, after the usual talk. In their speech they said they had heard that I never abandoned a trail; that when my food gave out I ate mule. That was the kind of a man they wanted to fight under; they were willing to eat mule too.

I am going to send six Ree scouts to Powder River with the mail; from there it will go with other scouts to Fort Buford. . . .

June 22d—11 A.M.

. . . I have but a few moments to write, as we move at twelve, and I have my hands full of preparations for the scout. . . . Do not be anxious about me. You would be surprised to know how closely I obey your instructions about keeping with the column. I hope to have a good report to send you by the next mail. . . . A success will start us all towards Lincoln. . . .

I send you an extract from General Terry's official order, knowing how keenly you appreciate words of commendation and confidence, such as the following: "It is of course impossible to give you any definite instructions in regard to this movement; and were it not impossible to do so, the Department Commander places too much confidence in your zeal, energy, and ability to wish to impose upon you precise orders, which might hamper your action when nearly in contact with the enemy."

THE END.